The Himalaya by the Numbers

A Statistical Analysis of Mountaineering in the Nepal Himalaya

Richard Salisbury
Elizabeth Hawley

Vajra Publications

Publisher
Vajra Publications
Jyatha, Thamel, P.O. Box 21779, Kathmandu, Nepal
Tel.: 977-1-4220562, Fax: 977-1-4246536
e-mail: bidur_la@mos.com.np
www.vajrabooks.com.np; www.vajrabookshop.com

Distributors
Vajra Book Shop
Kathmandu, Nepal

The Mountaineers Books
Seattle, Washington

Front Cover Photo: Kangchenjunga North Face (by Richard Salisbury)
Back Cover Photo: Elizabeth Hawley (by Billi Bierling)

ISBN 978-9937-506-63-2 (Hard Cover)
        978-9937-506-64-9 (Soft Cover)

Printed in Nepal

Contents

Introduction 5

Climbing Activity 9
   Yearly Activity 9
   Regional Activity 22
   Seasonal Activity 32
   Activity by Age and Gender 38
   Activity by Citizenship 43
   Team Composition 44
   Expedition Results 48
   Individual Climber Results 50

Ascent Analysis 55
   Ascents by Altitude Range 55
   Popular Peaks by Altitude Range 57
   Ascents by Climbing Season 62
   Ascents by Expedition Years 66
   Ascents by Day of the Year 79
   Ascents by Time of Day 83
   Ascents by Age Groups 88
   Ascents by Gender 94
   Ascents by Citizenship 99
   Ascents by Team Composition 101
   Ascents Rates from High Camp 106
   Average Expedition Duration and Days to Summit 116

Death Analysis 125
   Deaths by Peak Altitude Ranges 125
   Deaths on Popular Peaks 129
   Deadliest Peaks for Members 130
   Deadliest Peaks for Hired Personnel 134
   Deaths by Geographical Regions 137
   Deaths by Climbing Season 139
   Altitudes of Death 143
   Causes of Death 144
   Avalanche Deaths 150
   Deaths by Falling 158
   Deaths by Physiological Causes 166
   Deaths by Expedition Years 168
   Deaths by Age Groups 169
   Deaths by Gender 171
   Deaths by Citizenship 174
   Deaths by Team Composition 176
   Deaths Rates Above and Below High Camp 179
   Probability of Death on Everest on Summit Day 183
   Major Accidents 185

Oxygen and the 8000ers 191

Appendix A: Peak Summary 197
Appendix B: Supplemental Charts and Tables 208

Introduction

The Himalayan Database, published by the American Alpine Club in 2004, is a compilation of records for all expeditions that have climbed in the Nepal Himalaya. The data are based on the expedition archives of Elizabeth Hawley, a longtime journalist living in Kathmandu, and are supplemented by information gathered from books, alpine journals, magazines, and correspondence with Himalayan climbers.

The original data (published in CD format) cover all expeditions from 1905 through 2003 to more than 300 significant Nepalese peaks. Also included are expeditions to both sides of border peaks such as Everest, Cho Oyu, Makalu, and Kangchenjunga as well as to some smaller border peaks. Updates for the 2004 and subsequent climbing seasons are available free for download at *www. himalayandatabase.com* and can be applied to the original data set.

The analyses in this book draw primarily on information from *The Himalayan Database* and examine expedition climbing activity, ascents, and fatalities. The seasonal climbing summaries by Elizabeth Hawley written from 1985 to the present also contribute to the narrative portions of the book. The complete texts of these summaries are contained on *The Himalayan Database* CD.

For the analyses in this book, we cover 60 years of the history of climbing in Nepal divided into four parts:

    1900-1949 – the exploratory period
    1950-1969 – the expeditionary period
    1970-1989 – the transitional period
    1990-2009 – the commercial period

The early exploratory period is comprised primarily of expeditions to Everest in the 1920s and 1930s by the British and to the Kangchenjunga region during the 1930s by the Germans. These expeditions were few in number and do not contribute significantly to any meaningful analyses and thus are not included in the analyses.

The expeditionary period began in 1950 with the opening of Nepal to foreign expeditions. For the peaks higher than 8000m (the 8000ers), relatively large teams (8 or more members) used a military assault-style of climbing that employed many lowland porters to ferry in large stock-piles of equipment to base camp and then used hired high-altitude assistants or "Sherpas" to establish and cache higher camps until a final summit assault was mounted. Sherpas also accompanied the climbers to the top on all first ascents of the 8000ers in Nepal except for Annapurna, Lhotse, and Kangchenjunga.

The expeditionary period was also the beginning of the "super" expedition age that began with the large American and Indian Everest expeditions in 1963 and 1965 (both sent 60+ climbers and high-altitude assistants above base camp), continued into the 1970s with a very contentious international effort on Everest in 1971 (80+ persons) and the 1973 Italian Everest expedition (sending up 150+ persons and one helicopter), and culminating with 1989 USSR traverses of four summits of Kangchenjunga and the "extra-super" 1988 China-Japan-Nepal Friendship expedition that sent over 200 climbers and high-altitude assistants up the mountain from both sides and completed the first north-south traverses. The Chinese also contributed with two very large expeditions to the north side of Everest in 1960 and 1975 that sent up the mountain hundreds of climbers and porters (or "assistants" as they are called on Chinese expeditions).

During the transitional period from 1970 to 1989, alpine-style climbing slowly began to replace expeditionary-style climbing. Highly skilled climbers such as Reinhold Messner and Jerzy Kukuzcka using lightweight gear moved rapidly up and down the mountain with fewer fixed camps and with minimal or no high-altitude assistant support. After Messner and Peter Habeler's ascent of Everest without supplementary oxygen in 1978, climbing all peaks without oxygen became the ultimate goal of many elite climbers.

Expeditionary-style climbing continued on Everest as many of the largest expeditions were organized and funded for a nation's first attempt (the Japanese in 1970, the Yugoslavs in 1979, the Canadians and Soviets in 1982, and the Czechs in 1984). But new challenging routes that required greater technical skills were opened up on the great walls of the big peaks (the south face of Annapurna I in 1970, the southeast face of Cho Oyu in 1978, the Kangschung face of Everest in 1983, and finally the tragic efforts on the south face of Lhotse in the late 1980s). Highlighting the mid-1980s was the race to be the first to climb the fourteen 8000ers that was completed by Messner when he summited Makalu and Lhotse in the autumn of 1986. The 1980s was a very bold period that included many difficult climbs even during the cold and windy winter seasons, but with the result that many of the most talented climbers also perished.

The commercial era began in the early 1980s, when the German DAV (Deutscher Alpenverein) Summit Club under the leadership of Franz Kroell and Guenther Haerter organized the first commercial teams to Annapurna IV and Baruntse. Other groups soon followed and by the 1990s commercial Himalayan climbing was in full motion.

Ama Dablam, Cho Oyu, and Everest (which are referred to as the ACE peaks later in this book) became the prime target of commercial ventures; Ama Dablam because of its majestic splendor overlooking the Khumbu Valley, Cho Oyu being the "easiest" of the 8000m peaks, and Everest being the ultimate goal of many Himalayan mountaineers. Many of the earlier commercial outfitters, Alpine Ascents International (1990 Todd Burleson), Adventure Consultants (1990 Rob Hall & Gary Ball), Mountain Madness (1991 Scott Fischer), International Mountain Guides (IMG) (1991 Eric Simonson), Amical Alpin (1992 Ralf Dujmovits), and Himalayan Experience (1994 Russell Brice) are still operating today, although some are under new management due to climbing accidents involving the original founders (Gary Ball died on Dhaulagiri in 1993 and Rob Hall and Scott Fischer on Everest in 1996).

The Everest disaster that claimed 8 lives in 1996 did not deter interest in Everest and Himalayan climbing, but had almost the opposite effect of increasing interest to the point that now hundreds of climbers scramble to reach the summit each spring season. During the spring 2006 season, 480 climbers and high-altitude assistants reached the summit of Everest from both sides, and in the spring 2007 season over 600 summited.

The quest for the seven summits (the highest peak on each of the seven continents) for adventure climbers and the 14 8000ers for elite climbers has created a climate of "peak bagging." This along with the endless quests of "firsts" (being the first ethnic "x", the oldest or youngest "y", or overcoming obstacle "z") has added to the lure and congestion of Everest. All of this has also required some creative fund-raising efforts for those that could not afford to buy themselves a spot on a commercial expedition.

In addition to the "firsts", innovative and sometimes fatal variations became almost the norm – descents by skiing, snowboarding, and parapenting, speed ascents, a summit bivouac on Everest, etc.

The steady increase of climbing activity in Nepal was tempered by the Maoist insurgency from 1996 to 2008 that helped to divert many expeditions into the Khumbu and Annapurna regions and across the border to the Tibet while the more remote regions of Nepal experienced a serious decline, especially on the lower peaks.

The Nepalese government tried to counter this exodus by opening up over 100 new remote peaks to expeditions, but until Nepal's political stalemate is completely resolved, these peaks will be considered unsafe to approach. If and when this finally happens, a vast number of challenges will await those who truly yearn for a unique out of the way adventure.

Methodology

Analyses in this book are based on all expeditions from 1950 to 2009 to peaks officially open for mountaineering by the Nepal Ministry of Tourism plus a few other major peaks not officially open, as well as expeditions to the border peaks such as Everest, Cho Oyu, Makalu, and Kangchenjunga from the Chinese or Indian sides.

Expeditions prior to 1950 are excluded because they were few and far between and mostly originated outside of Nepal from either Tibet or Sikkim.

Expeditions to trekking peaks are excluded starting either in 1978 when the first 18 peaks were designated as such by the Nepal government, or in the year that they were subsequently added to the official list of trekking peaks. For trekking peaks, *The Himalayan Database* generally records only first ascents or unusual events such as new routes, exceptional climbs, or major accidents.

Expeditions to a few peaks entirely outside of Nepal such as Changtse and Kabru Dome are also excluded. Most attempts on those peaks were secondary goals for expeditions to another higher peak. Changtse was usually climbed (often illegally) from the North Col of Everest, and Kabru Dome was often a part of a larger Indian expedition to the Kabru massif on the Nepal-Sikkim border.

The ascent and death rates in the tables and charts are based separately on the number of members, hired personnel, or total climbers that went above base camp. In the past ascent rates often were based on the number of expeditions, and death rates were often calculated as a fraction of the number of summiters because data for the numbers of climbers venturing above base camp were not readily available until the publication of *The Himalayan Database*. By basing ascent and deaths rates on the numbers that went above base camp instead of summiter counts, we can now obtain correct rates instead of some of the wildly exaggerated rates presented in the past when some authors or web sites reported "death rates" exceeding 100%, i.e., giving a death rate of 150% for three deaths and two ascents on a peak or route.

The data in the tables throughout the book are extracted from *The Himalayan Database* using the reporting and analysis commands in the Himal program that manages the database. The data were then exported to Excel for further processing and charting. For the trend lines in the charts, 2 or 3-period moving averages or *n*-order polynomial curves are usually employed.

Yates' chi-square tests (formulated to give more accurate results for statistical significance when sample sizes are smaller) are used to calculate statistical significance of the results and those results are shown as "p-values" which indicate the probability of a given result occurring by randomly by chance. Most statisticians consider a p-value of 0.05 or smaller as being statistically significant, that is, there is less than a 5% probability that the result occurred by chance.

The data used for the analyses in this book correspond to *The Himalayan Database* data set with the 2009 Autumn-Winter Update applied to the database.

Additional Resources

Several research papers have been published that enhance the discussions in this book:

Paul G. Firth, et al., *Mortality on Mount Everest, 1921-2006: A Descriptive Study*, British Medical Journal, 11 December 2008

Raymond B. Huey, et al., *Effects of Age and Gender on Success and Death of Mountaineers on Mount Everest*, Biology Letters, 2 October 2007

Raymond B. Huey, et al., *Success and Death on Mount Everest*, American Alpine Journal, 2003

Xavier Eguskitza, et al., *Supplemental Oxygen and Mountaineering Deaths*, American Alpine Journal, 2000

They are available for download from the Himalayan Database web site at

www.himalayandatabase.com

Acknowledgements and Credits

The authors would like to thank Dr. Raymond B. Huey, Department of Biology, University of Washington, for his assistance with the statistical analyses presented in this book. His guidance and patience in reviewing our methodology has been an eye opening and a wonderful learning experience.

Comments, Corrections, and Suggestions

Comments, corrections, and suggestions are most welcome. Please send them to

hbn@himalayandatabase.com

They will be graciously considered for future editions of this book.

Climbing Activity

This chapter focuses on the climbing activity on the principle peaks in the Nepal Himalaya, those peaks officially open for mountaineering and a few additional peaks with significant activity. Expeditions to border peaks such as Everest, Cho Oyu, and Kangchenjunga are included for both sides of the Nepalese, Chinese, and Indian borders. Trekking peaks are omitted as well as peaks entirely outside of Nepal such as Changtse and Kabru Dome.

The tables and charts cover the period from 1950 through 2009 unless specified otherwise. Before 1950 there were few expeditions, almost entirely before World War II, and they were mostly from the Tibetan or Indian sides of the border.

Climbing activity is measured by the number of climbers and hired personnel that went above base camp, or advanced base camp in those cases where no technical skills are required to reach it, such as Chinese base camp at 5700m on the northwest ridge route of Cho Oyu and the normal advanced base camp at 6400m on the north side of Everest (climbing activity is measured from the traditional base camp at 5350m on the south side of Everest because all higher camps are above the dangerous and technically demanding Khumbu Icefall). The analyses examine climbing activity over time on a yearly basis, by geographic regions in Nepal, by climbing season (spring, autumn, and winter), by age and gender, and by team composition (the numbers of climbers and hired personnel per expedition).

Members of an expedition are those persons who are listed on the climbing permit and they are generally foreigners except for all-Nepalese or Chinese climbing teams. *The Himalayan Database* denotes expeditions that did not attempt to climb their objective peak and distinguishes those members that either did not reach base camp or did no climbing above base camp or advanced base camp; these groups are eliminated from the analyses.

Hired personnel are those who are paid by the expedition for their services. They may be lowland porters ferrying loads to base camp, base camp staff including liaison officers, and high-altitude assistants (usually Sherpas or Tibetans) who establish and stock higher camps, fix ropes, or serve as guides for the climbing members. Foreign guides and leaders on commercial expeditions are considered as members, not hired personnel. Hired personnel are not listed on Nepalese climbing permits, but are listed on Chinese permits, which causes some difficulty in distinguishing them from members on all-Chinese teams. *The Himalayan Database* tracks the numbers of hired personnel that went above base camp and these numbers are used in the analyses. Lowland porters and base camp staff figure only in the *Death Analysis* chapter later in this book.

Yearly Activity

Charts C-1a and C-1b show climbing activity for all peaks from 1950 to 1969 and 1970 to 2009 measured by the number of members that climbed above base camp (in **blue**).

In each of the years from 1950 to 1965, the number of members above base camp ranged from a low of 15 (1950, 1951, and 1957) up to 133 (1960), 139 (1954), and 143 (1964). The 139 count is actually inflated because one expedition led by Edmund

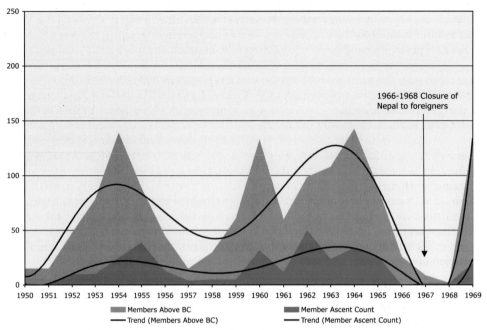

Chart C-1a: Climbing activity (members above base camp) and ascent counts
for all peaks from 1950-1969

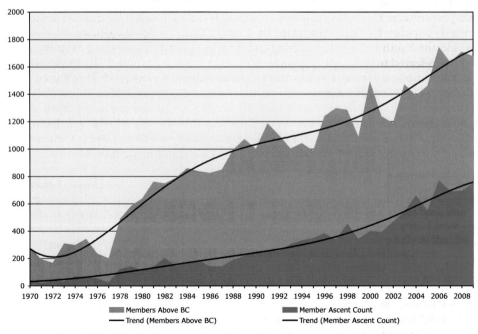

Chart C-1b: Climbing activity (members above base camp) and ascent counts
for all peaks from 1970-2009

10 Climbing Activity

Hillary attempted seven peaks in the spring of 1954 and another expedition led by the Frenchman Jean Franco attempted five peaks in the following autumn. The 133 count for 1960 is also somewhat inflated due to several teams attempting multiple peaks. If only the number of *different individuals* that went above base camp were counted, then the result would be a smoother increase from 1950 to 1964.

From 1966 to 1968, Nepal closed its peaks to foreign expeditions. Thus only the Chinese from Tibet and the Indians from Sikkim did any meaningful climbing; but a few unauthorized climbs of minor peaks were made within Nepal, often by American Peace Corps volunteers or trekking groups.

When Nepal reopened its peaks to foreigners in 1969, expeditions returned in larger numbers. In the spring of 1969 an American team led by Boyd Everett Jr. attempted Dhaulagiri with disastrous results (five members and two Sherpas were killed by an avalanche at their deposit camp). The following autumn Yuichiro Miura from Japan reconnoitered Everest in preparation for his famous "ski descent" in 1970 (which lost seven Sherpas in the Khumbu Icefall and with Miura narrowly escaping his own demise at the end of his long vertical downhill speed-run from the South Col). Miura's expedition is recounted in the book and movie, *The Man Who Skied Down Everest*.

Starting in 1978 climbing activity nearly quadrupled in the span of four years (from 203 members above base camp in 1977 to 763 in 1981). Teams from other countries including Eastern Europe now joined in with the many American, Western European, and Japanese teams already climbing in the Himalaya for several years. In addition, China opened is borders to foreign expeditions in 1979, first allowing access to Everest from the north, and then later in 1987 to Cho Oyu.

In the late 1980s-early 1990s, commercial climbing became more popular and many guided expeditions flocked to Ama Dablam, Cho Oyu, and Everest. Four routes became extremely popular: the southwest ridge on Ama Dablam, the northwest ridge on Cho Oyu, and the South Col-southeast ridge and North Col-northeast ridge on Everest, and these are referred to as the ACE commercial routes in subsequent text. In recent years, expeditions attempting these routes have exceeded the numbers on all other routes of all peaks in the Nepal Himalaya.

Charts C-2a–d show climbing activity for all peaks, the 6000ers, 7000ers, and 8000ers for all routes and for only the ACE commercial routes (in **magenta**). The difference between the two is the non-ACE climbing activity (the resulting **blue** band).

When separating out the ACE commercial routes for all peaks in Chart C-2a, there is a steady rise of non-ACE climbing into the early 1980s followed by a leveling out for the remainder of decade, then a slow decrease after the early 1990s when commercial climbing started in earnest as indicated by the narrowing of the gap between the two trend lines. The more rapid decline from 2003 onward may be result of the Maoist insurgency as the more remote areas became less attractive to foreign expeditions due to transportation hazards and increased extortion for money.

For the 6000ers, the 1980s was the most active period for climbing with a very busy year in 1982 due in part to five large expeditions to Bhrikuti (Austrian and Japanese-Nepalese), Kotang (two Indian), and Phurbi Chhyachu (Japanese), which accounted for 77 of the 231 members above base camp. Interest in the 6000ers was renewed after

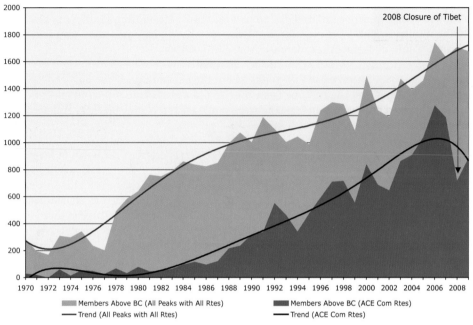

Chart C-2a: Climbing activity (members above base camp) for all peaks from 1970-2009
with Ama Dablam, Cho Oyu, and Everest commercial routes separated out

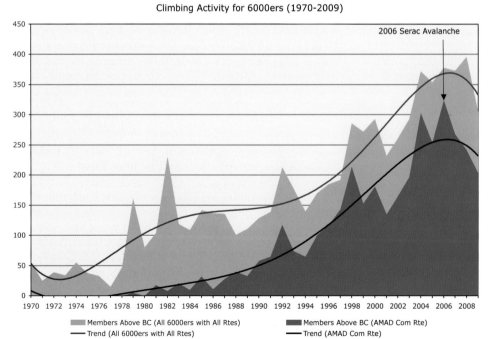

Chart C-2b: Climbing activity (members above base camp) for all 6000ers from 1970-2009
with the Ama Dablam commercial route separated out

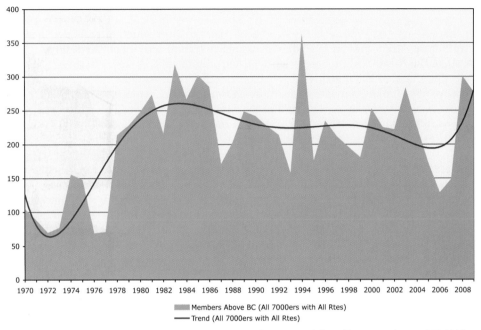

Chart C-2c: Climbing activity (members above base camp) for all 7000ers from 1970-2009
(there are no ACE commercial routes in the 7000ers)

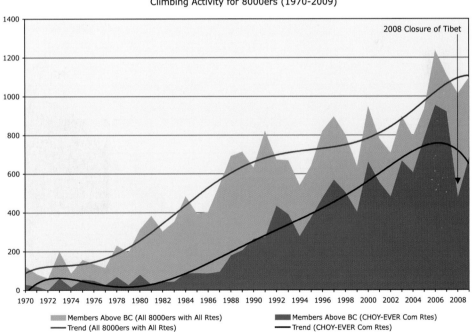

Chart C-2d: Climbing activity (members above base camp) for all 8000ers from 1970-2009
with the Everest and Cho Oyu commercial routes separated out

the Nepal government in 1997 started opening over 150 new peaks for mountaineering, many in the 6000m range.

For the 7000ers, the 1980s was the most active period, after which interest declined except for the large spike in 1994 due to: extensive Indian activity on the Kabru massif on the Nepal-Sikkim border with one expedition of 50 climbers to three Kabru peaks (for a total of 103 members above base camp), twelve expeditions to Pumori (60 above base camp), and nine expeditions to Baruntse (57 above base camp), all of which accounted for more than half of the climbers that season. There also was renewed interest in the early 2000s of some of the secondary commercial peaks such as Annapurna IV, Himlung, Pumori, and Tilicho.

For the 8000ers excluding the ACE commercial routes, the late 1980s was the most active period, after which there has been a steady decline. Only one new 8000m subpeak was added to the list of newly opened peaks, the very difficult and almost inaccessible middle summit of Lhotse (8410m), which was successfully climbed in 2001 from the South Col to the north ridge/face of Lhotse by a very talented Russian team led by Sergei Timofeev. The middle summit of Lhotse is unlikely to be climbed again unless there is an attempt to traverse the treacherous knife-edged ridge of the three Lhotse summits, Lhotse Main, Lhotse Middle, and Lhotse Shar.

Charts C-3a-c show climbing activity on Ama Dablam, Cho Oyu, and Everest.

On Ama Dablam from the mid-1970s through the 1980s, climbing activity was limited and spread out across various routes with the southwest ridge, north ridge, and south face being the most popular. However, since the early 1990s, almost all activity has

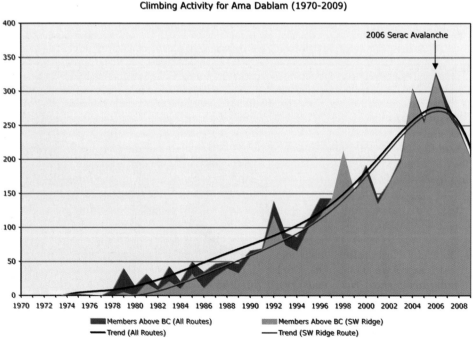

Chart C-3a: Climbing activity (members above base camp) on Ama Dablam
for all routes and the SW Ridge commercial route from 1970-2009

been on the southwest ridge route as indicated by the closeness of the two trend lines in Chart C-3a. Only a few climbers have ventured onto the northwest and northeast ridges, perhaps to escape "the crowds." In 2001 Rich Cross and the late Julian Cartwright climbed the entire length of the northwest ridge, the first time it had been done successfully. In 2006 a fatal serac avalanche discouraged many commercial operators from offering future expeditions to Ama Dablam (see the inset box, *2006 Serac Avalanche on Ama Dablam*, on pg. 107).

On Cho Oyu much of the early climbing activity was from the Gokyo Valley on the Nepal side because the original northwest ridge route climbed by the Austrian expedition in 1954 was inaccessible except for those daring few climbers who ventured illegally across the Nangpa La when Chinese border guards occasionally patrolling the area were absent. But once the northwest ridge route opened up from China in 1987, most climbers switched to this route (approaching from Tingri) as indicated by the convergence of the trend lines in Chart C-3b, because the alternative southwest ridge and south face of Cho Oyu were much too difficult and dangerous. Only three attempts have been made on the south side of Cho Oyu from the Gokyo Valley during the last ten years (two teams from South Korea in 2000 and a Slovenian team in 2006).

Climbing Cho Oyu from Tibet has in general been successful, but occasional incidents have upset the tranquility (see the inset box, *Gunfire on Nangpa La*, on pg. 22).

The early expeditions to Everest went for the traditional South Col and North Col routes, but then in the 1980s much of the activity ventured away from these two routes to the more challenging southwest face, north face, and west ridge routes as shown by the widening gap in the trend lines in Chart C-3c. The larger, more nationalistic teams

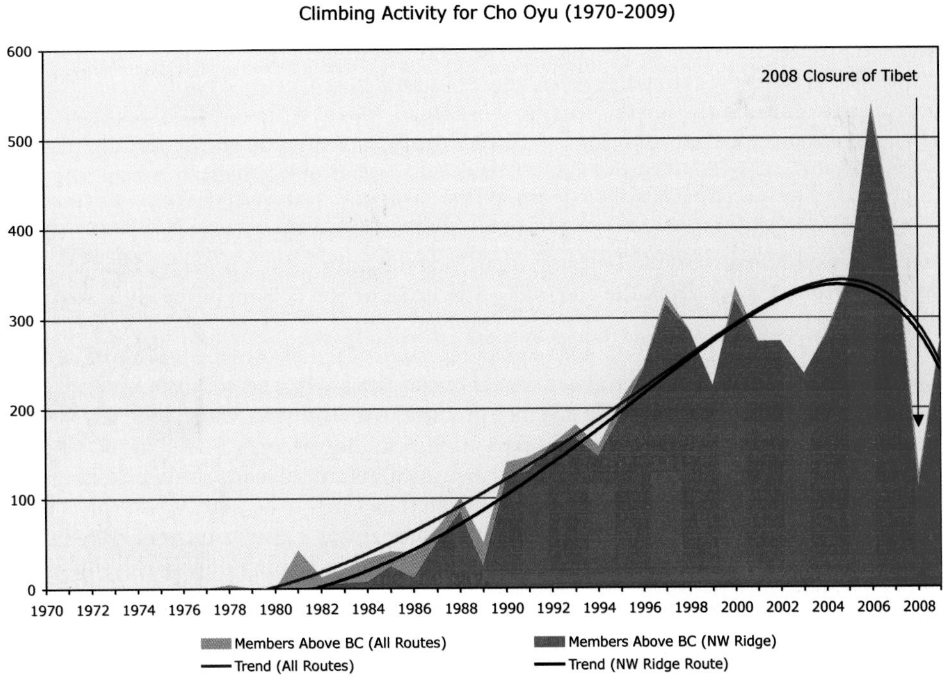

Climbing Activity for Cho Oyu (1970-2009)

Legend: Members Above BC (All Routes) — Members Above BC (NW Ridge) — Trend (All Routes) — Trend (NW Ridge Route)

Chart C-3b: Climbing activity (members above base camp) on Cho Oyu for all routes and the NW Ridge commercial route from 1970-2009

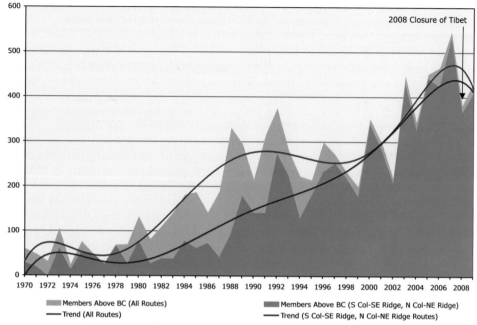

Chart C-3c: Climbing activity (members above base camp) on Everest
for all routes and the S Col-SE Ridge and N Col-NE Ridge commercial routes from 1970-2009

had already succeeded via the traditional South Col route and smaller alpine-style teams of elite climbers looking for more difficult challenges were now replacing them. In fact during the late 1980s, these other routes had slightly more activity than the traditional routes as this was just before commercial climbing became popular. But by the late 1990s, these other routes were almost abandoned. Currently only occasional attempts are made on the north face and west ridge, two of which ended disastrously during snowboard/ski descents (Marco Siffredi disappeared while snowboarding down the Hornbein Couloir in 2002 and skier Tomas Olsson fell to his death after pulling out an anchor in the Great Couloir in 2006). The east side is currently almost entirely ignored due to the difficult and dangerous ice seracs on the Kangschung face. The only remaining unclimbed route is "fantasy ridge," a steep knife-edged icy ridge that joins into the northeast ridge from the east side of Everest at the bottom of the Kangschung Glacier.

Chart C-3d compares the climbing activity between the north and south commercial routes of Everest after the opening of Tibet in 1980 to foreigners. After 1996, the north side became more popular due in part to the smaller permits fees charged by the Chinese government and the increased number of commercial operators sponsoring expeditions to the north. But this dramatically changed in spring 2008 when the Chinese closed Everest to make way for the Olympic Torch expedition that carried the torch to the summit to promote the Olympic games held in Beijing during the summer of 2008. Coincidental political unrest in Tibet extended this closure until September 2008 which affected many of the planned autumn Cho Oyu expeditions. Further unrest in spring 2009 affected both Everest and Cho Oyu expeditions that year. The result was a sharp increase in 2008-2009 of expeditions to the south side of Everest and a switch of many commercial Cho Oyu expeditions to Manaslu.

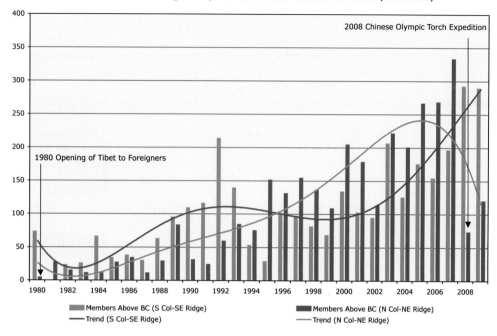

Chart C-3d: Comparison of climbing activity (average members above base camp) between the S Col-SE Ridge and N Col-NE Ridge commercial routes on Everest from 1970-2009

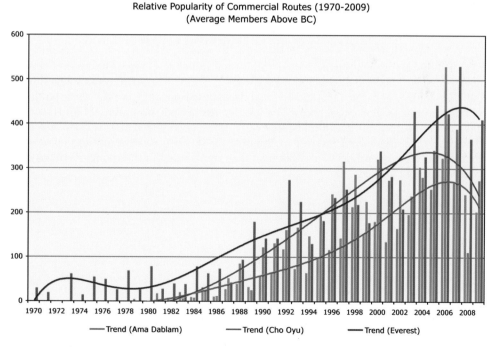

Chart C-3e: Relative climbing activity (average members above base camp) for the commercial routes on Ama Dablam, Cho Oyu, and Everest from 1970-2009

Chart C-3e shows the steady increase in popularity of the commercial routes (and commercial climbing) on Ama Dablam, Cho Oyu, and Everest. From 1997 to 2004, the activity on Cho Oyu leveled off, perhaps indicating that more commercial clients were attempting Everest without having prior experience on other 8000ers such as Cho Oyu, or perhaps due to fewer novice Everesters having both the time and finances to fund two 8000m expeditions and instead were training on less expensive peaks such as Aconcagua or Denali (or skipping high-altitude training altogether). From 2005 Cho Oyu activity again increased sharply until the 2008 closure of Tibet.

Table C-4 summarizes the current trends in climbing activity since the commercial period began in 1990. The compound annual growth rate of climbing activity from 1990 to 2009 for all peaks is 2.7%, but when the ACE commercial routes are removed, the annual growth rate is only 0.8%. Ama Dablam has shown the largest increase in activity with a 6.8% annual growth rate. Cho Oyu and Everest are not far behind, with 4.3% and 5.8% annual growth rates, respectively. Most everything else has shown very low annual growth rates.

	Members Above BC		Compound Annual Growth Rate
	1990	2009	
All Peaks	1004	1679	2.7
All Peaks w/o AMAD-CHOY-EVER Commercial Routes	682	792	0.8
6000ers	129	304	4.6
6000ers w/o AMAD Commercial Route	71	101	1.9
7000ers	242	277	0.7
8000ers	633	1098	2.9
8000ers w/o CHOY-EVER Commercial Routes	369	414	0.6
AMAD Commercial Route (SW Ridge)	58	203	6.8
CHOY Commercial Route (NW Ridge)	122	273	4.3
EVER Commercial Routes (S Col-SE Ridge, N Col-NE Ridge)	142	411	5.8

**Table C-4: Current trends in climbing activity from 1990-2009
(compound annual growth rate of members above base camp)**

Charts C-5a-f show climbing activity on all routes and on the standard routes of the other Nepalese 8000ers: Kangchenjunga, Makalu, Lhotse, Manaslu, Annapurna I, and Dhaulagiri I. For Cho Oyu and Everest, the standard routes are the same as the commercial routes illustrated above. During the last decade, most activity for the other 8000ers has been on the standard routes; only Annapurna I continues to show much divergence. Perhaps recent interest in climbing all fourteen 8000ers and the increase of commercial activity on Lhotse and Manaslu has contributed to the rising popularity of standard route climbing.

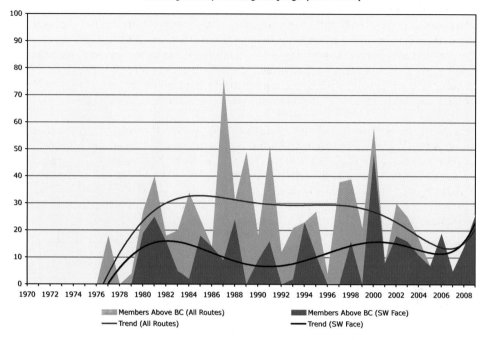

**Chart C-5a: Climbing activity (members above base camp) on Kangchenjunga
for all routes and the SW Face standard route from 1970-2009**

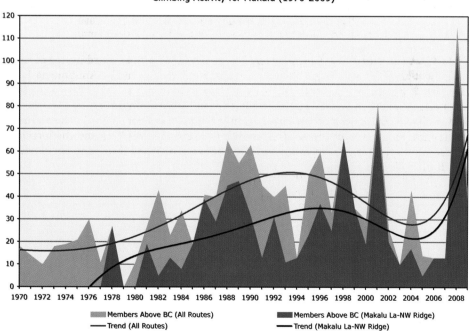

**Chart C-5b: Climbing activity (members above base camp) on Makalu
for all routes and the Makalu La-NW Ridge standard route from 1970-2009**

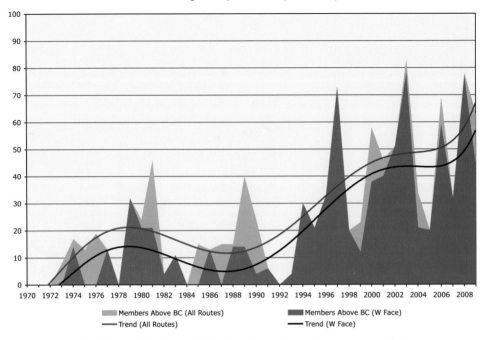

Climbing Activity for Lhotse (1970-2009)

Members Above BC (All Routes)   Members Above BC (W Face)
Trend (All Routes)   Trend (W Face)

**Chart C-5c: Climbing activity (members above base camp) on Lhotse
for all routes and the W Face standard route from 1970-2009**

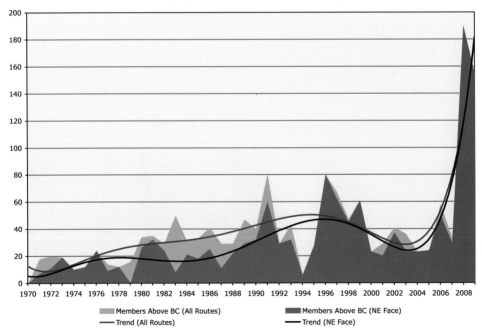

Climbing Activity for Manaslu (1970-2009)

Members Above BC (All Routes)   Members Above BC (NE Face)
Trend (All Routes)   Trend (NE Face)

**Chart C-5d: Climbing activity (members above base camp) on Manaslu
for all routes and the NE Face standard route from 1970-2009**

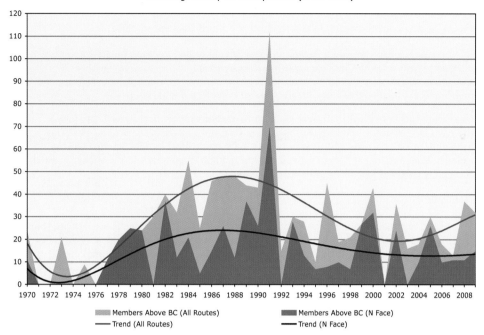

Chart C-5e: Climbing activity (members above base camp) on Annapurna I for all routes and the N Face standard route from 1970-2009

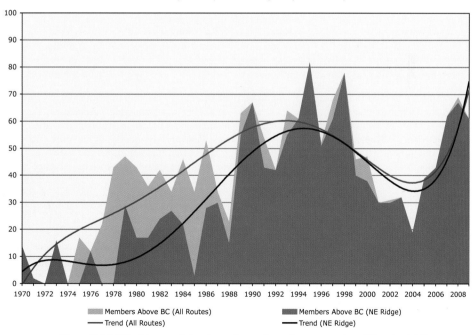

Chart C-5f: Climbing activity (members above base camp) on Dhaulagiri I for all routes and the NE Ridge standard route from 1970-2009

Gunfire on the Nangpa La

From *The Seasonal Stories* of Elizabeth Hawley – Summer-Autumn 2002

In autumn of 2002, a two-man American expedition planned to make the first ascent of Nangpa Gosum I in the Cho Oyu area, but they never got above base camp. Dave Morton and Jeff Lamoureux unexpectedly encountered three soldiers from China who had come into Nepal via the Nangpa La, a major pass between Nepal and Tibet.

The climbers had pitched their base camp at 5100m at the foot of the southeast face of their 7312m objective, and then on the 20th of September went around to its west side intending to look for a possible descent route via the north ridge. The Nangpa Gosum range is just south of the Tibet-Nepal border, if not actually on it, and the western end of Nangpa Gosum I is not far from the 5700m Nangpa La.

Suddenly they were fired on by two Chinese soldiers; it was the first incident of this kind ever to befall any mountaineers within Nepalese territory. The Americans were unharmed, but they immediately abandoned any thought of climbing. "It was scarier than any climbing I've ever done," Lamoureux said about their experience. Added Morton, "It was hard to figure out what their motive was, which made it more frightening."

Morton told how "a shot came at us and just missed us. We heard the bullet go right past our ears. ... We started running and there was another shot. We hid behind a rock and ditched our backpacks so we could run faster, then kept running. It seemed clear they were actually shooting towards us. There were about five shots total at us." The Chinese kept pursuing the Americans, who managed to escape by turning up a side glacier and hiding for several hours behind rocks. They got safely back to base camp, packed up their gear and spent the night hiking down to the nearest village, Thami.

The tents of Cho Oyu expeditions' advance base camps were on the other side of the border not far from the Nangpa La, and one of the leaders who were there at the time, Russell Brice, explained the background to the incident: three soldiers of the Chinese army, the People's Liberation Army (PLA), were searching for a group of about 20 Amdos, Tibetans from northwest Tibet. Since the Nangpa La is an important escape route for Tibetans fleeing their country, usually to passing through Nepal to join the Dalai Lama in northern India, a unit of the PLA is permanently posted close to Cho Oyu base camp on a highway.

The three soldiers found a woman lying down near the pass; she probably was a decoy, for when they went to look at her closely, they were unexpectedly attacked by Amdos, who hit them over the head with rocks and stole two of their guns before escaping across the pass into Nepal. The three soldiers, two of who were Tibetans themselves while only one was Han Chinese, chased after them the next day. The night after that the two Tibetan soldiers came back across the Nangpa La and slept in one of Brice's advance base camp tents. They had no sleeping bags, warm clothing or food.

On the third day, 15 to 20 more soldiers arrived at advance base camp looking for the same group of Amdos. Some searched the moraine, some went to the Nangpa La and returned to advance base. Three of them spent the night in Brice's tent and the rest slept in tents of a joint Japanese-Chinese women's Cho Oyu expedition. Next day the soldiers went back to their encampment near the road.

Later that morning shots were heard at advance base camp, fired by the Han Chinese soldier from the original trio who was now crawling, dragging himself through the snow and firing to attract attention. Brice, his Sherpas and some Tibetans employed as Sherpas by the women's expedition went to investigate and brought the unfortunate soldier into camp. Brice speculates that the Americans were caught in crossfire between the Amdos and the PLA.

Regional Activity

To analyze climbing activity by geographical regions, we divide the Nepal Himalaya into seven regions:

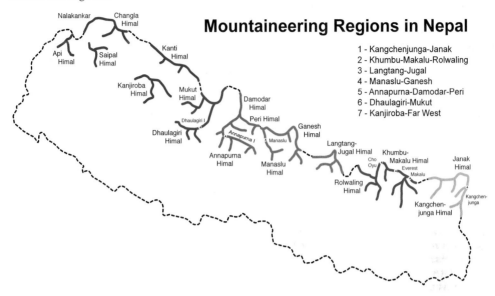

Mountaineering Regions in Nepal

1 - Kangchenjunga-Janak
2 - Khumbu-Makalu-Rowaling
3 - Langtang-Jugal
4 - Manaslu-Ganesh
5 - Annapurna-Damodar-Peri
6 - Dhaulagiri-Mukut
7 - Kanjiroba-Far West

The regional locations of all of the peaks are given in Appendix A. The weather patterns and snow conditions differ from region to region with certain regions having more favorable and safer climbing conditions depending on the season. Subsequent chapters on ascent and death analyses probe deeper into these regional differences.

Charts C-6a–g show climbing activity on a regional basis from 1970 to 2009.

During the 1960s and early 1970s, expeditions to the **Kangchenjunga-Janak** region were limited mostly to Japanese exploratory teams to the peaks northwest of the Kangchenjunga massif and to Indian expeditions to the peaks in the Kabru range along the Sikkim border south of Kangchenjunga. More teams went into the region beginning in the mid-1970s.

Two large traverse teams to the Kangchenjunga massif highlighted the 1980s. In 1984 a 26-climbing-member Japanese team led by Katsuhiko Kano traversed from the south summit to the central summit, camped for a night at 8250m and then continued on to the main summit on the next day. Their planned finish to Yalung Kang was aborted when support parties were unable to deliver oxygen and supplies to the 3-man traverse team after the main summit was attained. Separate parties also went directly to the central and main summits. This team put a total of 35 members above base camp for the three peaks (with some members climbing multiple peaks).

The four-summit traverse of the Kangchenjunga massif was completed in 1989 by a 32-person USSR team led by Eduard Myslovsky with 24 climbers, 3 film crew, and one Sherpa attaining a total of 85 summits for the four peaks. The team completed the traverse from Yalung Kang to the south summit in both directions, with two 5-member

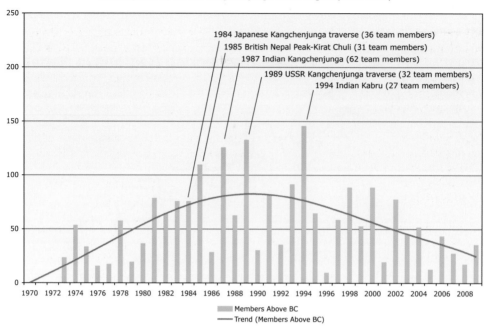

Chart C-6a: Climbing activity (members above base camp) for the
Kangchenjunga-Janak region from 1970-2009

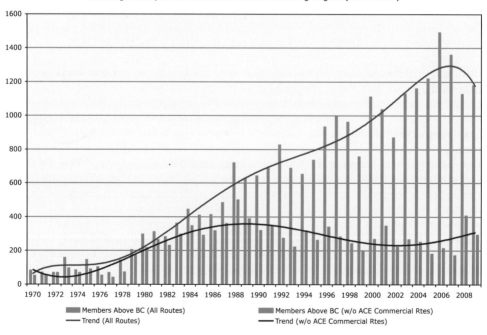

Chart C-6b: Climbing activity (members above base camp) for the
Khumbu-Makalu-Rolwaling region from 1970-2009

teams meeting at 1:20 p.m. on 1 May between the main and central summits (see the inset box, *A Contrast of Russian Styles*, on pg. 47).

Between the two traverse expeditions a very large 62-person Indian Army expedition led by Major General Prem Lal Kukrety attempted Kangchenjunga from the Sikkim side in the spring of 1987. Six climbers summited on two different days, but all three of the first group were blown off the northeast spur during descent and one member of the second group also fell to his death near the summit. This was the largest team ever to attempt Kangchenjunga.

The **Khumbu-Makalu-Rowaling** region attracted many of the earliest teams after Nepal opened up to foreigners in 1950. Everest was the primary magnet for British, Swiss, German and American teams in the 1950s and 1960s, but early British-Scottish-New Zealand teams led by Eric Shipton, Edmund Hillary, and Thomas Weir also explored many of the surrounding valleys from Rowaling to Makalu.

A dubious milestone of Khumbu activity occurred in 1973 when an Italian Everest expedition sent 56 climbers, 88 Sherpas and one helicopter above base camp. 5 members and 3 Sherpas summited and all safely returned except for the helicopter which crashed near camp 2 while ferrying supplies over the Khumbu Icefall. Pieces of the abandoned craft finally began to emerge from the base of the icefall just above base camp in 1984 after being carried down through the icefall for eleven years by the slow moving glacial tide.

Since the 1990s, the Khumbu area has had explosive growth with most of it on the commercial routes of Ama Dablam, Cho Oyu, and Everest. But when these commercial routes are subtracted out, the overall pattern is similar to the other regions with the highest activity in the 1980s, but at much larger numbers averaging between 200-400 climbers per year on the non-commercial routes. During the last few years, Khumbu has been the easiest area to travel to and the safest in terms of Maoist interference with expeditions as very few rebels operated successfully above the Lukla airstrip, the gateway into Khumbu. Generally expeditions were approached for "donations" only in the outlying Makalu and Rowaling areas.

Other than a few American expeditions to Ganchempo and Urkinmang in the 1970s, the **Langtang-Jugal** region was mostly ignored until the 1980s. This region has no 8000ers except for Shishapangma, which is entirely in Tibet and was off limits to foreigners until 1980; thus there was no strong attraction to Langtang-Jugal for the more skilled climbers seeking the highest peaks. The two most attractive peaks, Langtang Lirung (7227m) and Dorje Lhakpa (6966m), did not have their first ascents until 1978 and 1981, respectively.

In 1982, the most active year, five Japanese teams went to Langtang-Jugal. Two of those teams (16 persons to Phurbi Chhyachu and 12 persons to Langshisa Ri) were very large by normal standards for the region as most teams tended to be small private groups of climbing friends. In 1990, the Nepal Mountaineering Police also mounted a large 19-person training expedition to Ganchempo. Other than a strong autumn 1999 season, recent activity has been low. The very skilled Slovenian climber Tomaz Humar attempted to solo the south face of Langtang in October 2009, but perished after a fall that left him stranded with a broken leg and spine and little hope of rescue.

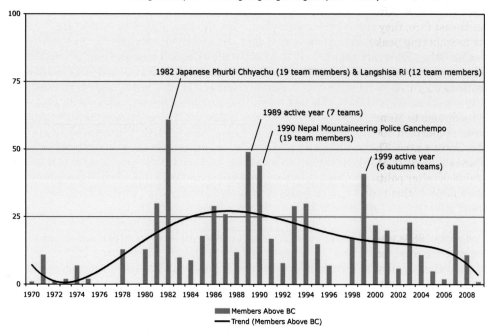

Climbing Activity for the Langtang-Jugal Region (1970-2009)

**Chart C-6c: Climbing activity (members above base camp) for the
Langtang-Jugal region from 1970-2009**

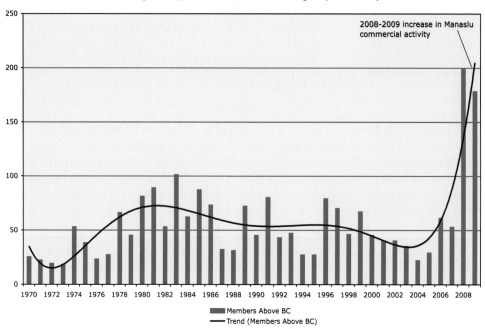

Climbing Activity for the Manaslu-Ganesh Region (1970-2009)

**Chart C-6d: Climbing activity (members above base camp) for the
Manaslu-Ganesh region from 1970-2009**

The Japanese were also very active in the **Manaslu-Ganesh** region from the 1950s to the early 1980s. After making the first ascent of Manaslu in 1956 via the now-standard northeast face, they turned their attention to the difficult west wall in 1971 and to its neighboring peaks, Peak 29 and the Himalchuli's, and then finally to the Ganesh peaks. Other European teams also mounted expeditions to Ganesh Himal in the 1980s when activity to the region was at its highest. But since then, Ganesh has fallen out of favor as only five teams have climbed there during the last twelve years (1997-2009).

Expeditions to Manaslu peak itself remained steady until 1996, as it is one of the coveted fourteen 8000m peaks, before subsiding a bit because of Maoist influence in the Gorkha area. The first teams that the Maoists began "taxing" were inbound for Manaslu in 2000. Many commercial operators began switching to Manaslu in 2008 and 2009 after political unrest in Tibet caused permission for Cho Oyu to become unreliable. If this trend continues, the northeast face of Manaslu may become the "new" popular commercial route in the future.

The early 1980s were the most active period for the **Annapurna-Damodar-Peri** region with most expeditions going to the Annapurnas and Tilicho south of the Marshyangdi Valley and Thorung La. Many of these peaks are easily accessible, provide good opportunities for small teams, and present significant challenges for more skilled climbers, especially climbing Annapurna I via the south face or by longer Roc Noir-Annapurna east summit route.

Tilicho and Annapurna IV have had limited commercial interest, but deep snow and avalanche danger have posed problems especially on the northern approach to Tilicho

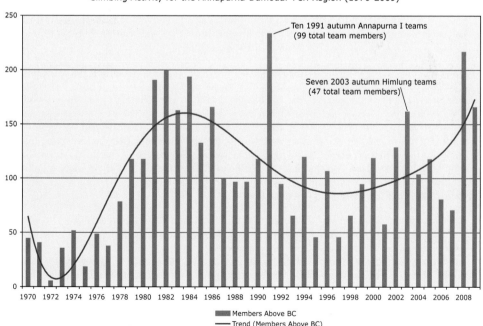

Chart C-6e: Climbing activity (members above base camp) for the Annapurna-Damodar-Peri region from 1970-2009

Api-Bobaye-Nampa Trilogy

From *The Seasonal Stories* of Elizabeth Hawley – Autumn 1996

The first ascent of Bobaye, a 6808m mountain in the far west of Nepal, was accomplished in alpine style by one member alone from a Slovenian team that set out to scale simultaneously three western peaks, all by new routes in alpine style, and they succeeded in their ambitious objective on all three; in fact, on Bobaye the soloist made the first attempt via any route. This expedition of ten climbers led by Roman Robas established a central base camp for their climbs of the three mountains, two better-known peaks, Api and Nampa, which had been successfully climbed in earlier years, as well as the virgin Bobaye. The three stand near each other in a triangle with Bobaye south of Nampa and southeast of Api. No Sherpas, no fixed ropes, no fixed camps figured in these ascents, none of which took longer than four days from depots at the feet of their mountain faces to their respective summits.

Bobaye was scaled by Tomaz Humar, who began his climb from a depot at 4300m on 1 November at 2:00 a.m. by crossing a glacier in deep snow on his hands and knees because of fear of hidden crevasses. Then he moved onto the west face and into a small diagonal couloir, where he had to hurry because its 80-degree slope was a chute for pieces of ice from a frozen waterfall. He traversed the face towards the northwest ridge; he wanted to bivouac on the ridge, but deep soft snow made his progress very slow, so at 3:00 p.m. he bivouacked on the face at 5500m in an ice cave under seracs

The next day Humar resumed his ascent at 5:30 a.m., reached the northwest ridge and crossed over onto the mixed ice and rock of the northwest face, came to a rock band with thin ice cover at 6500m, then a col (saddle) between Bobaye's middle and main summits and finally up the last 30-40 vertical meters or 150 linear meters on the north ridge from the col to the highest point at 1:00 p.m. Most of his ascent had been on terrain slanting at 60 to 90 degrees.

At the summit he had clear weather although gusts of wind were blowing snow horizontally, and it was very cold. In his descent he took a different, more direct line via the west pillar and west face, avoiding the extremely difficult northwest face, and was back in his bivouac at 4:00 p.m. This was 27-year-old Humar's first solo climb.

Nampa stands north of Bobaye. Here two other Slovenians, Matija Jost and Peter Meznar, pioneered a new route via the central couloir of its southwest face, and on 3 November they made the second ascent of the 6755m mountain on the fourth day of their assault. They began their climb from their 4200m depot at 10:00 p.m. on the 31st of October, and just above a large crevasse at 4500m they entered an ice couloir. They needed two hours to surmount the first 300 vertical meters of the 50-degree couloir, but they had to spend nine hours on the next very steep (85-degree) 400m section. At the top of the gully, at 5500m, they rested for four hours on the rocks of a ridge to the left of the top of the couloir, climbed for three hours on the ridge, then stopped again and now, at 6:00 p.m. on 1 November, made their first bivouac at 5600m and went to sleep.

Next day they started late at 10:00 a.m., continued up the ridge and bivouacked at 6300m at 6:00 p.m. Finally on 3 November they gained the summit after coming close to the west ridge and joining the route by which a Japanese team in the spring of 1972 had made the mountain's first ascent. They were at the top at 9:50 a.m., descended by the west ridge and briefly by the north face to 5800m, where they found a Japanese piton and rope, and on down to their final bivouac at 8:00 p.m. at 4800m on rock below a col on the west ridge.

Three more members of the expedition set out on 1 November for an ascent of the highest of the Slovenians' peaks, 7132m Api, which is west of Nampa, on a route that had been attempted by a British team in the autumn of 1992. (Led by Robert Brown, the five Britons had to abandon their climb because of heavy snowfall and lack of time after they had reached 6000m. The Slovenians found some of their pitons and rope.) The British called the feature they climbed the south face, but the Slovenians believe it is more accurately described as the southeast face, and they completed the British route. They were the fifth expedition to summit Api by any route.

Dusan Debelak and Janko Meglic completed their ascent of Api on the fourth day of their push up the face. Tomaz Zerovnik started out with them, but became sick during the night at their third bivouac at 6050m and was unable to make the final day's climb to the top. On their last day, 4 November, Debelak and Meglic began at 1:00 a.m., traversed beside a crevasse and moved up the snow face in very cold wind blowing the loose snow of frequent small avalanches at them, which made breathing difficult. Finally they came to rock covered by thin ice and then arrived at the western plateau and from there climbed the last 20 vertical meters (100 linear meters) to the top at 3:30 p.m. They descended the same route, moving fast in strong wind, and slept that night in the bivouac where Zerovnik had waited for them. They had crowned their expedition's plans to summit three mountains with the third success.

near Lake Tilicho where many teams have been turned back without even reaching their base camps.. The north side of Annapurna I and the Nilgiris are also difficult to approach due to the steep trails along the Mristi Khola and over the Thulobugin Pass.

After 1986 due to avalanche hazards on difficult routes, interest in the Annapurna region declined for about 10 years except for the autumn season of 1991 when ten teams went to Annapurna I (a record season for that peak). Over the last ten years, interest has again been renewed with a number of peaks opening up in the Damodar and Peri Himals north of the Marshyangdi River. In autumn 2003 seven teams went to Himlung, which is now gaining popularity for commercial climbing. Trekking parties are also venturing into the Damodar area and Saribung has become a popular target for them along its non-technical routes, both from the north and south sides.

The Japanese dominated in the **Dhaulagiri-Mukut** region during the first half of the 1970s. Their high activity in 1970 was the result of three multipeak Japanese expeditions to the Dhaulagiri 7000ers, while in 1975 six different Japanese teams climbed in the region.

By the late 1970s, other nationalities ventured into the area. In 1979, the record year for the region, 18-person Spanish and Polish teams attempted Dhaulagiri I, a 20-person Japanese team climbed three Dhaulagiri 7000ers, and a 27-person German DAV (Deutscher Alpenverein) Summit Club commercial expedition repeated the club's success on Putha Hiunchuli the previous year with a 26-person team. But since the 1970s, Dhaulagiri II, III, IV, and V have been seldomed attempted, with no attempts at all on Dhaulagiri III and IV since 1980 due to avalanche hazards.

Interest in the Dhaulagiri-Mukut region remained steady before trailing off after 2000. Most of the recent activity has been confined to Dhaulagiri I and other peaks accessible from the Kali Gandaki valley. Maoist presence has discouraged approaching through Dolpo from the west or up the Myagdi Khola from Beni.

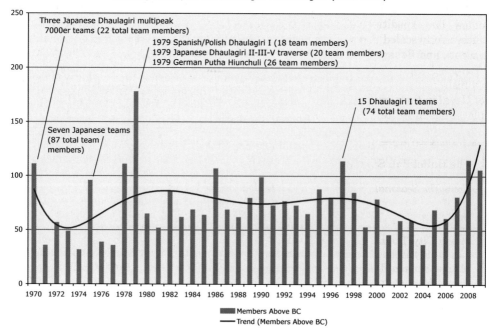

Climbing Activity for the Dhaulagiri-Mukut Region (1970-2009)

Chart C-6f: Climbing activity (members above base camp) for the Dhaulagiri-Mukut region from 1970-2009

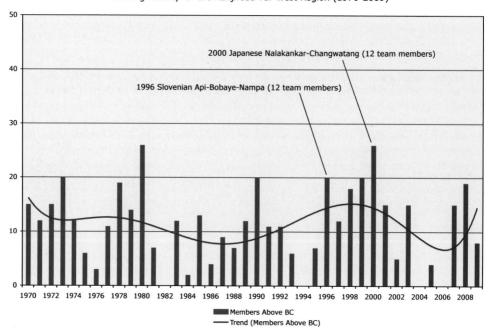

Climbing Activity for the Kanjiroba-Far West Region (1970-2009)

Chart C-6g: Climbing activity (members above base camp) for the Kanjiroba-Far West region from 1970-2009

The **Kanjiroba-Far West** region generally has experienced very low activity except in 1996 and 2000. But in both these cases, the two spikes in Chart C-6g are the result of only two expeditions. A 12-person Slovenian expedition in 1996 led by Roman Robas successfully scaled three peaks in the Api Himal: Api Main (6th ascent), Nampa (2nd ascent), and Bobaye (1st ascent solo by Tomaz Humar, see the inset box, *Api-Bobaye-Nampa Trilogy*, on pg. 28); and a 12-person Japanese expedition led by Tamotsu Ohnishi explored several peaks of the Nalakankar region in the far northwest corner of Nepal in the summer of 2000. Over the last decade Ohnishi has continued his explorations in western Nepal and has published several accounts and maps in Japan.

The Hallelujah Summit?

From *The Seasonal Stories* of Elizabeth Hawley – Autumn 1997

A planned climb that did not actually happen was an attempt on Everest from the Nepalese side by three Mexicans and a Costa Rican under the leadership of Mrs. Ana Mendez from Mexico City. Their expedition was called *Summit for Peace – Everest 1997*, and their intention was to pray at the highest point on earth for peace in the world and against poverty. As Mrs. Mendez explained, "The top of the world is a symbol of the world. By standing on the top of the world, I intercede with God for the world." She said that 50 million people around the world from a large number of Christian organizations would pray with her team as they held a brief ceremony on the summit. She acknowledged that none of the four climbing members including herself had known much about climbing one year before, so they had done some "intensive training" in Mexico and Peru.

However Mrs. Mendez never received a permit from the Nepalese authorities to set foot on Everest, and her party never moved above base camp. She claimed her Kathmandu trekking agent robbed her; the agent said she never produced the funds for the permit and instead made a concerted effort to convince officials that disasters would strike Nepal if they could not pray at the summit, and they should not be charged any fee for their vital services to the country; the tourism ministry said no permit was issued because only part of the $50,000 royalty fee was offered by a representative of the team (not the agent).

So Mrs. Mendez's group fascinated others at base camp by their unprecedented activities. One Spanish leader reported that they explained their goal was to take the devil away from the summit of Everest so that God could come to Nepal and the Hindu and Buddhist people of Nepal could be evangelized. They wrote with an ice axe on seracs near base camp "Jesus Lives," and they made an altar in the ice at which they prayed every day. Even before they reached base camp, they were praying, he said: it took them six hours to travel the final normal one hour's walk into camp because they frequently fell on their knees in prayer. They found a big hole on the way to camp, and they said this was the gateway to Hell; they prayed to God to close it. (He did not.) When they didn't receive their climbing permit, they declared that base camp was just as good a site as the summit for their purposes.

Seasonal Activity

The primary climbing seasons in the Nepal Himalaya are spring and autumn when the bulk of the expeditions come during the good-weather months from March to May and September to November. Most commercial expeditions climb during these two periods. The winter season from December to February only has had occasional activity when a few brave and hardy souls are willing to endure the cold winter winds either for the additional challenge or to avoid the prime-season crowds on the more popular peaks. The summer monsoon season from June to August has minimal climbing except for a few exploratory expeditions to the drier climates of the far western areas. The summer season is ignored in our analyses.

Charts C-7a–b show climbing activity on a seasonal basis from 1970 to 2009 for the spring and autumn seasons. Overall only the spring season shows a steady increase due to the rapid rise in spring expeditions to Ama Dablam and Everest (see Charts C-8b and C-8d). The autumn season activity has held steady since 1990 with the increase in Cho Oyu expeditions through 2007 and the switch to Manaslu since 2008 (see Charts C-8c and C-5d) offsetting the general decline in autumn expeditions to other peaks. Expeditions to non-ACE peaks are now less than half of what they were at the beginning of the 1990s.

Winter climbing as shown in Chart C-7c hits its peak in 1984 and 1985 with 18 Japanese and South Korean teams doing a variety of peaks many of which are technically quite challenging. But the big story in winter climbing for the 1980s was the Polish teams that included Jerzy Kukuczka who made the second winter ascent

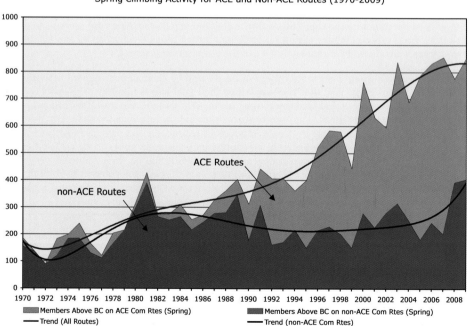

Chart C-7a: Climbing activity (members above base camp) for spring season for the ACE commercial and non-ACE commercial routes from 1970-2009

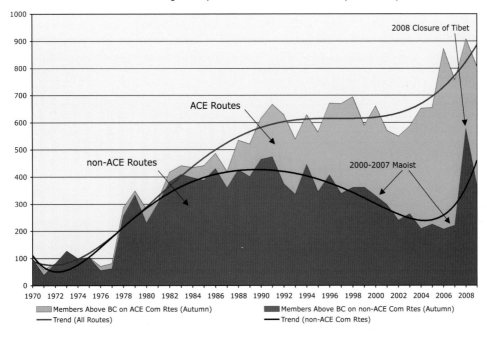

Autumn Climbing Activity for ACE and Non-ACE Routes (1970-2009)

2008 Closure of Tibet

ACE Routes

non-ACE Routes

2000-2007 Maoist

Members Above BC on ACE Com Rtes (Autumn)
Members Above BC on non-ACE Com Rtes (Autumn)
Trend (All Routes)
Trend (non-ACE Com Rtes)

Chart C-7b: Climbing activity (members above base camp) for autumn season for the ACE commercial and non-ACE commercial routes from 1970-2009

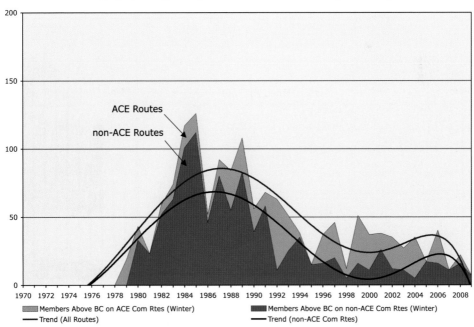

Winter Climbing Activity for ACE and Non-ACE Routes (1970-2009)

ACE Routes

non-ACE Routes

Members Above BC on ACE Com Rtes (Winter)
Members Above BC on non-ACE Com Rtes (Winter)
Trend (All Routes)
Trend (non-ACE Com Rtes)

Chart C-7c: Climbing activity (members above base camp) for winter season for the ACE commercial and non-ACE commercial routes from 1970-2009

Climbing Activity 33

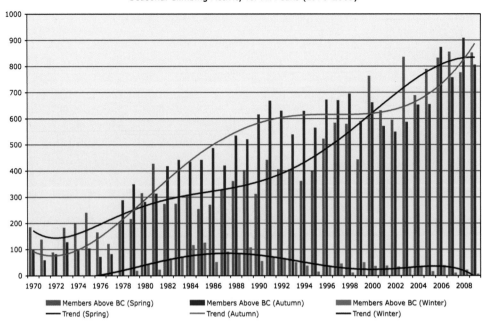

**Chart C-8a: Seasonal climbing activity (members above base camp)
for all peaks from 1970-2009**

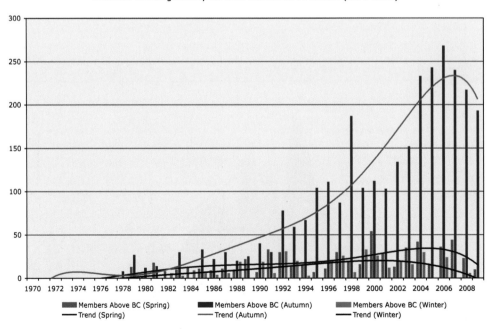

**Chart C-8b: Seasonal climbing activity (members above base camp)
for Ama Dablam (all routes) from 1970-2009**

34 Climbing Activity

Seasonal Climbing Activity for Cho Oyu on All Routes (1970-2009)

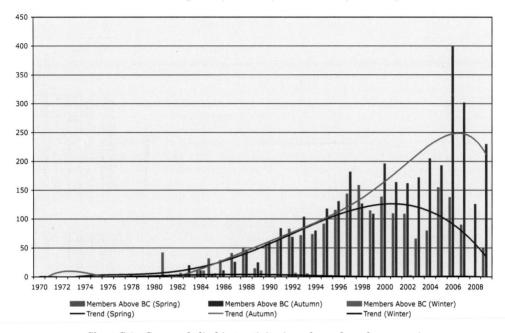

**Chart C-8c: Seasonal climbing activity (members above base camp)
for Cho Oyu (all routes) from 1970-2009**

Seasonal Climbing Activity for Everest on All Routes (1970-2009)

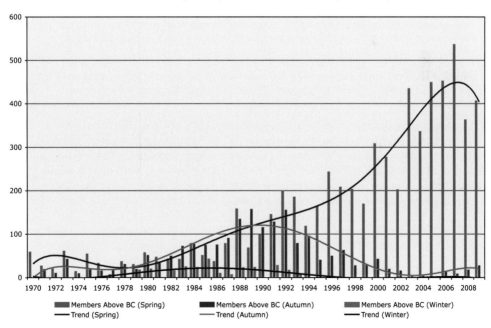

**Chart C-8d: Seasonal climbing activity (members above base camp)
for Everest (all routes) from 1970-2009**

A Bloody Confrontation

From *The Himalayan Database* notes of Elizabeth Hawley

The winter of 1989-90 featured the first battle between two expeditions, the Belgian-French and South Korean teams on Cho Oyu. The Belgian team was attempting the southeast face and had established camps and fixed lines up to 7200m. The South Korean team, originally permitted for the southwest ridge, made no attempt to climb their route, but came over to the Belgian route. The Sherpas for the Korean team used Belgian fixed ropes without asking and made their C1 at same Belgian site.

On December 18, Alain Hubert and Regis Maincent of the Belgian team went to the Korean's C1 to talk to the Koreans about sharing the route. But the Koreans they spoke to did not understand and did not agree. So the Belgians said they would next day remove their own rope and on this day (Dec 18) they cut on Korean rope at bottom of the route, which made the Koreans and their Sherpas very angry. On the 19th the Korean's Sherpas replaced the cut rope and Belgians took down their own short section of ropes, so then the Korean's Sherpas fixed entire route. On evening of the 19th (6:00 p.m.) three Koreans (including the deputy leader) and seven Korean Sherpas came over to the Belgian BC to fight. The deputy leader said to Hubert and Maincent, the only Belgian team members in BC, "I kill you" and two Koreans with sticks and two Sherpas with fists attacked Hubert and Maincent. In the hour-long fight that ensued, Maincent received a head wound that bled, and a rope was tied around his neck and his arms were pinned behind his back. He fell over and was able to free his hands from the insecure knots.

The Europeans fled in the night, hobbling away with the aid of their ski poles, leaving their own two Sherpas at camp, fearing the Koreans would return and again attack with their larger members. They reached Gokyo early in morning and then continued on down. "I never imagined such a thing could happen," said Hubert of the fight. "Mountain climbing should never turn into a battlefield."

The Korean leader, Lee Ho-Sang, denies that any Koreans took part in the fracas, but he does agree that in the hour-long fight Maincent received a head wound that bled, and that a rope was tied around Maincent's neck and his arms were pinned behind his back.

A week later Ang Lhakpa Sherpa of the Korean expedition reached the highest point of 7800m alone; he then fell 200m and a big snow avalanche immediately carried away his body. The other Sherpas refused to continue climb, and the Koreans then gave up.

---

of Dhaulagiri I in January 1985 via the northeast ridge, the first winter ascent of Cho Oyu three weeks later via the southeast pillar route, the first winter ascent of Kangchenjunga in January 1986 via the southwest face, and finally the first winter ascent of Annapurna I in February 1987 via the north face. All were done with no supplementary oxygen and minimal or no Sherpa support. A late November 1986 ascent of Manaslu was sandwiched in between these climbs.

Since the early 1990s winter climbing has declined to almost nil; now very little winter activity occurs on the ACE peaks except for a few expeditions to Ama Dablam.

Chart C-8a shows the climbing activity of these three seasons on a comparative basis. During the 1980s and 1990s the autumn season (shown in **red**) was the most popular by a wide margin, but in recent years the spring season (shown in **blue**) has equalled the autumn season boosted primarily by the large numbers attempting Everest (see Chart C-8d).

Charts C-8b-d show the seasonal patterns for Ama Dablam, Cho Oyu, and Everest. Everest has become increasingly popular in the spring while the autumn season has declined to almost nil due to more favorable spring-time weather conditions and the ability to more accurately forecast the window of opportunity for a summit attempt when the prevailing winds are shifting from the winter to the summer monsoon seasonal patterns.

Many commercial outfitters now allocate their climbing resources and guides to the spring season to meet the growing Everest demand and schedule their Ama Dablam, Cho Oyu, and Manaslu trips for the autumn season. This has led to severe crowding on the southwest ridge route on Ama Dablam as the limited campsites cannot easily accommodate the increased traffic; this is not such a severe problem on Everest, Cho Oyu, and Manaslu as the terrain is more forgiving of larger crowds.

Table C-9 gives the seasonal climbing activity by regions. As shown in Chart C-9, the eastern regions of Nepal attract more spring climbers, whereas the central and western regions attract more autumn climbers. During the Maoist insurgency, the western part of Nepal was heavily influenced by rebel control which accounts for much of the decline in non-ACE autumn climbing shown in Chart C-7b.

Region	Spring	Summer	Autumn	Winter
Kanjiroba-Far West	152	49	296	7
Dhaulagiri- Mukut	1231	22	1842	65
Annapurna-Damodar-Peri	1309	64	2739	230
Manaslu-Ganesh	1056	0	1243	98
Langtang-Jugal	284	0	372	76
Khumbu-Makalu-Rolwaling	12475	182	12112	966
Kangchenjunga-Janak	1412	0	781	63
Totals	17919	317	19385	1505

Table C-9: Members above base camp by region for all peaks from 1950-1989

Comparative Spring-Autumn Climbing Activity by Region for All Peaks from 1950-2009

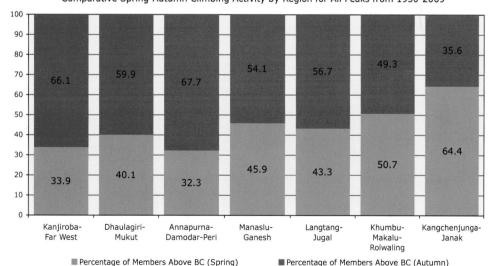

Chart C-9: Comparative spring-autumn climbing activity by region
for all peaks from 1950-2009

Activity by Age and Gender

Table C-10 and Charts C-10a-b show the average ages and age group distributions for all members and women members above base camp for all peaks from 1950 to 1989 and from 1990 to 2009 with the ACE commercial routes separated out for the latter period. For the 1950-1989 period, the majority of the climbers were in their late twenties to early thirties with a more rapid decline for those in their late thirties and older.

	All	Men	Women
1950-1989 All Peaks	32.50	32.49	32.63
1990-2009 w/o ACE Com Rtes	37.67	37.73	37.10
1990-2009 ACE Com Rtes	38.79	39.03	36.92
1990-2009 AMAD Com Rtes	38.49	38.76	36.54
1990-2009 CHOY Com Rtes	39.30	39.51	39.51
1990-2009 EVER Com Rtes	38.54	38.77	36.51

Table C-10: Average ages for members above base camp

More recently for the 1990-2009 period, the average age of climbers has both increased and spread out over a wider age range with more climbers in their forties, fifties, and older as noted by the shift of the apexes and the widening of the bell curves in the charts. This increase is even more pronounced when looking at climbers tackling the ACE commercial routes.

Women members follow a similar pattern with slightly younger average ages and a higher propensity to climb the ACE commercial routes, especially for women above the age of 30.

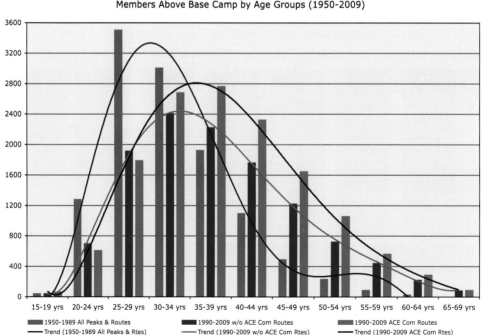

Chart C-10a: Members above base camp from 1950-1989 (all peaks & routes) and from 1990-2009 (all peaks with ACE commercial routes separated out)

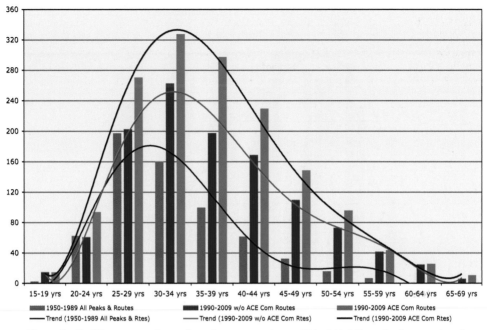

Chart C-10b: Women members above base camp from 1950-1989 (all peaks & routes) and from 1990-2009 (all peaks with ACE commercial routes separated out)

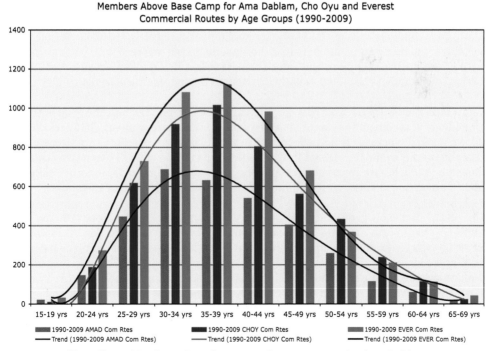

Chart C-10c: Members above base camp from 1990-2009 for Ama Dablam, Cho Oyu, and Everest commercial routes

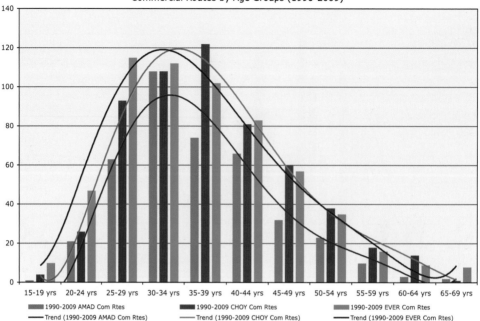

Chart C-10d: Women members above base camp from 1990-2009 for Ama Dablam, Cho Oyu, and Everest commercial routes

Charts C-10c-d show the age group distribution for all members and women members above base camp for each of the ACE commercial peaks from 1990 to 2009. For all members, the numbers of climbers and their average ages increase with peak altitude with Everest attracting more and older climbers than Cho Oyu and Ama Dablam. For women, the numbers are more equally distributed among the three peaks.

Chart C-11a shows gender activity for all peaks from 1970 to 2009 in the form of the percentage of members that went above base camp that were women. That period has shown a steady increase from under 5% to nearly 14% in the percentage of women climbing in the Himalaya, except for the spike in the spring of 1975 when two large Japanese and Chinese Everest teams put the first women, Junko Tabei (south side) and Phantog (north side), on the summit of Everest within 11 days of each other.

Charts C-11b-d show gender activity on the ACE commercial routes from 1990 to 2009. On these routes, the percentages of women above base camp on Ama Dablam and Cho Oyu generally have fluctuated in the 8% to 15% range, except for the recent 2007 spike above 20% in activity on Cho Oyu due in part to a large Croatian expedition with 18 women hoping to summit. Everest activity has been a bit more erratic. Two large Everest women's expeditions, a South Korean team led by Ji Hyun-Ok and an Indian expedition led by Bachendri Pal, sending a total of 30 women above base camp, account for the dramatic spike in 1993. The smaller spike in 2002 is a result of a drop off in number of men on commercial teams that year, not an increase in the number of women.

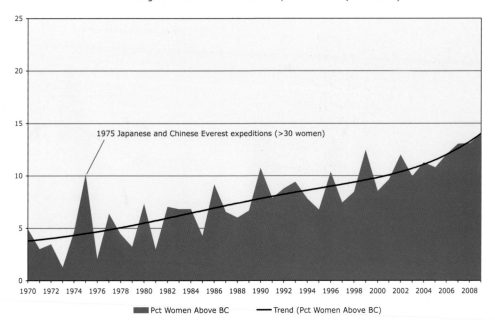

Percentage of Women Above Base Camp on All Peaks (1970-2009)

1975 Japanese and Chinese Everest expeditions (>30 women)

■ Pct Women Above BC ── Trend (Pct Women Above BC)

Chart C-11a: Percentage of women in members above base camp on expeditions for all peaks from 1970-2009

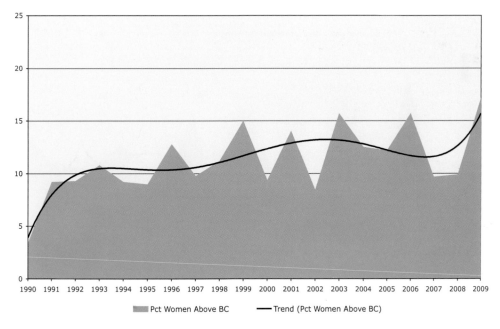

Percentage of Women Above Base Camp on Ama Dablam Commercial Rte (1990-2009)

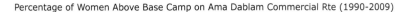

■ Pct Women Above BC ── Trend (Pct Women Above BC)

Chart C-11b: Percentage of women in members above base camp on expeditions for the Ama Dablam commercial route from 1990-2009

Percentage of Women Above Base Camp on Cho Oyu Commercial Rte (1990-2009)

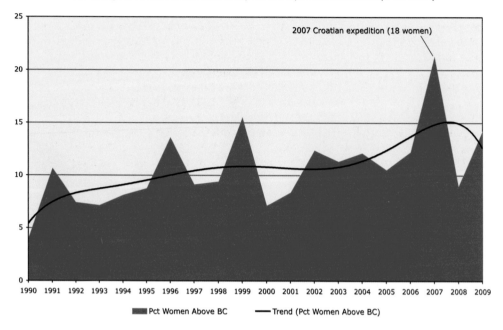

Chart C-11c: Percentage of women in members above base camp on expeditions
for the Cho Oyu commercial route from 1990-2009

Percentage of Women Above Base Camp on Everest Commercial Rtes (1990-2009)

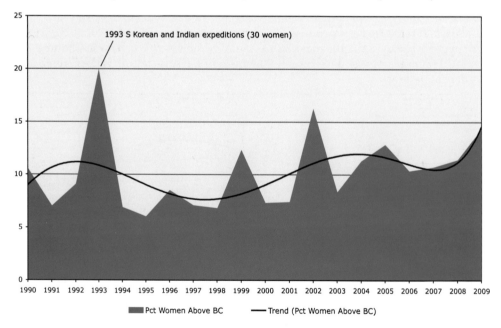

Chart C-11d: Percentage of women in members above base camp on expeditions
for the Everest commercial routes from 1990-2009

During the 1970-80s, several successful large all-women's expeditions occurred: the Japanese 1975 Everest expedition led by Eiko Hisano, the 1978 American Annapurna I expedition led by Arlene Blum, and the 1982 American Ama Dablam expedition led by Sue Giller. But by the mid-1990s, many of the more talented women climbers were beginning to climb for their own personal goals such as being the first women of a particular nationality to climb Everest or the seven summits, or to be the first woman to complete the 14 8000ers. Some of the more notable women were Wanda Rutkiewicz, Julie Tullis, Alison Hargreaves, Ginette Harrison, Chantal Mauduit, and Go Mi-Sun, all of whom perished pursuing their dreams; others are still active: Gerlinde Kaltenbrunner, Edurne Pasaban, Nevis Meroi, and Oh Eun-Sun with some newer faces on the horizon such as Kinga Baranowska. These women are becoming more in line with some of their male counterparts in terms of individual vs. team climbing.

Activity by Citizenship

Tables C-12a-b show climbing activity by citizenship for the 1950-1989 and 1990-2009 periods and for the 1990-2009 period with the ACE commercial routes separated out.

During the 1950-1989 period, Japanese climbers dominated the Nepal Himalaya by a wide margin, most likely due to the popularity of climbing in Japan and the relative closeness of the Himalaya. Many Japanese universities and towns had climbing clubs that often organized outings to Nepal especially for the sub-8000m peaks. Indian climbers although very close to Nepal tended to concentrate on their own local peaks in the Ladakh, Lahaul, Kumaon, and Garwhal areas. Many of the larger Indian expeditions to Nepal were organized and sponsored by the Indian military services.

Since 1990 climbers from other countries have surpassed the Japanese in numbers. On the ACE commercial routes, the Americans and the British are the most numerous, wheras the French and Japanese dominate the non-ACE routes. Several French commercial companies have organized trips to peaks such as Baruntse, Himlung, and other smaller peaks in the Damodar Himal north of Annapurna. Japanese climbing clubs still remain active and often send groups to Nepal, especially into the Khumbu and Rolwaling areas.

All Peaks 1950-1989					All Peaks 1990-2009				
Country	Mbrs	Pct	Women	Pct	Country	Mbrs	Pct	Women	Pct
Japan	2900	22.6	126	17.8	USA	3026	11.5	316	11.5
France	1044	8.1	109	15.4	France	2164	8.2	352	12.8
USA	1011	7.9	110	15.5	UK	2142	8.2	189	6.9
UK	922	7.2	36	5.1	Japan	1906	7.3	247	9.0
S Korea	667	5.2	16	2.3	Spain	1893	7.2	143	5.2
Spain	648	5.0	25	3.5	Germany	1563	5.9	184	6.7
W Germany	643	5.0	43	6.1	S Korea	1550	5.9	90	3.3
Italy	640	5.0	24	3.4	Italy	1368	5.2	98	3.6
Poland	563	4.4	38	5.4	Switzerland	1062	4.0	141	5.1
Switzerland	558	4.3	41	5.8	Austria	924	3.5	109	4.0
Austria	466	3.6	9	1.3	Russia	728	2.8	36	1.3
India	404	3.1	20	2.8	India	681	2.6	55	2.0
Yugoslavia	360	2.8	13	1.8	Australia	618	2.4	72	2.6
Czechoslovakia	267	2.1	17	2.4	Canada	541	2.1	57	2.1
All Countries	12853		709		All Countries	26273		2749	

Table C-12a: Members and women above base camp by citizenship from 1950-1989 and 1990-2009 for the most active countries

ACE Commercial Routes 1990-2009					All Other Peaks and Routes 1990-2009				
Country	Mbrs	Pct	Women	Pct	Country	Mbrs	Pct	Women	Pct
USA	2207	18.2	233	19.9	France	1326	9.4	228	14.5
UK	1383	11.4	129	11.0	Japan	1269	9.0	139	8.8
Spain	983	8.1	70	6.0	Spain	910	6.4	73	4.6
France	838	6.9	124	10.6	S Korea	873	6.2	37	2.3
Germany	764	6.3	84	7.2	USA	819	5.8	83	5.3
Italy	748	6.2	54	4.6	Germany	799	5.7	100	6.3
S Korea	677	5.6	53	4.5	UK	759	5.4	60	3.8
Japan	637	5.3	108	9.2	Italy	620	4.4	44	2.8
Switzerland	524	4.3	77	6.6	Switzerland	538	3.8	64	4.1
Austria	473	3.9	52	4.4	Austria	451	3.2	57	3.6
Australia	375	3.1	43	3.7	Russia	377	2.7	17	1.1
Canada	363	3.0	43	3.7	India	353	2.5	13	0.8
Russia	351	2.9	19	1.6	Slovenia	265	1.9	8	0.5
India	328	2.7	42	3.6	Australia	243	1.7	29	1.8
All Countries	12132		1173		All Countries	14141		1576	

Table C-12b: Members and women above base camp by citizenship from 1990-2009 for the most active countries separated by ACE commercial routes and all other peaks and routes

Early on most teams were of one nationality or related nationalities. In the 1970s, a few large international teams were assembled to climb Everest, but due to their large size they tended to break down into smaller subgroups along national lines often with unfortunate interpersonal consequences (the 1971 International Everest expedition led by Norman Dhyrenfurth is a prime example where twelve different nationalities were unable to function together as one cohesive team). As smaller alpine-style groups became more prevalent, they often looked past nationality and instead looked at the compatibility, climbing resumes, and friendships of the individual members. Today most of the larger commercial expeditions are international. Still some friction can occur between teams (see the inset box, *A Bloody Confrontation*, on pg. 36).

Team Composition

Team composition is one of the first decisions that a team leader faces when organizing a Himalayan expedition: how many members should be on the team, and if hired personnel are to be used, in what capacity and in what numbers. Over the years teams have varied from solo attempts or small alpine-style attempts up to very large military-style sieges with hundreds of members, hired personnel, and overland porters. Both styles have succeeded, or failed in part due to either a lack of manpower or an excess of people creating their own logistical nightmares. This section tries to shed some light on the issues of team composition.

Charts C-13a-b illustrate the changes in team composition (the numbers of members and hired personnel above base camp) over the last 40 years. Chart C-13c shows the ratio of hired personnel to members.

For all peaks, the average team member size shows a steady decline from a high of 11 members in 1976-77 to fewer than 5 members from 2004-2005 onward. Everest shows a more dramatic decline from 34 members in 1972-73 to fewer than 5 members from 2004-2005 onward. Since 2000 Everest has followed the norm for all peaks.

For all peaks, the average numbers of hired personnel employed shows a steeper decline from a high above 8 hired per expedition in the mid-1970s to about 2.5 hired

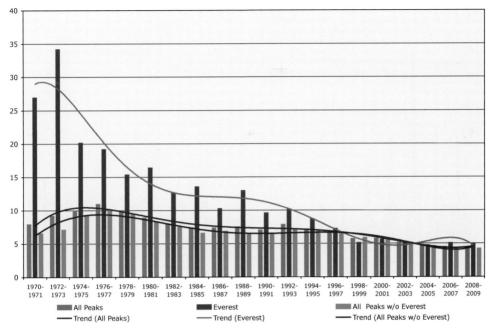

Chart C-13a: Average expedition team sizes (members above base camp) from 1970-2009

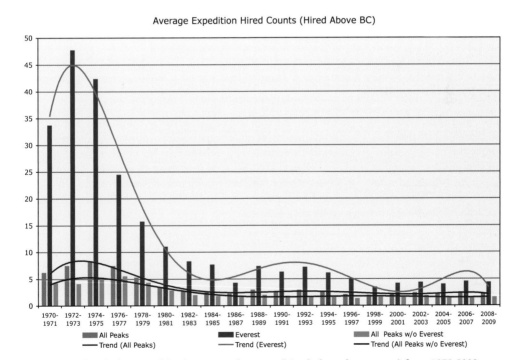

Chart C-13b: Average hired personnel counts (hired above base camp) from 1970-2009

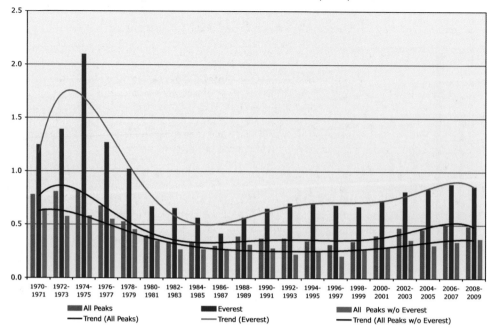

Average Ratios of Hired to Members Above BC per Expedition

Chart C-13c: Average ratios of hired to members above base camp from 1970-2009

per expedition by the early 1980s. For Everest a more dramatic decline has occurred from nearly 50 per expedition in the early 1970s to fewer than 10 per expedition after 1980 and a further decline to fewer than 5 per expedition by the mid-1990s.

The ratio of hired personnel to members for all peaks was the highest in 1973-1974 at nearly 2.5 hired for every member and dropped to it lowest of about .3 hired for every member in the mid-1980s.

The ratio of hired to members for Everest was above 2.0 in 1974-75 and dropped to .4 in 1986-87, but then has been on a steady increase mostly likely due to the increased employment of Sherpas or Tibetans by commercial expeditions for client safety. Often on summit day, many commercial clients are assigned their own Sherpa or Tibetan assistant for added safety, whereas others may have designated assistants for the entire climb. Team composition is further discussed in the following chapters with regards to climbing success and fatality issues.

A Contrast of Russian Styles

From *The Seasonal Stories* of Elizabeth Hawley – Spring 1989 and Spring 1994

The most dramatic first ascent on a first attempt by a given nationality in the spring of 1989 was certainly the Soviet conquest of all the peaks of Kangchenjunga in a remarkable display of effective logistical planning of a complex mountaineering undertaking, combined with good luck with the weather over an extended period of time and with excellent performance at very high altitudes by a very strong climbing team. The expedition's leader and 1982 conqueror of Everest, Eduard Myslovsky, was in charge of 32 Soviet men and 17 climbing Sherpas supplied with about three tons of food, fuel, tents, oxygen bottles, rope, batteries and all the rest of the gear that 600 porters carried for them to base camp.

Kangchenjunga's main axis is from north to south with the highest of its summits, 8586m, at the northern end; it also extends westward from this main summit to its second-highest peak, the west summit (8505m) that is also known as Yalung Kang. The expedition's principal goal was to send climbers from the west summit to the main (north) summit and thence along the summit ridge southward via the central peak (8482m) to the south summit, which at 8476m is the lowest of the four principal peaks, while at the same time another group would be making their own traverse from south to central to north summits and finally to the western one.

First the team methodically made their route up the southwest side of the mountain and set up two camps along the way to the plateau known as the Great Shelf at an altitude of 7250m, where they placed their advance base camp. From here they then proceeded to make three higher routes: one towards the col (saddle) between the west and main summits, another towards the col between the main and central summits, and the third up a rib to the west face of the south summit. Along each of these three higher routes they pitched two camps, making a total of six camps above the Great Shelf, and the camps were stocked with supplies of food, fuel, oxygen and other items for the final summit assaults. The three very highest camps were set at altitudes of 8200-8250m.

It was only after all these routes and camps had been put in place that permission was given for the first summit assault. Exactly one month after base camp at 5350m had been occupied on 9 March, four Soviet mountaineers stood on atop the main summit, the first Soviet men ever to scale any Kangchenjunga peak. Their conquest on 9 April was followed by two other summit parties of four men each to the central and south summits on 15 April, eight other members to the main summit on the 16th, four others to the south summit on the 17th, and on the 29th the central and west summits were scaled by three men who went to both these peaks and by two others to the main summit only.

The stage was now set for the climax of the whole effort: on 30 April a five-member team consisting of Anatoli Boukreev, Sergei Bershov, Evgeni Vinogradski, Alexander Pogorelov and Mikhail Turkevich, set out from the 5th camp on the route between the west and main summits to begin a traverse of the four peaks that would be completed next day, May Day, at the south summit and down through its camps 5 and 4, disassembling these camps as they went, and finishing at 7:00 that evening in camp 3 on the Great Shelf. Meanwhile also on 1 May another traverse team of five members, Grigori Luniakov, Vladimir Koroteev, Vasili Elagin, Vladimir Balyberdin and Zijnur Khalitov, set out from the south camp 5 and headed north; their traverse would end on 2 May on the west summit, Yalung Kang, and down its high route to the Great Shelf. The two traverse teams had crossed paths at 2:10 p.m. on May Day while they were on the summit ridge between the central and south peaks

The route of the Soviets' traverses followed the summit ridges the entire distance between the main summit and the south one, but between the west peak (Yalung Kang) and the main (north) summit, climbers left the top ridge at the col between them and descended the face to sleep at the western camp 5 at about 8200m before climbing up again to complete their ascents of all four of the summits.

The May Day traverses were clearly the high point of the entire climb. But the effort was not completely over, for as a sort of unplanned encore, on 3 May three more mountaineers, two Soviets and a Nepalese Sherpa, went to the main summit, the expedition's 26th to 28th climbers to gain that peak. Then that really was the end.

The expedition's accomplishments, in summary, were:

- They made the first traverse of all four summits, and furthermore a total of ten climbers for the first time made two simultaneous traverses in opposite directions.
- The two traverse teams followed the summit ridges most of the distance. This was in contrast to the only previous traverse of Kangchenjunga in the spring of 1984, when 30 Japanese, aided by 31 climbing Sherpas, sent two Japanese from south to central to main summits, but did not keep to the top ridge between the central and main peaks, and made no attempt to scale Yalung Kang.
- Six Soviet members scaled the main summit twice.
- New route variations were pioneered.
- A number of the 85 individual summit successes – but none of the traverses – were achieved without the use of bottled oxygen.

The spring 1994 Russian Ama Dablam team was led by Vladimir Bachkirov, who had conquered Annapurna I in 1991 and Everest in 1993 on more sizable expeditions and via known routes. Now he and his three compatriots, Sergei Bogomolov, Dima Botov, and Sergei Golubtsov, achieved the first Russian ascent of Ama Dablam in one continuous ascent with no fixed camps. After acclimatizing to 6000m on the south side for six days and returning to Pangboche for a rest, on 21 April they placed a base camp on the Nare Glacier and climbed the southeast face (to the right of the eastern of two ridges that run south from the summit) onto the southeast (or east-southeast) ridge. They had to make altogether six bivouacs as they moved up because the route was steep (average 50 degrees, sometimes vertical). There were many rock towers, and they could climb only for three or fours each morning before clouds rolled in and snow began to fall, limiting visibility to 20 meters ("it was necessary to see where to go"). Their bivouacs were on narrow ice ledges, on a steep ice slope, and in a snow cave, and they were held up for two days at their last 6700m bivouac due to bad weather. After spending two hours on the summit on 28 April, from where they could see from maybe Annapurna or Manaslu in the west to Kangchenjunga in the east, they descended 200 meters into the fog and emerged onto the glacier below on 29 April, utterly exhausted. They had little food left on descent; had only four ropes which they used only for belaying; and climbed in "pure alpine-style." The route was rather difficult especially where there were unstable seracs or very hard ice, but the main problem was the weather. There were many avalanches: only small ones on this route ("we chose the route correctly"), but big ones 100 meters to the right.

Expedition Results

Table C-14 lists the primary reasons that *expeditions* have terminated, both successfully and unsuccessfully for all peaks from 1950 to 2007. An expedition may terminate for multiple reasons, often as a result of a series of adverse events. For this analysis, only a single primary reason is assigned to each expedition. Individual members also have their own reasons for terminating their climbs; those reasons are discussed in the following section.

As shown in Tables C-14 and C-15, bad weather and bad conditions are the primary causes of expedition failure with over 26% (14.9+11.5) total for all peaks in all seasons.

Winter as expected was the most difficult for climbing with over a 34% (23.8+10.4) failure rate, while spring was the most favorable for climbing with only a 22.5% (15.0+7.5) failure rate. All other causes for expedition failure total approximately 19%. Within that group, accidents average in the 3-4% range while route difficulties and lack of team strength are in the 5% range.

Bad weather and bad conditions are more prevalent in the central Nepal regions of Dhaulagiri, Annapurna, and Manaslu with Manaslu being the worst especially in the autumn seasons. The accident rates are also higher for the Manaslu-Ganesh region due to avalanching after the heavy snows of the summer monsoon season as shown in Table C-15. If avalanche accidents were included with bad conditions, the Manaslu autumn rate of 39.7% would be even higher.

Periodically, massive storms fueled by large cyclones in the Bay of Bengal strike Bangladesh and then move up into the Himalaya and cause havoc with expeditions. One such storm that occurred is described in the inset box, *The Epic Storm of November 1995*, at the end of this chapter on pg. 53.

Reason for Expedition Termination	All Seasons		Spring		Autumn		Winter	
	Cnt	Pct	Cnt	Pct	Cnt	Pct	Cnt	Pct
Success (Main Peak)	3478	54.7	1662	57.8	1671	52.9	116	44.6
Partial Success (Attained Subpeak only)	74	1.2	27	0.9	45	1.4	2	0.8
Unrecognized Success Claim	18	0.3	9	0.3	8	0.3	1	0.4
Bad Weather (Storms, High Winds)	948	14.9	431	15.0	447	14.2	62	23.8
Bad Conditions (Deep Snow, Avalanches)	733	11.5	217	7.5	471	14.9	27	10.4
Accident (Death or Serious Injury)	209	3.3	83	2.9	113	3.6	12	4.6
Illness, AMS, Exhaustion, or Frostbite	276	4.3	151	5.2	116	3.7	8	3.1
Lack of Supplies or Equipment	138	2.2	69	2.4	57	1.8	12	4.6
Lack of Time	71	1.1	32	1.1	36	1.1	3	1.2
Route Too Difficult, Lack of Strength	325	5.1	141	4.9	163	5.2	17	6.5
Did not reach BC	0	0.0	0	0.0	0	0.0	0	0.0
Did not attempt climb	0	0.0	0	0.0	0	0.0	0	0.0
Attempt rumored	0	0.0	0	0.0	0	0.0	0	0.0
Other	86	1.4	55	1.9	30	1.0	0	0.0
Totals	6356	100.0	2877	100.0	3157	100.0	260	100.0

Table C-14: Reasons of expedition termination for all peaks from 1950-2009
(most common reasons shown in red)

For seasonal differences in success rates, the probability of success in winter at 44.6 is significantly lower than in spring and autumn seasons ($p=.0001$).

For seasonal differences in failure rates, bad weather (storms, high winds) occurring in the winter season (23.8) and bad conditions (deep snow, avalanching) occurring in the autumn season (14.9) are significantly higher than the other seasons ($p=.0002$ and $p=<.0001$, respectively). Winter is the time of cold, high winds coming down from the Tibetan plateau and autumn is more prone to avalanching from the snow pack built up by late monsoon storms.

The seasonal differences in failure rates for the other causes of termination generally are not significant.

100% − %success − %bad weather − %bad conditions = %all other causes

All Seasons $100.0 - 54.7 - 14.9 - 11.5 = 18.9$
Spring $100.0 - 57.8 - 15.0 - 07.5 = 19.7$
Autumn $100.0 - 52.9 - 14.2 - 14.9 = 18.0$
Winter $100.0 - 44.6 - 23.8 - 10.4 = 21.2$

	Bad Weather		Bad Conditions		Bad Weather & Conditions Combined		Accidents		Route & Strength Difficulties		Success	
	Cnt	Pct	Cnt	Pct	Cnt	Pct	Cnt	Pct	Cnt	Pct	Cnt	Pct
All Peaks, All Seasons	948	14.9	733	11.5	1681	26.4	209	3.3	325	5.1	3478	54.7
All Peaks, Spring	431	15.0	217	7.5	648	22.5	83	2.9	141	4.9	1662	57.8
All Peaks, Autumn	447	14.2	471	14.9	918	29.1	113	3.6	163	5.2	1671	52.9
All Peaks, Winter	62	23.8	27	10.4	89	34.2	12	4.6	17	6.5	116	44.6
Regions, All Seasons												
Kanjiroba-Far West	7	7.5	14	15.1	21	22.6	3	3.2	11	11.8	45	48.4
Dhaulagiri-Mukut	67	13.3	93	18.5	160	31.9	22	4.4	27	5.4	248	49.4
Annapurna-Damo-Peri	101	15.3	132	20.0	233	35.3	43	6.5	45	6.8	285	43.2
Manaslu-Ganesh	86	22.3	62	16.1	148	38.3	26	6.7	23	6.0	147	38.1
Langtang-Jugal	10	7.3	16	11.7	26	19.0	10	7.3	22	16.1	64	46.7
Khumbu-Maka-Rolw	633	14.8	378	8.8	1011	23.6	93	2.2	171	4.0	2542	59.5
Kangchenjunga-Janak	44	14.5	38	12.5	82	27.1	12	4.0	26	8.6	147	48.5
Regions, Spr/Aut												
Kanjiroba, Spring	2	7.4	4	14.8	6	22.2	2	7.4	5	18.5	8	29.6
Kanjiroba, Autumn	5	9.3	10	18.5	15	27.8	1	1.9	4	7.4	28	51.9
Dhaulagiri, Spring	27	13.0	31	14.9	58	27.9	14	6.7	13	6.3	108	51.9
Dhaulagiri, Autumn	38	13.8	61	22.1	99	35.9	7	2.5	13	4.7	129	46.7
Annapurna, Spring	26	12.8	35	17.2	61	30.0	13	6.4	10	4.9	103	50.7
Annapurna, Autumn	63	15.7	87	21.6	150	37.3	29	7.2	26	6.5	164	40.8
Manaslu, Spring	39	23.2	21	12.5	60	35.7	9	5.4	10	6.0	73	43.5
Manaslu, Autumn	39	19.6	40	20.1	79	39.7	16	8.0	11	5.5	69	34.7
Langtang, Spring	5	9.4	4	7.5	9	17.0	4	7.5	9	17.0	28	52.8
Langtang, Autumn	4	5.8	11	15.9	15	21.7	5	7.2	11	15.9	28	40.6
Khumbu, Spring	309	15.0	112	5.5	421	20.5	38	1.8	80	3.9	1249	60.8
Khumbu, Autumn	279	13.8	235	11.6	514	25.4	47	2.3	86	4.2	1203	59.4
Kangchenjunga, Spr	23	14.1	10	6.1	33	20.2	10	6.1	14	8.6	93	57.1
Kangchenjunga, Aut	19	14.4	27	20.5	46	34.8	27	20.5	12	9.1	50	37.9

Table C-15: Reasons of expedition termination by season from 1950-2009

Individual Climber Results

Table C-16 gives the reasons and explanations for *individual climber* terminations. Often individuals will terminate their climbs for a combination of reasons. For our analysis, only the primary reason is used. This section analyses those members that went above *base* camp, and those members that went above *high* camp on a summit bid. Members that did not reach base camp or stayed at base camp are not included in these analyses; hired personnel are also excluded.

Table C-17 lists the reasons that individual climbers have terminated above *base* camp, both successfully and unsuccessfully, for all peaks from 1990 to 2009 (*The Himalayan Database* has the most complete data for this period).

Chart C-17 shows the termination rates for *unsuccessful* members above *base* camp for all peaks from 1990 to 2009. Bad weather and bad conditions cause the most problems in spring and autumn, while route difficulty is an additional factor in winter, which perhaps accounts for the drop-off in the winter success rate as the routes become more difficult due to hard-ice conditions.

Table C-18 narrows the above list of reasons to those individual climbers that terminated on a summit bid above *high* camp, both successfully and unsuccessfully.

Chart C-18 shows the termination rates for *unsuccessful* members above *high* camp. Bad weather and bad conditions continue to dominate along with the added factors of exhaustion and frostbite/coldness and in winter slower climbing speeds and later morning starts due to extreme coldness.

Reason	Definition
Success	Success on main peak
Subpeak	Success on subpeak
Bad Weather	Storms, high winds
Bad Conditions	Deep snow, avalanching or avalanche danger, falling rock or Ice
Accident	Death or injury to self or others
Altitude/AMS	AMS symptoms, difficultly breathing or other altitude issues
Exhaustion	Exhaustion, fatigue, weakness or lack of motivation
Frostbite/Cold	Frostbite, snowblindness or coldness
Other Illnesses	Non-AMS illnesses (coughs, flu, diarrhea, minor injuries or pains, etc.)
Lack of Supplies	Lack of supplies/support or equipment problems
O2 System	O2 system failure
Too Difficult	Route difficulty, intimidation or insufficient ability
Too Late/Slow	Too late in day or climbing too slow
Assisting Others	Assisting, guiding, supporting or accompanying others
Rte Preparation	Route/camp preparation or fixing rope
Lack of Time	Insufficient time left for expedition
No Climb/Intent	Did not climb or intend to summit
Other	Other (left early for family emergencies, disagreements, etc.)
Unknown	Reason unknown
Unspecified	Unspecified failure (insufficient information available about member)

Table C-16: Reasons for termination of individual members

Above Base Camp Termination Reason	All Seasons		Spring		Autumn		Winter	
	Cnt	Pct	Cnt	Pct	Cnt	Pct	Cnt	Pct
Success	9201	35.0	4239	35.1	4693	35.3	197	27.9
Subpeak	119	0.5	46	0.4	73	0.5	0	0.0
Bad Weather	2740	10.4	1283	10.6	1335	10.0	96	13.6
Bad Conditions	2317	8.8	665	5.5	1554	11.7	64	9.1
Accident	482	1.8	166	1.4	298	2.2	18	2.5
Altitude/AMS	759	2.9	342	2.8	387	2.9	20	2.8
Exhaustion	1203	4.6	575	4.8	593	4.5	28	4.0
Frostbite/Cold	505	1.9	249	2.1	247	1.9	9	1.3
Other Illnesses	962	3.7	500	4.1	448	3.4	11	1.6
Lack of Supplies	347	1.3	168	1.4	165	1.2	14	2.0
O2 System	86	0.3	76	0.6	10	0.1	0	0.0
Too Difficult	797	3.0	293	2.4	420	3.2	72	10.2
Too Late/Slow	348	1.3	185	1.5	144	1.1	19	2.7
Assisting Others	338	1.3	172	1.4	160	1.2	6	0.8
Rte Preparation	92	0.4	62	0.5	27	0.2	1	0.1
Lack of Time	79	0.3	32	0.3	47	0.4	0	0.0
No Climb/Intent	554	2.1	372	3.1	161	1.2	12	1.7
Other	398	1.5	201	1.7	185	1.4	10	1.4
Unknown	1160	4.4	676	5.6	452	3.4	30	4.2
Unspecified	3786	14.4	1772	14.7	1897	14.3	99	14.0
Totals	26273	100.0	12074	100.0	13296	100.0	706	100.0

Table C-17: Reasons for termination of individual members above *base* camp
for all peaks from 1990-2009

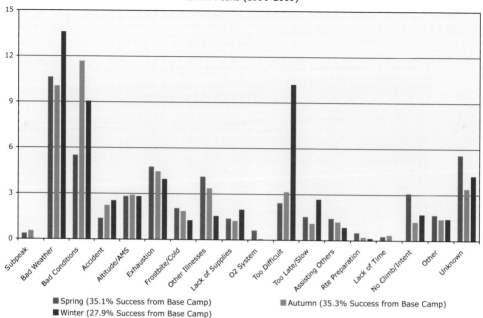

Chart C-17: Seasonal termination percentages for unsuccessful members above *base* camp
for all peaks from 1990-2009

Above High Camp Termination Reason	All Seasons		Spring		Autumn		Winter	
	Cnt	Pct	Cnt	Pct	Cnt	Pct	Cnt	Pct
Success	9201	72.2	4239	69.8	4693	74.6	197	71.1
Subpeak	119	0.9	46	0.8	73	1.2	0	0.0
Bad Weather	811	6.4	506	8.3	283	4.5	18	6.5
Bad Conditions	444	3.5	161	2.7	265	4.2	7	2.5
Accident	112	0.9	39	0.6	69	1.1	4	1.4
Altitude/AMS	113	0.9	48	0.8	62	1.0	2	0.7
Exhaustion	450	3.5	227	3.7	208	3.3	8	2.9
Frostbite/Cold	403	3.2	215	3.5	185	2.9	3	1.1
Other Illnesses	134	1.1	70	1.2	63	1.0	1	0.4
Lack of Supplies	77	0.6	47	0.8	30	0.5	0	0.0
O2 System	71	0.6	62	1.0	9	0.1	0	0.0
Too Difficult	226	1.8	87	1.4	121	1.9	15	5.4
Too Late/Slow	285	2.2	152	2.5	114	1.8	19	6.9
Assisting Others	137	1.1	85	1.4	49	0.8	3	1.1
Rte Preparation	6	0.0	0	0.0	6	0.1	0	0.0
Lack of Time	1	0.0	0	0.0	1	0.0	0	0.0
No Climb/Intent	1	0.0	0	0.0	1	0.0	0	0.0
Other	55	0.4	29	0.5	25	0.4	0	0.0
Unknown	89	0.7	57	0.9	32	0.5	0	0.0
Unspecified	0	0.0	0	0.0	0	0.0	0	0.0
Totals	12735	100.0	6070	100.0	6289	100.0	277	100.0

Table C-18: Reasons for termination of individual members above *high* camp
for all peaks from 1990-2009

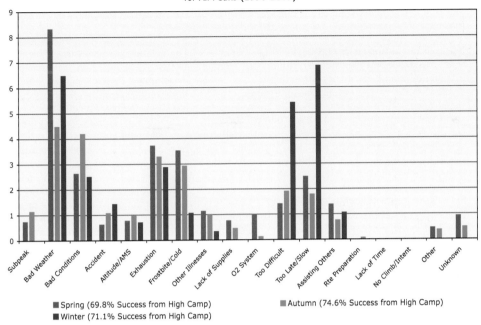

Seasonal Termination Rates for Unsuccessful Members Above High Camp
for All Peaks (1990-2009)

Spring (69.8% Success from High Camp)   Autumn (74.6% Success from High Camp)
Winter (71.1% Success from High Camp)

Chart C-18: Seasonal termination percentages for unsuccessful members above *high* camp for all peaks from 1990-2009

The Epic Storm of November 1995

From *The Seasonal Stories* of Elizabeth Hawley – Autumn 1995

Ama Dablam had enjoyed an exceptional season. 67 climbers from 17 teams gained the summit of Ama Dablam by its usual route on the southwest ridge. Leaders returning from Ama Dablam commented on how smooth relations were amongst the large international community on their mountain, a situation that was a very pleasant surprise for many of them, including Russell Brice, who amazed others by his ascent that began from camp 1 at 5200m at 6:00 a.m., just after an early breakfast, put him on the top at 9:20 a.m., and got him safely back to base camp at 4600m in time for lunch at 1:00 p.m. "It was just a nice day out for me, a half-day holiday" from his work as leader of a small team.

Brice's summit day, 8 November, was the final day that anyone got to the summit of Ama Dablam. The last teams to arrive in Nepal to attempt any peak in the autumn season, which officially ends on the 15th of November, were three for Ama Dablam, and they paid a price for coming so late and therefore not having time to spare to wait out bad weather. One of them, six Italians and an Austrian, had come to base camp two days before and had pitched their first high camp that day but returned to base to sleep. Another, a Spanish party, arrived at base camp the next day, the 9th, to start their climb, and the third, a French group, had a summit-attack party in their highest camp, poised for a push to the top on the 9th.

But on the 9th an unusually large snowstorm began about noon and by the time it ended in the night of the 10th, it had dumped a remarkable two meters of fresh snow at base. Brice knew how much had fallen because only the top of his toilet tent was visible above it. He suddenly found himself hard at work during these days shoveling snow off his team's tents and taking hours to dig out a path to the start of the ridge so other climbers could get safely down to base. Everyone who was in base camp remained snowbound there until the morning of the 11th, when the Italian-Austrian group, the Spaniards and some of Brice's own members plowed their way out to the village of Pangboche.

Up on the mountain on the 9th were eight Frenchmen who had planned to attack the summit that day. Brice, an experienced Himalayan climber, advised them by radio to descend immediately, and down they struggled with difficulty for 12 hours through half a meter of snow on the ridge to their first high camp, a descent that would normally take perhaps seven hours. Then they were stuck in camp 1 on the 10th; their leader, Michel Cormier, spent two hours to go to the Italians' tent not far away to fetch food and return to his camp. On the 11th they managed to reach an intermediate camp, but could go no farther in the very deep snow. Finally by the 12th, Brice, his teammate who was still in base camp and two of Cormier's members who had summited on the 8th and had safely descended to base before the height of the storm, had dug out a trail up from base and were able to rescue Cormier and his party. These Frenchmen, who came down the last part of the ridge on their backsides or crawling while dragging their sacks of belongings to the point where they met Brice's party and the trail, suffered no frostbite from their ordeal, but Cormier felt that if they had spent one more night above base camp, they would have had frostbitten feet.

The French team left base on the 13th for Pangboche on their trek down to an airfield for a flight to Kathmandu. The Italians went back to base camp that day from Pangboche to retrieve their tents and gear left at camp 1 but made no attempt to go higher. The Spaniards also returned to base on the 13th; they established their own camp 1 on the 14th with the intention of trying to go on to the summit. But on the 15th, when their leader, Jorge Clariana, and Gyalbu Sherpa tried to reach the site for camp 2, they were unable to gain more than 500 meters altitude before they decided that the snow on the ridge was still too deep and the avalanching falling onto their intended route was too dangerous to continue. Their climb was finished.

The world's television, radio and newspapers carried many stories about this epic storm, and especially about the tragedy in the Gokyo Valley, northwest of Ama Dablam and its Khumbu Valley, where a massive avalanche smothered a tiny village called Panga and killed almost all of the people in a Japanese trekking group sleeping there; all 13 Japanese trekkers and 10 of their 11 Nepalese staff (guide, cook and porters), plus two local residents, were killed. Farther east, at the site of the north Kangchenjunga base camp, another Japanese trekking group was hit by the heavy snowfall, and here three Japanese and four Nepalese died while six Japanese survived. In the Manang region, just north of the great Annapurna massif in north-central Nepal, a landslide caused by constant rains buried a cluster of houses and lodges, and here six foreign trekkers (a German, an Irishwoman, a Briton and three Canadians) and some of the local residents also died. No mountaineering expedition members were lost, but the climbing season had come to an abrupt and dramatic end.

Ascent Analysis

This chapter analyzes ascents of the principle peaks in the Nepal Himalaya, those peaks officially open for mountaineering and a few additional peaks with significant activity. Border peaks such as Everest, Cho Oyu, and Kangchenjunga are included for expeditions from the Nepalese, Chinese, and Indian sides of the border. The tables and charts cover the period from 1950 through 2009 unless specified otherwise.

Ascents are analyzed by several different categories: peak altitude, climbing season, day of year, time of day, historically over time, age, citizenship, and gender. Ascent rates are given for the most popular peaks. Ascents are also analyzed by team composition, that is, the number of members and hired personnel on an expedition and the ratio between the two.

Ascent rates are calculated only for members above base camp because ascent rates cannot be reasonably calculated for hired personnel as many of them went above base camp with no intention of attempting the summit, but only fulfilling their assigned roles of ferrying loads, establishing higher camps, or fixing ropes.

Disputed ascents, as marked in *The Himalayan Database*, are counted in the ascent totals. Claimed, but unrecognized ascents, and ascents of subpeaks are excluded from the ascent totals. Multiple ascents by the same climber on the same peak in the same season are only counted once.

Tables at the end of this chapter show the average duration and the minimum and maximum days to the summit for successful expeditions for many popular peaks.

Ascents by Altitude Range

Table and Chart A-1 show member ascent rates from 1950 to 1989 and 1990 to 2009 for all peaks in altitude ranges from 6000m to 8850m in 500m increments.

Peak Altitude	1950-1989 All Peaks with All Routes			1990-2009 All Peaks with All Routes			1990-2009 All Peaks And Routes excluding Ama Dablam-Cho Oyu-Everest Commercial Rtes		
	Above BC	Ascent Cnt	Ascent Rate	Above BC	Ascent Cnt	Ascent Rate	Above BC	Ascent Cnt	Ascent Rate
6000-6499m	573	270	47.1	690	361	52.3	690	361	52.3
6500-6999m	1607	606	37.7	4469	2166	48.5	1090	328	30.1
7000-7499m	2429	571	23.5	3654	997	27.3	3654	997	27.3
7500-7999m	1804	294	16.3	789	92	11.7	789	92	11.7
8000-8499m	3052	492	16.1	8854	2891	32.7	3834	875	22.8
8500-8850m	3388	398	11.7	7817	2692	34.4	2075	470	22.7
Totals	12853	2631	20.5	26273	9199	35.0	12132	3123	25.7

Table A-1: Member ascents for peak altitude ranges (6000-8850m)

As shown in Chart A-1, member ascent rates for all peaks from 1950 to 1989 (the **blue** line) are the highest at 47.1% for the lower 6000m+ peaks and then drop steadily to 11.7% as peak height increases to 8500m+ suggesting as would be expected that the higher the peak, the more difficult it is to summit.

Member Ascent Rates by Peak Altitude

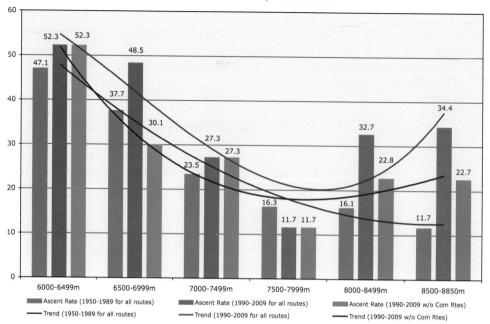

Ascent Rate (1950-1989 for all routes) Ascent Rate (1990-2009 for all routes) Ascent Rate (1990-2009 w/o Com Rtes)
Trend (1950-1989 for all routes) Trend (1990-2009 for all routes) Trend (1990-2009 w/o Com Rtes)

Chart A-1: Member ascent rates by peak altitude between 1950-1989 and 1990-2009

Member Ascent Rates for Ama Dablam, Cho Oyu, Everest
(Commercial vs Non-Commercial Routes)

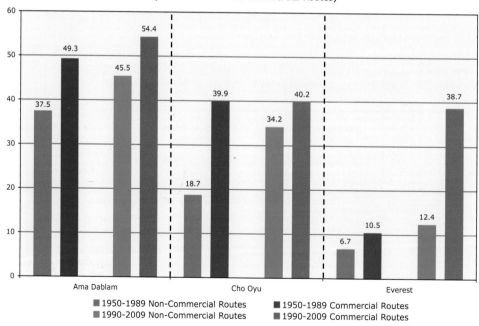

■ 1950-1989 Non-Commercial Routes   ■ 1950-1989 Commercial Routes
■ 1990-2009 Non-Commercial Routes   ■ 1990-2009 Commercial Routes

Chart A-2: Member ascent rates for Ama Dablam, Cho Oyu, and Everest

The ascent rates in the above and subsequent charts in this chapter represent the percentage of climbers that summited for each category in the chart.

The center and rightmost columns of Table A-1 show member ascent rates from 1990 to 2009 for all peaks including and excluding expeditions on the commercial routes of the three most popular peaks, Ama Dablam (southwest ridge), Cho Oyu (northwest ridge), and Everest (South Col-southeast ridge and North Col-northeast ridge).

In Chart A-1, the red columns and trend line show ascent rates during the 1990-2009 period for all peaks and routes, and the **green** columns and trend line show ascent rates during the 1990-2009 period factoring out the commercial routes on Ama Dablam, Cho Oyu, and Everest. The difference between the red and green trend lines illustrates the impact of commercial climbing after 1990 as the red trend line is substantially higher than the green trend line. Commercial climbing, which has become increasingly popular since 1990, has contributed significantly to the numbers of climbers going above base camp (nearly 54% of all climbers above base camp were on the commercial routes of one of these peaks from 1990 to 2009).

Table and Chart A-2 shows the member ascent rates for Ama Dablam, Cho Oyu, and Everest during the 1950-1989 and 1990-2009 periods. Segregating out the commercial routes for the 1950-1989 period does not substantially affect the member ascent rates during that earlier period because those expeditions did not concentrate so much on previously climbed routes, but were more eager to explore new unclimbed routes. Since 1990 many of the more skilled climbers are pursuing quests for the seven summits or the fourteen 8000ers and thus want to climb Everest and Cho Oyu as quickly and simply as possible, whereas most commercial clients do not have the skills for the more difficult non-commercial routes.

	Non-Commercial Routes			Commercial Routes		
1950-1989	**Above BC**	**Ascent Cnt**	**Ascent Rate**	**Above BC**	**Ascent Cnt**	**Ascent Rate**
Ama Dablam	200	75	37.5	217	107	49.3
Cho Oyu	203	38	18.7	263	105	39.9
Everest	1307	88	6.7	1253	131	10.5
1990-2009						
Ama Dablam	167	76	45.5	3379	1838	54.4
Cho Oyu	152	52	34.2	5020	2016	40.2
Everest	829	103	12.4	5742	2222	38.7

Table A-2: Member ascents for Ama Dablam, Cho Oyu, and Everest

The low ascent rate for the non-commercial routes on Cho Oyu during the 1950-1989 period is due to several failed attempts on the southeast face and along the east ridge from Ngojumba Kang. These routes were seldom attempted after the northwest ridge route opened up from Tibet in 1987. In fact, the last (and only successful) attempt along the east ridge was in 1991 by the Russians (see the inset box, *Cho Oyu by the East Ridge*, on pg. 62).

Popular Peaks by Altitude Range

Chart A-3 gives member ascent rates for the most popular peaks in Nepal, those peaks with 750 or more members above base camp (roughly equivalent to 75+ expeditions).

Member ascent rates for two commercial peaks, Ama Dablam at 52.9% and Cho Oyu at 39.2%, are higher than the mean (average) of 30.2% for all peaks (in black), whereas the ascent rate for Everest is lower at 27.9%.

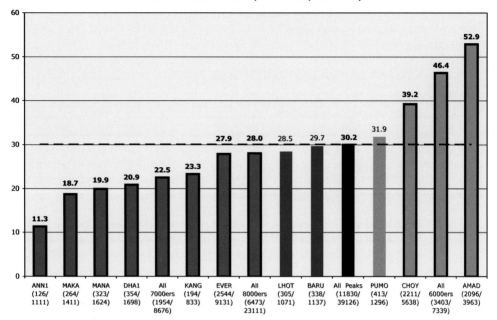

Chart A-3: Member ascent rates for popular peaks from 1950-2009
with more than 750 members above base camp
(the ascent rate is above the column bar; the ascent / above BC counts are below)
(see Appendix A for the definitions of the peak symbols in this and subsequent charts)

In the above chart and in the three charts that follow for the most popular 6000ers, 7000ers, and 8000ers for members, the columns outlined in black represent peaks or groups of peaks that statistically have either significantly higher (in blue) or lower (in red) ascent rates than the mean ascent rate for all peaks (in **black**). Statistical significance means that there is less than a 5% probability that the result occurred by chance. For the non-outlined peaks, the ascent rates can be considered as only anecdotal evidence of higher or lower ascent rates than the mean rate for all peaks.

Member ascent rates for all of these peaks or groups are significantly higher or lower (statistically) than the 30.2% mean ascent rate for all peaks except for Lhotse, Baruntse, and Pumori that have rates very close to the mean ascent rate for all peaks.

The next group of charts shows member ascent rates grouped by 6000m, 7000m, and 8000m altitudes for the most popular peaks in Nepal. Ama Dablam, Cho Oyu, and Everest are further separated out by their commercial and non-commercial routes.

Chart A-4 shows the 6000m peaks with 50 or more members above base camp. The Ama Dablam southwest ridge commercial route accounts for 49.0% of the members above base camp and 57.2% of the member ascents for all 6000m peaks. If this route were omitted from the counts, the overall ascent rate for the other 6000ers would drop from 46.4% to 39.0%.

Two of the peaks in Chart A-4, Langshisa Ri and Cholatse, were reclassified as trekking peaks in 2002. Expeditions to those peaks after that date are not counted in the 6000m totals. Also expeditions to Dhampus (71.4% ascent rate) and Saribung (85.1%) are not included as they are no longer tracked in *The Himalayan Database* because these peaks are very easy and often climbed illegally by trekking groups.

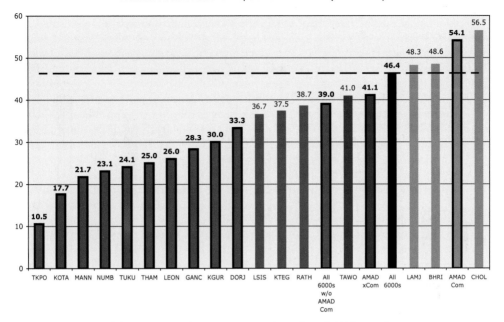

Chart A-4: Member ascent rates for selected 6000m peaks
with 50+ members above base camp from 1950-2009

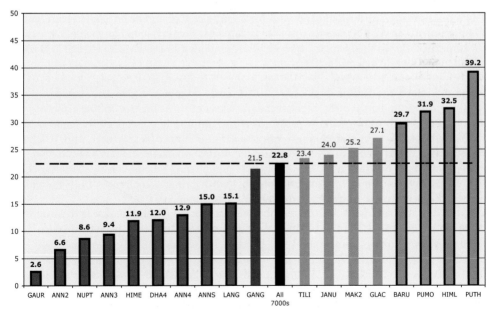

Chart A-5: Member ascent rates for selected 7000m peaks
with 100+ members above base camp from 1950-2009

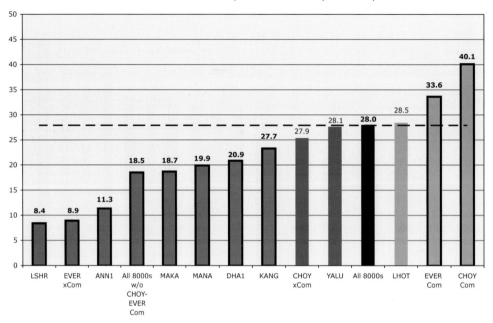

Member Ascent Rates for Popular 8000m Peaks (1950-2009)

**Chart A-6a: Member ascent rates for selected 8000m peaks
with 150+ members above base camp from 1950-2009**

Member ascent counts and ascent rates for Manaslu include ascents to both the true summit (8163m) and the fore-summit (8125m). The last pitch to the true summit is often extremely dangerous due to high winds and unstable ice cornices, hence many climbers have stopped at the fore-summit and have considered that a sufficient success and historically have reported their climbs as successful.

Tawoche, Lamjung, and Bhrikuti do not have significantly higher or lower ascent rates than the mean for all 6000ers because their rates are very close to the mean. Langshisa Ri, Kangtega, Rathong, and Cholatse with few members above base camp are still too close to the mean to be significant.

Chart A-5 shows the 7000m peaks with 100 or more members above base camp. Himlung and Pumori have the highest member ascent rates for the 7000ers and are often attempted by commercial expeditions with Himlung being especially popular for French groups. Many commercial groups also attempt Baruntse, Pumori, and Tilicho. Annapurna IV was also a target of commercial teams in the 1980s, but has not been since then due to its often heavy snow pack. Gangapurna, Tilicho, Jannu, Makalu II, and Glacier Dome do not have significantly higher or lower ascent rates than the mean for all 7000ers because their rates are very close to the mean.

At 2.6% Gaurishankar has one of the lowest ascent rates in the entire Nepal Himalaya with only 3 of 25 teams being successful, the last in 1985, and all by the southwest face. The peak requires very technical ice climbing skills and presents many hazards from falling ice and rocks. The American John Roskelley, the first summiter in 1979, returned with his son Jess in 2005 to try the northeast ridge from the Tibetan side; but they were defeated at only 5450m by a ridge of unstable rocks with huge icicles hanging from them—"like a house of cards" reported John, and "the difficulties got even worse as the ridge went higher."

60 Ascent Analysis

Member Ascent Rates for 8000m Standard and Non-Standard Routes (1950-2009)

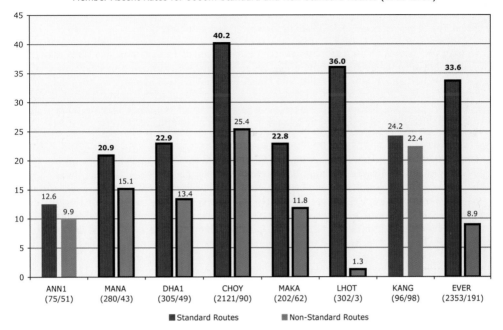

Chart A-6b: Member ascent rates for 8000m standard and non-standard routes from 1950-2009
(the ascent rates are above the column bars; the ascent counts are below)
(column pairs outlined in black indicate statistically significant differences
in ascent rates between the standard and non-standard routes)

8000m Standard Routes:		
ANN1 – N Face	CHOY – NW Ridge	KANG – W Face
MANA – NE Face	MAKA – Makalu La-NW Ridge	EVER – S Col-SE Ridge,
DHA1 – NE Ridge	LHOT – W Face	N Col-NE Ridge

Chart A-6a shows member ascent rates for the 8000m peaks with 150 or more members above base camp. The Cho Oyu and Everest commercial routes by far enjoy the highest member ascent rates (40.1% and 33.6%), whereas the lowest ascent rates are on Lhotse Shar (8.4%), the Everest non-commercial routes (8.9%), and Annapurna (11.3%). Interestingly for the 8000m peaks, Cho Oyu is also the safest, whereas Lhotse Shar and Annapurna are the most dangerous (see the *Death Analysis* chapter). Yalung Kang, Cho Oyu (non-commercial routes), and Lhotse are too close to the mean for all 8000ers to be statistically significant.

Chart A-6b shows member ascent rates for the standard and non-standard routes on the eight major 8000m peaks in Nepal. The standard routes are significantly easier on all of them except for Annapurna 1 and Kangchenjunga. For Annapurna I, all routes are very difficult (and dangerous); for Kangchenjunga, variations of the north face are nearly as popular and successful as the southwest face.

The member ascent rates for all peaks are given in Appendix A. However, most of those peaks that are not depicted in the previous charts do not have ascent and member above base camp counts high enough to be statistically significant when comparing them to the mean ascent rates for all peaks in their respective groups.

Ascents by Climbing Season

Chart A-7 shows member ascent rates by climbing season for all peaks.

The member ascent rates the autumn season of 30.7% and the winter season of 20.9% are statistically significantly higher and lower than the mean ascent rate of 30.2% for all seasons. The spring ascent rate of 28.5% is too close to the mean rate to be significant. But the summer ascent rate of 28.1% is insignificant in spite of the much lower ascent rate than the mean due to the small number of members above base camp. Most of the summer expeditions were either to Cho Oyu or Everest from the Tibetan side in the 1980s, or were summer explorations of northwest Nepal by Tamotsu Ohnishi. For these reasons, the summer season is excluded from the analyses in remainder of this section.

Table A-8 shows member ascent counts and rates for selected peaks and peak ranges for the spring, autumn, and winter climbing seasons.

The overall differences between spring and autumn season are small, but when examined on a peak by peak or region by region basis, they are more significant.

Chart A-8 compares member ascent rates for selected peaks and peaks ranges for the spring and autumn climbing seasons. Overall, the spring member ascent rates are higher for the 8000m peaks except for Cho Oyu, and lower for the 6000m and 7000m peaks.

Table and Chart A-9a show member ascent counts and rates by season broken out by geographic regions for all peaks.

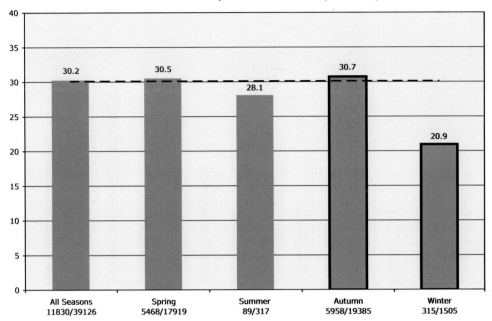

Chart A-7: Member ascent rates by climbing season for all peaks from 1950-2009
(the ascent rate is above the column bar; the ascent / above BC counts are below)

The columns outlined in black in the above chart represent seasons that statistically have either significantly higher or lower ascent rates than the mean ascent rate for all seasons. Statistical significance means that there is less than a 5% probability that the result occurred by chance. For the non-outlined peaks, the ascent rates can be considered as only anecdotal evidence of higher or lower ascent rates than the mean rate for all seasons.

	Spring			Autumn			Winter		
	Above BC	Ascent Cnt	Ascent Rate	Above BC	Ascent Cnt	Ascent Rate	Above BC	Ascent Cnt	Ascent Rate
All Peaks	17919	5468	30.5	19385	5958	30.7	1505	315	20.9
6000ers	1725	659	38.2	4993	2477	49.6	502	198	39.4
7000ers	2779	570	20.5	5630	1330	23.6	255	50	19.6
8000ers	13415	4239	31.6	8762	2151	24.5	748	67	9.0
KANG	673	170	25.3	133	21	15.8	27	3	11.1
MAKA	805	213	26.5	544	49	9.0	62	2	3.2
LHOT	724	239	33.0	315	65	20.6	32	1	3.1
EVER	6720	2336	34.8	1985	189	9.5	275	13	4.7
CHOY	2164	720	33.3	3390	1465	43.2	56	18	32.1
MANA	723	158	21.9	819	152	18.6	82	13	15.9
ANN1	455	74	16.3	512	46	9.0	139	6	4.3
DHA1	788	213	27.0	846	130	15.4	62	9	14.5
AMAD	621	190	30.6	2989	1747	58.4	353	159	45.0
BARU	295	63	21.4	832	271	32.6	10	4	40.0
PUMO	392	119	30.4	848	278	32.8	56	16	28.6

Table A-8: Member ascents by season for selected peaks from 1950-2009

The results indicate that the spring season is more favorable in the central and far eastern regions of Nepal, areas that are prone to heavy monsoon snowfall and avalanching, whereas the autumn season is more favorable in the Khumbu-Makalu-Rolwaling and in the far western regions of Nepal. The Khumbu region is still slightly

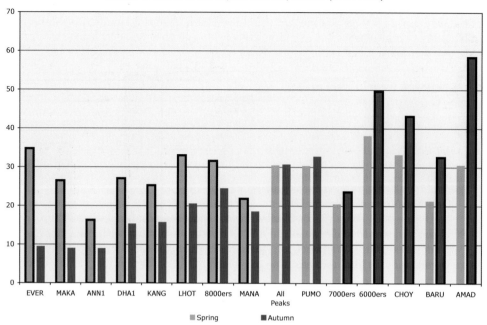

Chart A-8: Member ascent rates for selected peaks by season from 1950-2009
(ranked from left to right by favorability from spring to autumn)

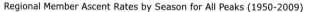

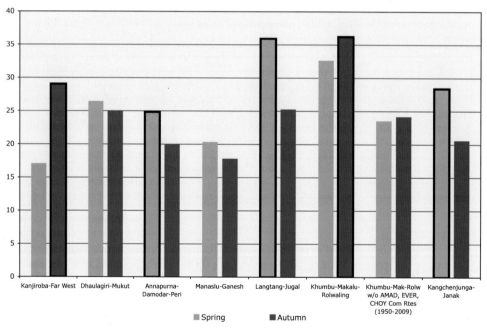

Chart A-9a: Regional member ascent rates by season for all peaks from 1950-2009

The columns outlined in black in the above and following charts represent seasons that statistically have significantly higher ascent rates than the opposing season for that region.

	Spring			Autumn			Winter		
	Above BC	Ascent Cnt	Ascent Rate	Above BC	Ascent Cnt	Ascent Rate	Above BC	Ascent Cnt	Ascent Rate
Kanjiroba-Far West	152	26	17.1	296	86	29.1	7	2	28.6
Dhaulagiri-Mukut	1231	326	26.5	1842	460	25.0	65	12	18.5
Annapurna-Damodar-Peri	1309	325	24.8	2739	546	19.9	230	22	9.6
Manaslu-Ganesh	1056	215	20.4	1243	222	17.9	98	14	14.3
Langtang-Jugal	284	102	35.9	372	94	25.3	76	13	17.1
Khumbu-Makalu-Rolwaling	12475	4073	32.6	12112	4389	36.2	966	247	25.6
Kangchenjunga-Janak	1412	401	28.4	781	161	20.6	63	5	7.9
Totals	**17919**	**5468**	**30.5**	**19385**	**5958**	**30.7**	**1505**	**315**	**20.9**
Khumbu-Makalu-Rolwaling w/o ACE Com Rtes	4354	1027	23.6	4953	1198	24.2	483	77	15.9

Table A-9a: Regional member ascents by season for all peaks from 1950-2009

Regional Member Ascent Rates by Season for 6000ers & 7000ers (1950-2009)

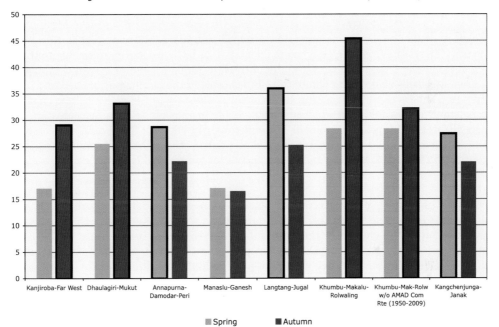

Chart A-9b: Regional member ascent rates by season for the 6000m and 7000m peaks from 1950-2009

	Spring			Autumn			Winter		
	Above BC	Ascent Cnt	Ascent Rate	Above BC	Ascent Cnt	Ascent Rate	Above BC	Ascent Cnt	Ascent Rate
Kanjiroba-Far West	152	26	17.1	296	86	29.1	7	2	28.6
Dhaulagiri-Mukut	443	113	25.5	996	330	33.1	3	3	100.0
Annapurna-Damodar-Peri	827	237	28.7	2191	487	22.2	89	15	16.9
Manaslu-Ganesh	333	57	17.1	424	70	16.5	16	1	6.3
Langtang-Jugal	284	102	35.9	372	94	25.3	76	13	17.1
Khumbu-Makalu-Rolwaling	1924	546	28.4	5754	2610	45.4	541	213	39.4
Kangchenjunga-Janak	541	148	27.4	590	130	22.0	25	1	4.0
Totals	**4504**	**1229**	**27.3**	**10623**	**3807**	**35.8**	**757**	**248**	**32.8**
Khumbu-Makalu-Rolwaling w/o AMAD Com Rte	1404	398	28.3	3006	964	32.1	213	62	29.1

Table A-9b: Regional member ascents by season for the 6000m and 7000m peaks from 1950-2009

Ascent Analysis 65

more favorable in autumn when the expeditions to Ama Dablam, Cho Oyu, and Everest are factored out (Ama Dablam and Cho Oyu are best in autumn, whereas Everest is best in spring as shown in Table A-8).

Table and Chart A-9b show member ascent counts and rates by season broken out by geographic regions for the 6000m and 7000m peaks.

When only peaks under 8000m are considered, the Annapurna-Damodar-Peri, Langtang-Jugal, and Kangchenjunga-Janak regions remain significantly more favorable in the spring because the Manaslu-Ganesh region is skewed by the higher spring success rates on Manaslu (see Charts A-8 and A-9a). The Dhaulagiri-Mukut region becomes significantly more favorable in the autumn when the high spring success rate on Dhaulagiri I is factored out.

Ascents by Expedition Years

Chart A-10 shows member ascent rates by expedition years in 5-year steps for all peaks. The results from the early years from 1950 to 1970 are more erratic due to the lower numbers of expeditions, especially in the late 1960s when Himalayan climbing was suspended in Nepal and before the Chinese side of the border was opened to foreign climbers in 1980. From the 1970s onward, the data in Chart A-10 show more consistent results as the trend lines show a steady increase in member ascents and ascent rates for all peaks combined. The widening gap between the ascents rates for the ACE commercial routes (in **green**) and all peaks without the ACE commercial routes (in **red**) illustrates the increasing success of commercial climbing since the mid-1980s.

Many of the larger expeditions from the earlier years often had members that went above base camp to assist the primary summit team with the knowledge that they would never have a chance for the summit themselves. But in recent times with commercial climbs dominating the popular peaks, nearly all the paying members have summit dreams, otherwise they would not pay the high expedition fees.

Chart A-11 shows member ascent rates over time broken out by altitude. The rates for the 6000ers and 7000ers are relatively even over time, 40-50% for the 6000ers and 20-25% for the 7000ers. Only for the 8000ers has there been a steady increase since 1970, starting at about 5% in 1970 and increasing to 40% after 2005, again illustrating the increasing success rates on Cho Oyu and Everest.

Charts A-12a-c give a more detailed view of member ascent rates since 1970 when segregating out the ACE commercial routes. These commercial peaks show a more rapid increase in ascent rates during the last 15 years. For the 6000ers until 2000, a gradual decrease in ascent rates actually occurred when Ama Dablam is removed; since 2000 that ascent rate has increased possibly due to recent emphasis on exploratory expeditions to the newly opened 6000m peaks. For the 7000ers, the recent rise in ascent rates from 2007 to 2009 is due in part to renewed interest in Baruntse, Himlung, and Putha Hiunchuli by commercial and small private groups as alternatives to Cho Oyu as these three peaks are considered less difficult than many of the other 7000ers and 8000ers. For the 8000ers, an increase in ascent rates occurs for peaks other than Cho Oyu and Everest, most likely due to the increasing interest in climbing all of the fourteen 8000ers.

Member Ascent Rates for All Peaks (1950-2009)

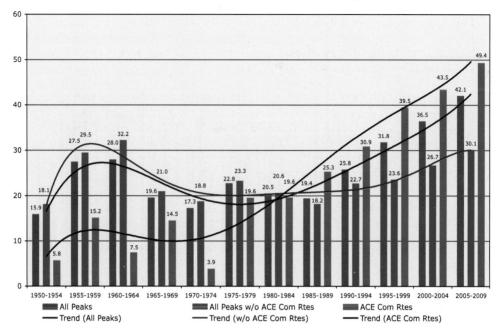

Chart A-10: Member ascent rates by expedition year for all peaks from 1950-2009

Member Ascent Rates for All 6000ers, 7000ers, and 8000ers (1950-2009)

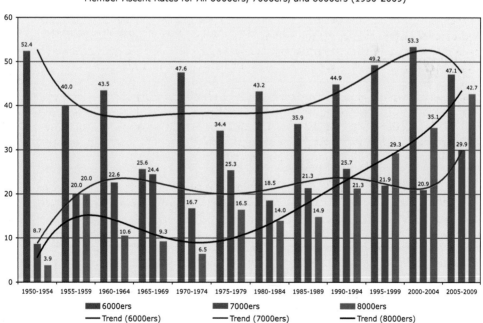

Chart A-11: Member ascent rates by expedition year for 6000ers, 7000ers, and 8000ers from 1950-2009

Ascent Analysis 67

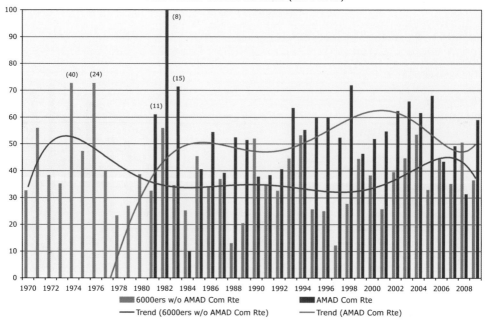

Chart A-12a: Member ascent rates by expedition year for
6000ers and Ama Dablam from 1970-2009

Members ascent counts are given in parentheses in this and the following charts for instances where the ascent rates are much higher than the trend line.

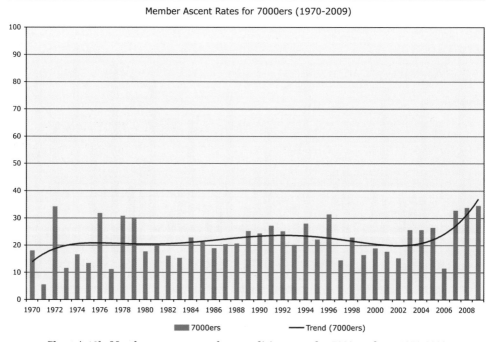

Chart A-12b: Member ascent rates by expedition year for 7000ers from 1970-2009

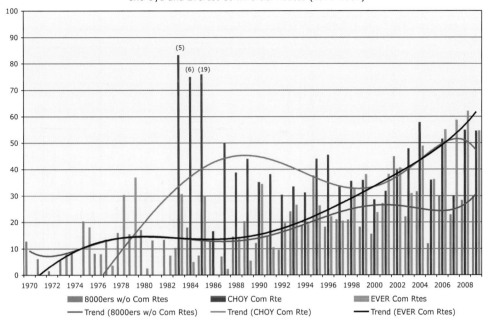

Member Ascent Rates for 8000ers and
Cho Oyu and Everest Commercial Routes (1970-2009)

**Chart A-12c: Member ascent rates by expedition year for
8000ers, Cho Oyu, and Everest from 1970-2009**

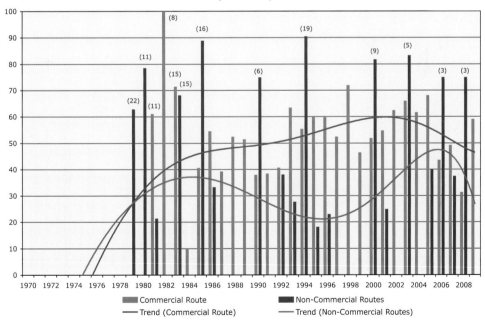

Commercial vs. Non-Commercial Routes Member Ascent Rates for Ama Dablam
(1970-2009)

**Chart A-13a: Member ascent rates by expedition year for commercial (SE Ridge)
and non-commercial routes on Ama Dablam from 1970-2009**

Ascent Analysis 69

Commercial vs. Non-Commercial Routes Member Ascent Rates for Cho Oyu
(1970-2009)

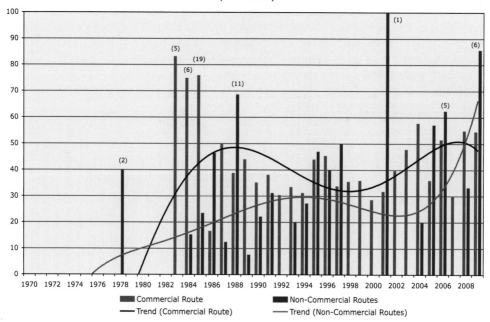

**Chart A-13b: Member ascent rates by expedition year for commercial (NW Ridge)
and non-commercial routes on Cho Oyu from 1970-2009**

Commercial vs. Non-Commercial Routes Member Ascent Rates for Everest
(1970-2009)

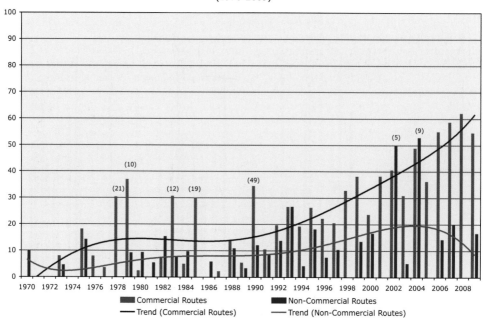

**Chart A-13c: Member ascent rates by expedition year for commercial (S Col & N Col)
and non-commercial routes on Everest from 1970-2009**

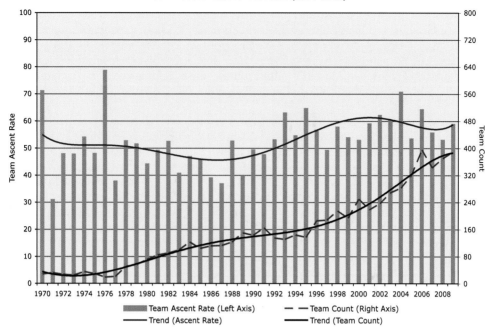

Chart A-14: Team ascent rates by expedition year for all peaks from 1970-2009

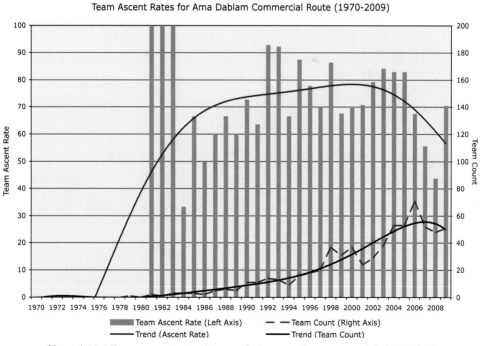

Chart A-15a: Team ascent rates by expedition year for commercial (SW Ridge) route on Ama Dablam from 1970-2009

Team Ascent Rates for Cho Oyu Commercial Route (1970-2009)

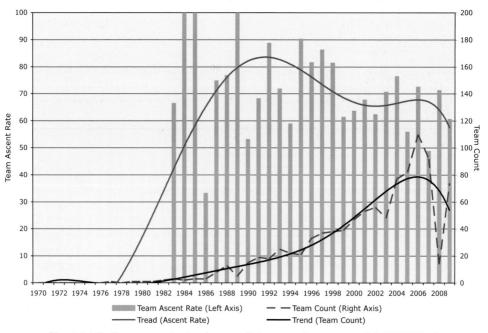

Chart A-15b: Team ascent rates by expedition year for commercial (NW Ridge) route on Cho Oyu from 1970-2009

Team Ascent Rates for Everest Commercial Routes (1970-2009)

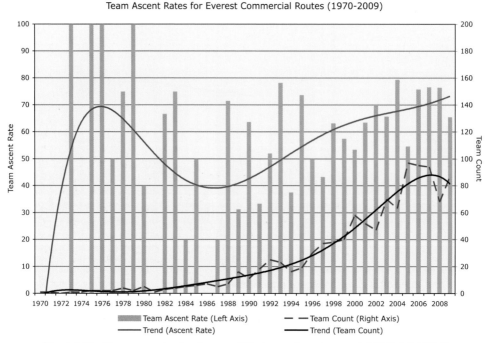

Chart A-15c: Team ascent rates by expedition year for commercial (S Col & N Col) routes on Everest from 1970-2009

Charts A-13a-c compare member ascent rates on Ama Dablam, Cho Oyu, and Everest since 1970 for the commercial routes and the non-commercial routes. Ama Dablam and Cho Oyu show recent increases in member ascent rates for the non-commercial routes; for Everest, the ascent rates are relatively flat for the non-commercial routes.

Before 1980, minimal interest was shown in the southwest ridge of Ama Dablam, and from China the northwest ridge of Cho Oyu was closed to foreigners. But from 1980 to 1986, the majority of expeditions to Cho Oyu still crossed over the Nangpa La illegally from Nepal; it wasn't until 1987 foreign expeditions began approaching from Tingri in Tibet after a few border incidents with Chinese soldiers discouraged the southern approach (see the inset box, *High Tension on Cho Oyu*, on pg. 74).

Charts A-14 and A-15a-c compare team counts and ascent rates for all peaks and for the commercial routes on Ama Dablam, Cho Oyu, and Everest since 1970. For all peaks the team counts have increased from about 20 expeditions per year in the early 1970s to nearly 400 per year in recent years (see the right scale of Chart A-14); but the team ascent rates during this period have remained relatively steady in the 50-60% range (see the left scale of Chart A-14). For the ACE commercial routes, the yearly team counts have dramatically increased for each peak indicating the enormous popularity of commercial climbing. Team ascent rates for Everest have steadily increased to about 75%, whereas in the last few years they have declined a bit for Ama Dablam and Cho Oyu perhaps due to the bad weather that plagued Nepal during the 2005-2007 autumn seasons when most of the Ama Dablam and Cho Oyu expeditions occurred. Cho Oyu experienced a particularly sharp decline in 2008 when Tibet was closed until late summer causing many commercial operators to cancel both their spring and autumn expeditions due to the uncertainty of obtaining permits in a timely fashion.

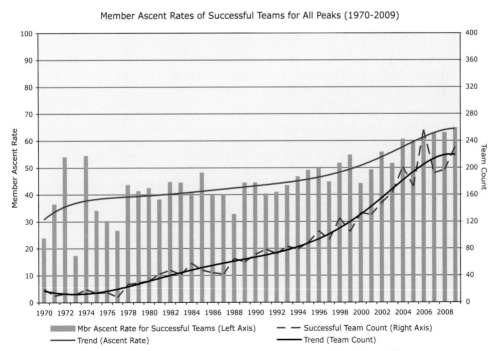

Chart A-16: Member ascent rates by expedition year for successful teams
for all peaks from 1970-2009

High Tension on Cho Oyu

From The Seasonal Stories of Elizabeth Hawley – Spring 1987

Tension arose when three climbing teams went to essentially the same route on the west side of Cho Oyu without knowing in advance that anyone else was going to be there. Two teams, Americans and Chileans, received permits from the Nepalese government for the south and southwest sides, but from the start each actually intended to follow the so-called Tichy route, named for the pioneering Austrian mountaineer who led the first ascent of Cho Oyu in 1954. The Tichy route lies mostly on the Tibetan side of the mountain, but is easily accessible from Nepal across the unguarded border. A third expedition, composed of 29 European alpinists, did have permission for this route: their permit came from the Chinese authorities, and a Chinese liaison officer accompanied them.

The Chileans and the Americans had some friction in Kathmandu before they set out for the mountain. The South Americans felt that they were the only team from Nepal's side who were authorized to be anywhere near the Tichy route, but they finally agreed in Kathmandu to let the North Americans come on the route too if they paid part of the Nepalese government's peak fee. According to the Chileans, the Americans agreed to this, but never kept their part of the bargain. Finally, when these two parties got onto Cho Oyu and encountered the Europeans from Tibet, new differences arose. The Europeans and their Chinese official objected to the presence of unauthorized climbers, and this in turn led to Chilean annoyance at the Americans, who they believed had been unnecessarily provocative by pitching a camp right under the noses of the Chinese and Europeans.

Despite all these disagreements, some men did manage to scale Cho Oyu. Two Chileans and two Nepalese Sherpas accompanying them succeeded in going to the summit on 29 April together with two Europeans. For the Chileans and their leader Mauricio Purto, it was the first Chilean ascent of any 8000m peak, and they were the first from their country ever to have climbed in Nepal. For the Europeans on a commercial expedition, it was a series of successes in which 13 members reached the summit over seven different days, the last on 12 May. But for the Americans, there was failure to get higher than 7600m.

The Chinese did more than remove the Americans advance base, if indeed they did that. On April 25, when the four Americans were moving up the mountain from advance base, one of them, leader Robert Watters, who had been the last to leave their camp, heard shouting from below and went back to investigate. He found himself confronted by two Chinese officials at the camp. He waved to his three teammates to continue on up while he turned his attention to the Chinese request for his permits from the Nepalese authorities. After he had handed over these documents and then, on their demand, his passport, he was told by the Chinese to follow them down, apparently to go to a People's Liberation Army camp near the Europeans' base. As the trio descended, Watters suddenly turned away from the top trail the two Chinese were following ahead of him, and he hastily crossed back in Nepal, abandoning his passport and permits. (The other Americans descended a few days later in a snowstorm and did not meet the officials.)

Watters was not the only person to have his documents seized by the Chinese. Two of the Chileans found them at one of their camps and handed over their Nepalese permits when the Chinese gave urgency to their order by pulling out their knives.

It sems likely that the Chinese government will draw the attention of the Nepalese authorities, with whom they have cordial relations, to these violations of the border. The Europeans' leader, Marcus Schmuck has already lodged a protest. The Nepalese probably will ban Watters and Purto, and perhaps their teammates, from climbing again in Nepal for several years, and they may also stop granting permission to climb Cho Oyu from its southwestern side if not from all sides in Nepal.

Member Ascent Rates of Successful Teams for Ama Dablam Com. Route (1970-2009)

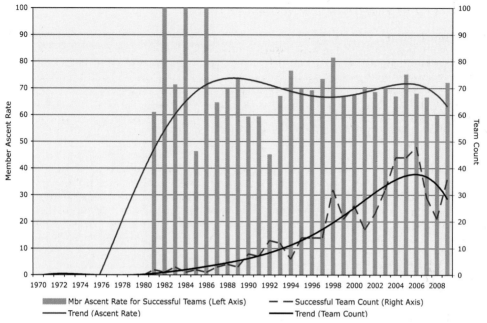

**Chart A-17a: Member ascent rates by expedition year for successful teams
for commercial (SW Ridge) route on Ama Dablam from 1970-2009**

Member Ascent Rates of Successful Teams for Cho Oyu Commercial Route (1970-2009)

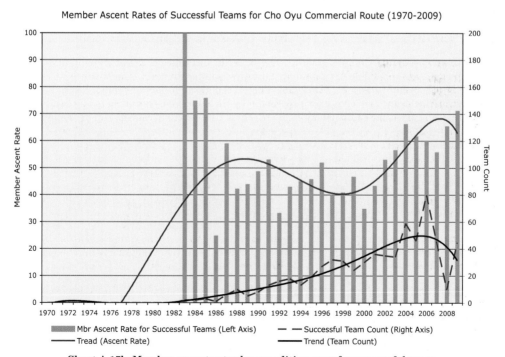

**Chart A-17b: Member ascent rates by expedition year for successful teams
for commercial (NW Ridge) route on Cho Oyu from 1970-2009**

Member Ascent Rates of Successful Teams for Everest Commercial Routes (1970-2009)

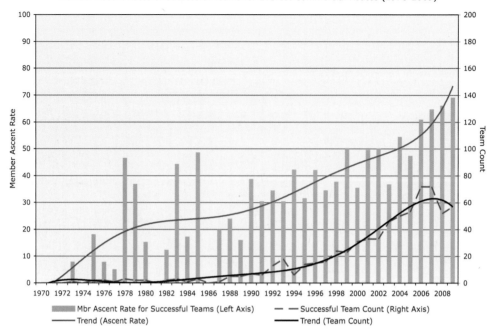

Chart A-17c: Member ascent rates by expedition year for successful teams for commercial (S Col & N Col) routes on Everest from 1970-2009

Yearly Seasonal Ascent Rates for All Peaks (1970-2009)

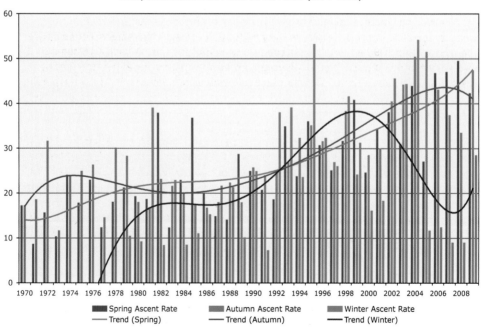

Chart A-18: Yearly seasonal ascent rates for all peaks from 1970-2009

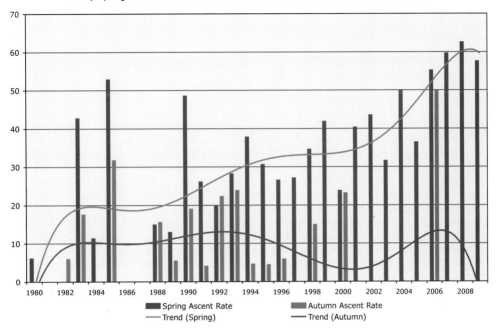

Chart A-19: Yearly spring vs. autumn ascent rates for the Everest South Col and North Col commercial routes from 1980-2009

Charts A-16 and A-17a-c compare member ascent rates and team counts for successful expeditions for all peaks and for the commercial routes on Ama Dablam, Cho Oyu and Everest since 1970. For all peaks, the percentage of members summiting per successful team has increased steadily from about 30% in the early 1970s to over 60% in 2007; for Everest, the average percentage of members summiting per successful team ranges from under 25% in the 1970-80s to over 65% by 2009, with the bulk of the increase occurring after 1990 when Everest commercial climbing become popular, most probably as a result of commercial teams placing a greater emphasis on individual paying clients rather than a team effort to place a few chosen members on top. The member ascent rates for successful teams for Ama Dablam and Cho Oyu commercial routes consistently have been higher than the average rates for all peaks.

Chart A-18 shows the yearly seasonal ascent rates for all peaks from 1970 to 2009. The rates for the spring and autumn seasons are very similar with a general upward bias in recent years. The winter rates are similar to the spring and autumn rates from the early 1980s to the early 2000s. Before and after, a steep drop-off occurs in winter ascent rates because there were no attempts before 1979 and fewer attempts in recent years. The early 1990s were really the golden age of winter climbing when some of the most notable ascents were achieved such as the Japanese ascent of the southwest face of Everest (see the inset box, *Winter Perserverence on Everest*, on pg. 86).

The biggest variation between spring and autumn ascent rates occurs on the commercial routes for Everest as shown in Chart A-19 when the spring ascent rate began a strong upward bias starting in the early 1990s. Improved weather forecasting and increased route familiarity allowed commercial operators to better pinpoint the optimal summit days in mid-May which increased both the success counts and climber

Ascent Analysis 77

traffic at the high bottlenecks of the Hillary Step and the Second Step. The autumn ascent rate dropped off to zero after 2000, except for one successful south-side Everest skiing expedition in October 2006 that summited five members. The spring-autumn ascents rates for Ama Dablam and Cho Oyu do not show this same variation.

Which Way to the Summit?

From The Seasonal Stories of Elizabeth Hawley – Spring 2000

Lhotse saw some successes and some near-successes. The most notable success was that of the veteran Italian mountaineer Sergio Martini. He and his compatriot Fausto De Stefani went together to Lhotse in the autumn of 1997, and when they came back to Kathmandu, they said they had been so very near the top that they considered they could rightfully claim a successful ascent. They were unable to say exactly how near they had gotten because wind was blowing snow in their faces and they were in mist at the time, but they decided they were as close as they could possibly get to the summit without being blown away. "For me and my friend, we feel that we reached very, very near the summit," Martini said with De Stefani beside him. "We are convinced that with the bad weather and without fixed rope we could not have gone higher. In this condition, for us this is the summit. We know we were not at the very last point, but for us this is the summit."

But a South Korean climber, who followed in their footprints on the crusted snow three days later in clearer weather, did not consider that they actually gained the top. While Martini and De Stefani indicated they were perhaps only a few meters below it, Park Young-Seok claimed that their footprints stopped well before the top, perhaps 30 meters below a small fore-summit and 150 vertical meters below the highest summit.

Now in 2000 Martini was back again, and this time he definitely summited Lhotse. The point was a very important one for the Italian pair since they had claimed it as their 13th 8000m summit success, leaving only one more for each of them. They subsequently reached those last summits. Martini was now on an international permit with three other semi-independent climbers who were strangers to each other, but the four men climbed the normal west-face route together as one team without any Sherpas or artificial oxygen. Fifty-year-old Martini went to the top two days after one of others did, but then he was with two Slovenians who confirmed that he certainly summited, and so there is no longer any question of his having been to the tops of all 14 of the highest mountains.

Martini told Simone Moro, an Italian who was on Lhotse's close neighbor, Everest, and whose base camp was at the same place, that "now I am very satisfied because I took the pictures I could not take before, and I touched the summit and saw the middle summit," which one cannot see below the main peak.

To reach the very highest summit of Lhotse via the normal route on its west face, one climbs a well-defined couloir and then just below the top of it moves over onto the left-hand (or northern) of two peaks that appear nearly equal in height from the couloir. Two climbers this spring made the wrong choice and on 26 May climbed the right-hand one.

They were Miss Cathy O'Dowd from South Africa, who was leading her own small team and was a candidate to become the first South African atop Lhotse, and Sandy Allan, a British member of a much larger Everest-Lhotse expedition. They had some discussion about which was actually the higher peak, and Miss O'Dowd's Sherpa, Pemba Tenji, was sure it was the one to the left. He went up that one and reported he had summited it, but the other two decided to go up the one on the right because it appeared to be more interesting technically. They were on their respective peaks at nearly the same time. Miss O'Dowd and Allan believe that a number of other Lhotse summit claimants had also climbed the same peak as they.

Ascents by Day of the Year

Chart A-20a shows member ascents by the day of the year for all peaks from 1990 to 2009 illustrating that the most successful periods are mid to late May and October through early November.

Charts A-20b-d show member ascents for the 6000ers, 7000ers, and 8000ers without the ACE commercial routes. The 6000ers are more spread out, whereas the 7000ers and 8000ers become more concentrated as the peak altitude range increases.

Charts A-20e-f show the members ascents for the Ama Dablam and Cho Oyu commercial routes. The most successful dates for the southwest ridge route of Ama Dablam are late October through early November with the main thrust occurring from October 20-25 and a secondary thrust occurring in the first week of November. The most successful dates for the northwest ridge route of Cho Oyu are from September 24 through October 2, before the colder northern winds from Tibet arrive.

Chart A-20g shows member ascents for the two commercial routes on Everest from 1990 to 2009. May 16-24 is the most successful time for both the north and south sides of Everest; few ascents are made before May 8 and after May 30. The patterns for both sides of Everest are very similar indicating that weather plays a significant role even though the teams on both sides are climbing independently of each other.

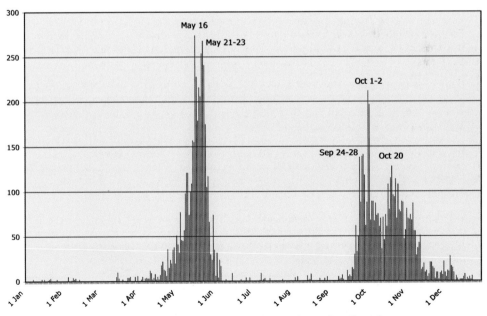

Member Ascents by Day of Year for All Peaks (1990-2009)

**Chart A-20a: Member ascents by day of year for all peaks
and all routes from 1990-2009**

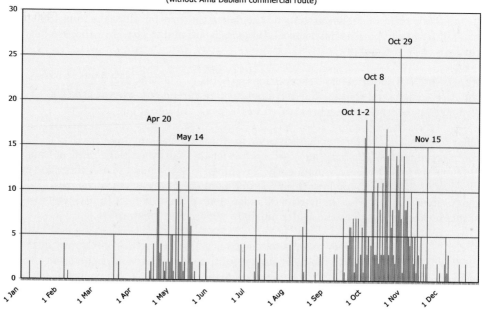

Member Ascents by Day of Year for 6000ers (1990-2009)
(without Ama Dablam commercial route)

**Chart A-20b: Member ascents by day of year for 6000ers
without Ama Dablam commercial route from 1990-2009**

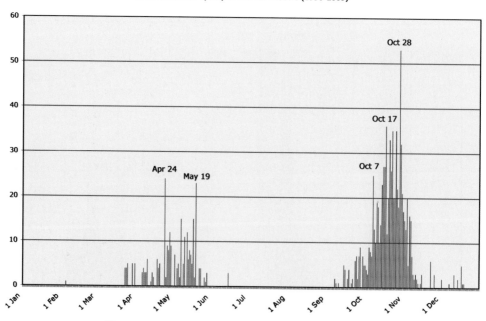

Member Ascents by Day of Year for 7000ers (1990-2009)

**Chart A-20c: Member ascents by day of year for 7000ers
from 1990-2009**

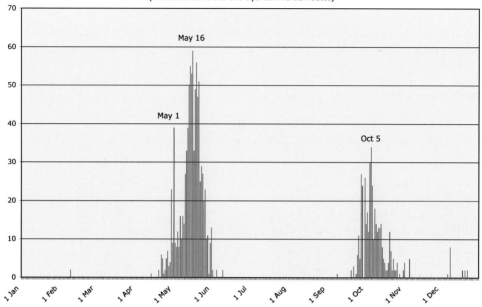

Chart A-20d: Member ascents by day of year for 8000ers without Cho Oyu and Everest commercial routes from 1990-2009

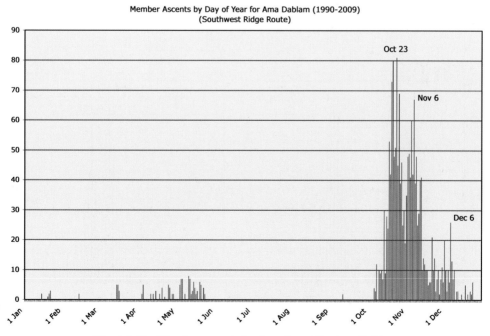

Chart A-20e: Member ascents by day of year for Ama Dablam southwest ridge route from 1990-2009

Ascent Analysis 81

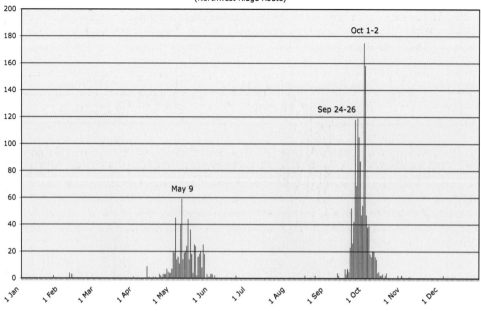

**Chart A-20f: Member ascents by day of year for Cho Oyu
northwest ridge route from 1990-2009**

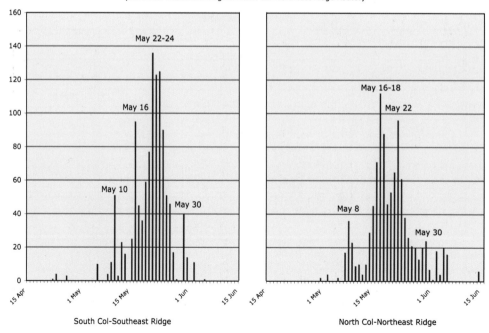

**Chart A-20g: Member ascents by day of year for Everest
commercial routes from 1990-2009**

Ascents by Time of Day

Chart A-21 shows member ascents by the time of day for all peaks and all routes from 1990 to 2009. The mean ascent time is approximately 11 a.m. with the bulk of ascents occurring between 6 a.m. and 4 p.m.

Chart A-22 breaks out the ascent times for the 6000ers, 7000ers, and 8000ers without the ACE commercial routes. As expected, the lower altitude peaks have earlier mean ascent times than the higher peaks: about 11 a.m.-12 p.m. for the 6000ers and 12-1 p.m. for the 7000ers and 8000ers.

Charts A-23a-c show the ascent times for the ACE commercial routes. Ama Dablam has a slightly later ascent time than the other 6000ers possibly due to more congestion on the ascent route, whereas Cho Oyu and Everest have much earlier mean ascent times than the other 8000ers: 9-11 a.m. for Cho Oyu and 8-9 a.m. for Everest. Everest actually breaks down into two surges: an early surge from 6-7 a.m. and a later surge from 9-11 a.m., with the later surge reflecting the crowding that often occurs at the Hillary Step and the Second Step.

For Everest, the times of ascent directly affect the likelihood of survival during descent (see the section *Probability of Death on Everest* in the *Death Analysis* chapter).

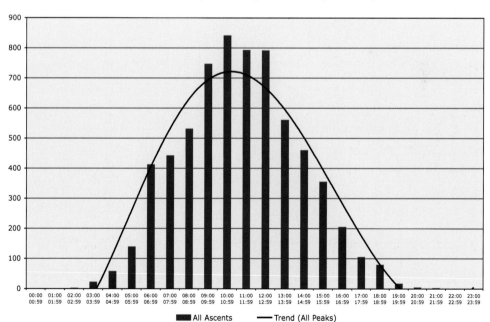

Chart A-21: Member ascents by time of day for all peaks and all routes from 1990-2009

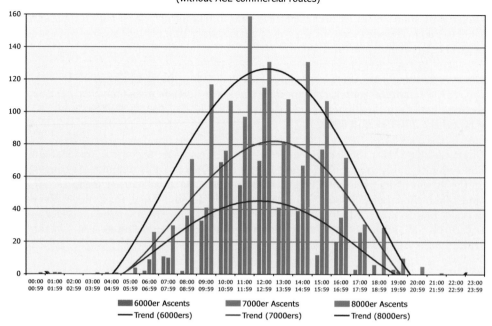

Chart A-22: Member ascents by time of day for 6000ers, 7000ers, and 8000ers without ACE commercial routes from 1990-2009

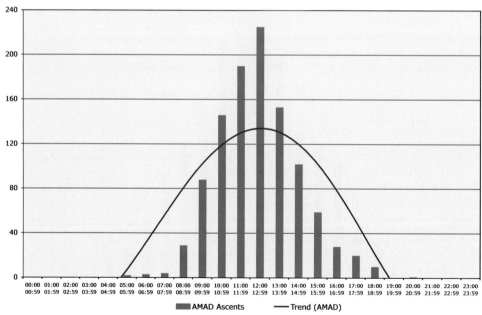

Chart A-23a: Member ascents by time of day for Ama Dablam Southwest Ridge route from 1990-2009

Member Ascents by Time of Day for Cho Oyu (1990-2009)
(Northwest Ridge Route)

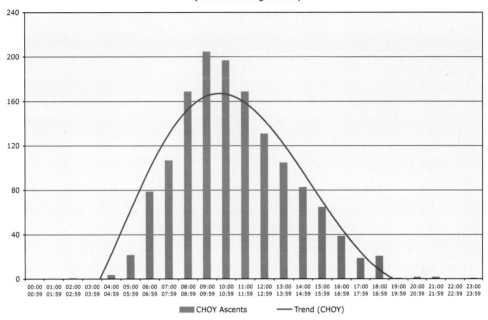

CHOY Ascents   —— Trend (CHOY)

**Chart A-23b Member ascents by time of day for Cho Oyu
Northwest Ridge route from 1990-2009**

Member Ascents by Time of Day for Everest (1990-2009)
(South Col-Southeast Ridge & North Col-Northeast Ridge Routes)

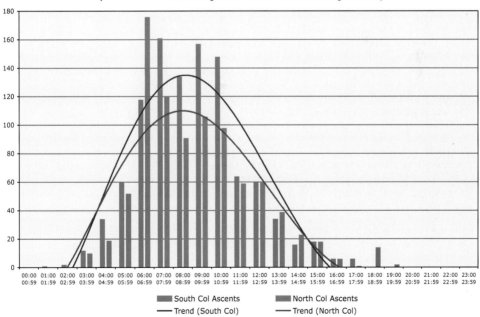

South Col Ascents   North Col Ascents
—— Trend (South Col)   —— Trend (North Col)

**Chart A-23c: Member ascents by time of day for Everest
for South Col-Southeast Ridge & North Col-Northeast Ridge routes from 1990-2009**

Winter Perserverence on Everest

From *The Seasonal Stories* of Elizabeth Hawley – Winter 1991-92, 1993-94

The winter of 1991-92 saw three teams on Everest, two South Korean and one Japanese, who struggled against terrible winter winds at very high altitudes via three different routes, and were never able to climb all the way to its summit.

The 16 Japanese climbers who were on Everest with 25 Nepalese Sherpas to help them, led by the Himalayan climbing veteran Kuniaki Yagihara, had set as their goal the first winter ascent of their mountain's formidable, exposed southwest face. This vast wall rises approximately 2400m from its foot in the high valley known as the Western Cwm, and it has been successfully scaled only three times, by British, Nepalese, Soviet and Czechoslovak climbers from 1975 to 1988, all in milder spring and autumn weather.

"Before the expedition, I had three fears: the cold, the wind and falling stones, but only the wind was a big problem: not so much cold, not so much stonefall," said Yagihara on return to Kathmandu after his team had spent three long months on the mountain. Although the low temperatures and falling stones did cause some slight injury – three members and a Sherpa suffered mild frostbite, and one member received a three-centimeter (slightly more than one-inch) cut on his cheek from a stone – it was the wind that defeated them. How strong was this force that halted four summit-attack parties at altitudes of about 8350m? The answer of the deputy leader, Yoshio Ogata, was not expressed in words but by a sound imitating the whoosh of a jet engine in full blast.

When Ogata and teammate, Fumiaki Goto, made their expedition's first attempt to set up a tent for the fifth high-altitude camp at 8350m on 21 December, the wind broke their tent poles, forcing them to descend without having established the camp. They had managed to climb a small distance above the campsite to what turned out to be the team's highest point, 8370m, before retreating.

Camp 5 was at last pitched on 8 January, slept in that night and again on the 15th, and reached for the last time on 29 January by two out of five members who had set out from camp 4 that day. Each time the climbers were confronted by devastating winds forcing their retreat. A total of seven tents, including two down at base camp, were torn apart. Although the expedition had taken 14 tons of cargo to base, they were beginning to run out of tents, and, more seriously, the Sherpas were becoming sufficiently demoralized by the constant battering by the gales that they were unwilling to carry more supplies of oxygen up to camp 5 for still another summit attack, which the Japanese wanted to mount when the winds seemed to diminish on 9 February.

So instead of trying one last time for camp 5 and the summit, the expedition decided on 9 February to abandon their effort. They had been climbing since 16 November, when they began making their route immediately above base camp through the Khumbu Icefall, where seracs were frequently falling and four Sherpas had to be permanently assigned to the task of repairing the route every day. Will Yagihara and Ogata try again? "I cannot say," was the reply each man gave in Kathmandu.

But the Japanese did return in the winter 1993-94 with a highly organized, well-financed, and abundantly equipped team with experienced leadership and 28 climbing Sherpas to help the seven Japanese climbing members reach the top of the world via one of its most difficult climbing routes, the vast southwest face, despite bitterly cold winter winds, and in the unusually short climbing period of only three weeks. The Japanese leadership were three Himalayan veterans: Kuniaki Yagihara, plus deputy leader Yoshio Ogata and climbing leader Hideji Nazuka. They carefully planned their effort, which actually began last autumn with the ascent by all seven Everest climbing members, plus Yagihara, five more compatriots and five of their Sherpas, of nearby Cho Oyu, which is very high but not very difficult by its normal route. Their successful climb of this mountain gave them good acclimatization to high altitudes; their use of artificial oxygen when they went to its summit minimized the likelihood of frostbite. They then spent three weeks resting in Kathmandu and southern lowland Nepal before returning to the high mountains.

When the Everest climbers arrived at base camp on 21 November, two of their Cho Oyu teammates had already established the camp and supervised the arrival of their 13 tons of food, tents and clothing for 50 people (seven Japanese climbers, leader and doctor at base camp, 28 high-altitude Sherpas, two head Sherpas and three Sherpa cooks at base and advance base, five kitchen helpers at base and three mail runners from and to base), plus all their equipment including a special light platform for their highest camp, 6000m of rope for fixing the route in the treacherous Khumbu Icefall and up much of the face, and 96 bottles of oxygen (65 were actually used).

Everest climbs usually take about six weeks. All seven of these Japanese climbers and their leader had experienced two grueling months of struggle in the winter of 1991-92 in their first attempt to scale the face. They were driven back then by fierce winds, and by the end of the two months, their Sherpas were no longer willing to continue the exertion to carry supplies to the highest camps. Now, this second time, the Japanese knew the route, which was the same line taken in the autumn of 1975 in the first successful ascent of the face by the British expedition led by Chris Bonington, and the one attempted by the Japanese themselves two years ago. They knew its problems, including what they needed to make a proper last camp at 8350m from which to make their final summit assault.

The Nepalese government's mountaineering regulations fix 1 December as the first day of the winter season. In the last half of November, the expedition's Sherpas made the route through the Khumbu Icefall with 50 ladders and 2000m of fixed rope, and carried supply loads to the top of it, the site of the first camp above base. At the same time the Japanese climbers made a quick climb of a small peak in the Everest region, Pokalde (5806m), which they all summited, and then they got down to their siege of Everest itself, well-acclimatized, fit and in good climbing condition. On 1 December, seven re-acclimatized members and a number of Sherpas moved up through the Icefall, and by that afternoon six of the Japanese were established in camp 2. Their epic climb had begun.

Winter is not usually a period of much snowfall, and for the Japanese there was only one day when new snow fell all day long. However on the face there was falling rock, which was blown loose from the mountain by the strong winds, and several climbers' headlamps and goggles were damaged, but no one was hurt. The problems were the wind and the cold. At base camp the temperature was minus 16 degrees Celsius; at 5:00 a.m. one day at the highest camp, camp 4 at 8350m, it was minus 36, and at the summit it probably was minus 45. The winds were especially fierce above the south summit – so fierce that the air was full of swirling snow blown off the mountain, making it impossible for the summiters to see Makalu not far away to the east.

Three pairs of Japanese reached the summit of Everest. "In winter the face is very easy to climb," says Ogata, "after route-making is finished." Between camp 2 at 6500m near the bottom of the face and the south summit (8750m), they had fixed their route with 3635m of rope. On the final difficult part of the entire climb, the Hillary Step on the southeast ridge, which they joined at the south summit, they had no need to fix any rope, for plenty had been left there by expeditions in previous seasons.

The successful summiters on the 18th, 20th and 22nd of December were Hideji Nazuka and Fumiaki Goto, Osamu Tanabe and Shinsuki Ezuka, Yoshio Ogata and Ryushi Hoshino. (The seventh climbing member had developed chest pains on reaching camp 4 on the 13th and was forced to abandon the climb.) With the use of bottled oxygen while sleeping and climbing at and above their two highest camps, the Japanese suffered no really serious damage from frostbite, although one member's fingers did get somewhat frostbitten. "We could not climb Everest in winter without oxygen and not lose all our fingers and toes," Yagihara said.

His team had achieved the first Japanese ascent of the face as well as its first ascent in wintertime by anyone. Yagihara and Ogata attributed their success to four factors: they had made a proper, complete camp 4 at 8350m; they were in good health and were well-acclimatized from their Cho Oyu and Pokalde climbs; they knew the route from their 1991-92 attempt; and they were under considerable psychological pressure to succeed this time. "Now I can go back to Japan," said Yagihara, stressing the word "now," following their success. Clearly another important factor was generous financing.

Ascents by Age Groups

Table and Chart A-24 show member ascent counts and rates by age groups in 5-year intervals. The table is divided into three sections: all peaks and routes from 1950 to 1989, and all peaks and routes from 1990 to 2009 including only and excluding the commercial routes on Ama Dablam, Cho Oyu, and Everest.

Age Groups	1950-1989 All Peaks with All Routes			1990-2009 Ama Dablam-Cho Oyu-Everest Commercial Routes Only			1990-2009 All Peaks and Routes excluding Ama Dablam-Cho Oyu-Everest Commercial Rtes		
	Above BC	Ascent Cnt	Ascent Rate	Above BC	Ascent Cnt	Ascent Rate	Above BC	Ascent Cnt	Ascent Rate
Unknown	1066	147	13.8	134	50	37.3	284	50	17.6
10-14	1	0	0.0	4	0	0.0	1	0	0.0
15-19	48	10	20.8	70	36	51.4	49	25	51.0
20-24	1288	271	21.0	614	284	46.3	705	174	24.7
25-29	3512	822	23.4	1799	809	45.0	1923	505	26.3
30-34	3016	662	22.0	2692	1244	46.2	2415	605	25.1
35-39	1932	386	20.0	2773	1275	46.0	2230	597	26.8
40-44	1105	207	18.7	2332	1016	43.6	1769	474	26.8
45-49	497	90	18.1	1653	656	39.7	1229	322	26.2
50-54	240	25	10.4	1066	381	35.7	728	187	25.7
55-59	95	8	8.4	570	183	32.1	448	101	22.5
60-64	35	2	5.7	295	101	34.2	228	44	19.3
65-69	13	0	0.0	95	29	30.5	91	27	29.7
70-74	3	0	0.0	38	10	26.3	28	10	35.7
75-79	2	1	50.0	6	2	33.3	4	2	50.0

Table A-24: Member ascents by age groups

Chart A-24 shows the difference between the 1950-1989 and 1990-2009 periods and the effects of commercial climbing when considering a climber's age.

During the 1950-1989 period (before commercial climbing), the optimal age for summiting was in the late 20s to early 30s as shown by the blue trend line in the chart. Above that age, the member ascent rate shows a slow steady decline as age increases into the 40s followed by a more rapid decline into the 50s and 60s. After age 65, no ascents were made.

During the 1990-2009 period for the ACE commercial routes (the red trend line), the optimal age shifts upward to the middle to late 30s with a slower decline as climbers age beyond 40. Also ascents were made by climbers in their late 60s and early 70s as shown by the red columns. There is also a very high ascent rate for very young climbers under age 20, but this is based on a relatively small sample size.

Member Ascent Rates by Age Groups (1950-2009)

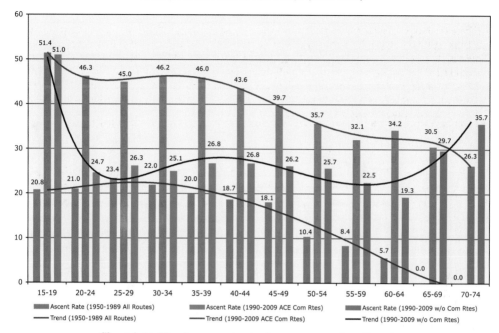

Chart A-24: Member ascent rates by age groups for all routes
between 1950-1989 (blue) and between 1990-2009 for
only ACE commercial routes (red) and excluding ACE commercial routes (green)

Member Ascent Rates for 6000ers, 7000ers, and 8000ers
All Peaks and Routes (1990-2009)

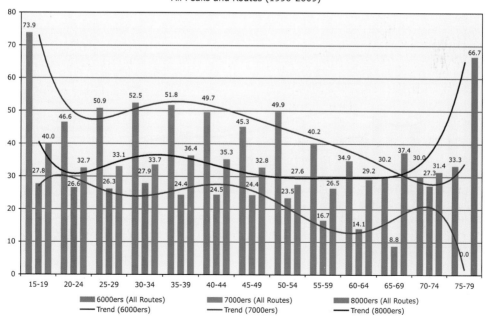

Chart A-25: Member ascent rates by age groups for
6000ers, 7000ers, and 8000ers from 1990-2009 for all peaks and routes

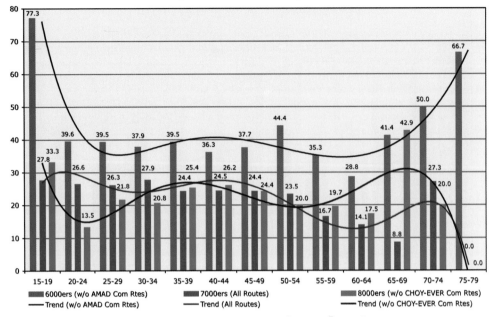

Member Ascent Rates for 6000ers, 7000ers, and 8000ers
Excluding ACE Commercial Routes (1990-2009)

**Chart A-26: Member ascent rates by age groups for
6000ers, 7000ers, and 8000ers from 1990-2009 excluding
commercial routes for Ama Dablam, Cho Oyu, and Everest**

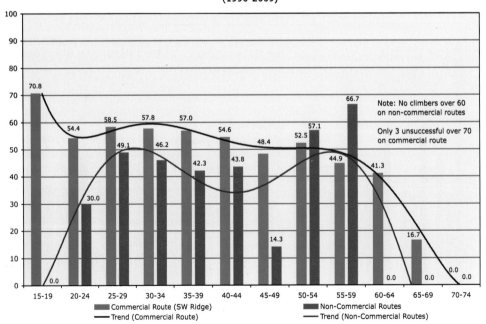

Ama Dablam Member Ascent Rates by Age Group
(1990-2009)

**Chart A-27a: Member ascent rates by age groups for the commercial (SW Ridge)
and non-commercial routes for Ama Dablam from 1990-2009**

90 Ascent Analysis

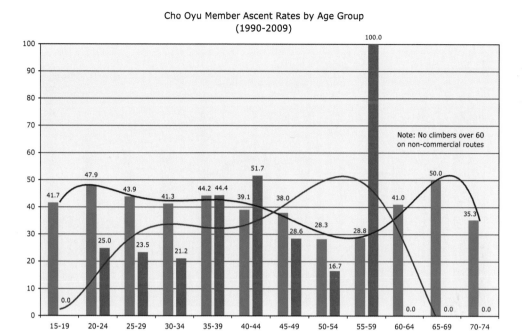

Chart A-27b: Member ascent rates by age groups for the commercial (NW Ridge) and non-commercial routes for Cho Oyu from 1990-2009

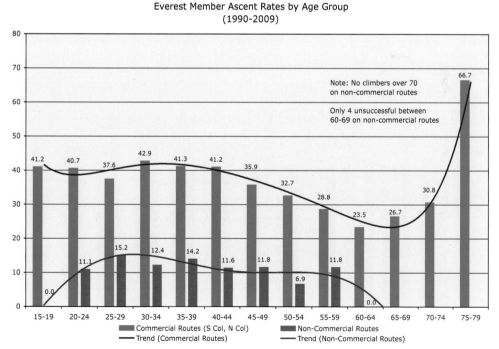

Chart A-27c: Member ascent rates by age groups for the commercial (S Col & N Col) and non-commercial routes for Everest from 1990-2009

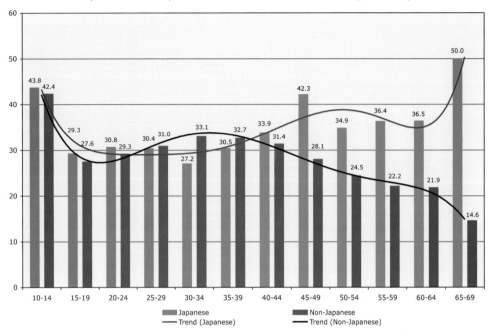

Chart A-28: Japanese vs. non-Japanese ascent rates for all peaks from 1950-2009

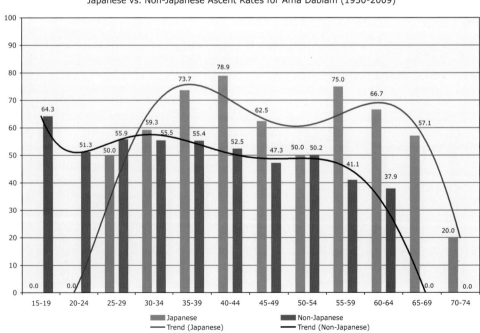

Chart A-29a: Japanese vs. non-Japanese ascent rates for Ama Dablam from 1950-2009

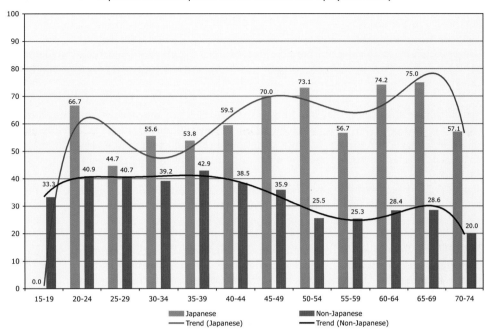

Japanese vs. Non-Japanese Ascent Rates for Cho Oyu (1950-2009)

Chart A-29b: Japanese vs. non-Japanese ascent rates for Cho Oyu from 1950-2009

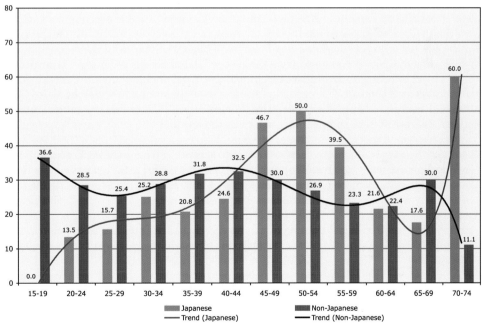

Japanese vs. Non-Japanese Ascent Rates for Everest (1950-2009)

Chart A-29c: Japanese vs. non-Japanese ascent rates for Everest from 1950-2009

Ascent Analysis 93

For the non-commercial routes during the 1990-2009 period (the **green** trend line), the optimal age shifts even higher into the late 30s to early 40s (see the discussion of Japanese climbers below).

Charts A-25 and A-26 compare member ascent rates for all peaks between the 6000ers, 7000ers, and 8000ers by age groups both including and excluding the Ama Dablam, Cho Oyu, and Everest commercial routes.

For the 6000ers, a noticeable flattening of the (**blue**) trend line occurs when the Ama Dablam southwest ridge route is excluded indicating higher ascent rates for climbers under 50. However, younger climbers under 20 seem to do very well on the 6000ers, perhaps due to better supervision by older and more experienced partners.

Charts A-27a-c compare the member ascent rates for Ama Dablam, Cho Oyu, and Everest by age groups for the commercial and non-commercial routes.

Chart A-28 shows Japanese vs. non-Japanese ascents rates for all peaks from 1950 to 2009. Beginning at age 50 the Japanese have substantially higher ascent rates than other nationalities; in fact the elder Japanese have higher ascent rates than their younger compatriots. Many of these ascents are by groups of Japanese seniors in excellent health with good climbing skills attempting peaks in the 6000-6500m range. The Japanese have sent the most climbers to the Nepal Himalaya of any nationality (see Table C-12a in the previous chapter); hence these ascent rates are not a result of low numbers with very skilled climbers such as for the Kazakhs or Slovenians.

For the oldest climbers, the Japanese do exceptionally well. 19 of the 28 summiters of all peaks that are of age 70 or older are Japanese. These ascents include six Cho Oyu summits and six Everest summits; the majority of the remainder are low 6000ers. Before 2008 the oldest summiter was Nobuo Akayama who at age 75 summited Arniko Chuli (6034m) and Yemelung Kang (6024m) in 2003. Other notable ascents were of Cho Oyu in 2002 by Ms. Toshiko Uchida (age 70) and of Everest in 2003 by Yuichiro Miura (age 70), who previously gained fame in 1970 as "the man who skied down Everest" and in 2006 by Takao Arayama (also age 70, but 3 days older than Miura). Miura vowed to return to Everest to recapture his record and did summit Everest in May 2008 at the age of 75, but a 76-year old Nepali Min Bahadur Sherchan also summited Everest a day earlier to capture the age record [Miura has vowed to return again to Everest in 2013 to retake his record at the age of 80].

Charts A-29a-c show Japanese vs. non-Japanese ascents rates for the ACE peaks. For Ama Dablam and Cho Oyu, Japanese have done better for most ages, whereas for Everest, they have done best at the middle ages (45-59) and the oldest ages (70-74).

Ascents by Gender

Table and Chart A-30 show member ascent rates by gender from 1950 to 1989 and 1990 to 2009.

The table and chart show that for all peaks men had significantly higher ascent rates than women during the 1950-1989 period (20.7% to 15.8%), but this advantage subsequently narrowed during the 1990-2009 period (35.1% to 34.6%) and became statistically insignificant.

	Men			Women			Male/ Female Ascent Ratio
	Above BC	Ascent Cnt	Ascent Rate	Above BC	Ascent Cnt	Ascent Rate	
All 6000ers (1950-1989)	2017	822	40.8	163	54	33.1	1.23
All 7000ers (1950-1989)	4003	832	20.8	230	33	14.3	1.45
All 8000ers (1950-1989)	6124	865	14.1	316	25	7.9	1.79
All Peaks (1950-1989)	12144	2519	20.7	709	112	15.8	1.31
All 6000ers (1990-2009)	4519	2244	49.7	640	283	44.2	1.12
All 6000ers w/o AMAD Com Rte (1990-2009)	1544	607	39.3	236	82	34.7	1.13
All 7000ers (1990-2009)	3954	989	25.0	489	100	20.4	1.22
All 8000ers (1990-2009)	15051	5014	33.3	1620	569	35.1	0.95
All 8000ers w/o CHOY-EVER Com Rtes (1990-2009)	5461	1242	22.7	448	103	23.0	0.99
All Peaks (1990-2009)	23524	8247	35.1	2749	952	34.6	1.01
All Peaks w/o ACE Com Rtes (1990-2009)	10959	2838	25.9	1173	285	24.3	1.07
Ama Dablam Com Rte (1990-2009)	2975	1637	55.0	404	201	49.8	1.11
Cho Oyu Com Rte (1990-2009)	4450	1786	40.1	570	230	40.4	0.99
Everest Com Rtes (1990-2009)	5140	1986	38.6	602	236	39.2	0.99
AMAD-CHOY-EVER Com Rtes (1990-2009)	12565	5409	43.0	1576	667	42.3	1.02

Table A-30: Member ascents by gender from 1950-1989 and 1990-2009

Statistical significances of ascent rates for men (M) and women (W):

1950-1989:

6000ers:	M (40.8), W (33.1), p=.068
7000ers:	M (20.8), W (14.3), p=.023
8000ers:	M (14.1), W (7.9), p=.002
All peaks:	M (20.7), W (15.8), p=.002

1990-2009:

6000ers:	M (49.7), W (44.2), p=.011
6000ers xAMAD:	M (39.3), W (34.7), p=.204
7000ers:	M (25.0), W (20.4), p=.031
8000ers:	M (33.3), W (35.1), p=.150
8000ers xCHOY, EVER:	M (22.7), W (23.0), p=.950
All peaks:	M (35.1), W (34.6), p=.672
All peaks xACE:	M (25.9), W (24.3), p=.248
AMAD Com Rte:	M (55.0), W (49.8), p=.052
CHOY Com Rte:	M (40.1), W (40.4), p=.956
EVER Com Rtes:	M (38.6), W (39.2), p=.821
All ACE Com Rtes:	M (43.0), W (42.3), p=.602

p-values for statistically significant differences (p <= .05) are shown in red above and their columns are outlined in black in Chart A-31. All others are statistically insignificant.

But when the commercial routes for Ama Dablam, Cho Oyu, and Everest are factored out for all peaks during the 1990-2009 period, the men have a slightly higher, but still insignificant, ascent rate (25.9% to 24.3%). Women have done the best on these commercial routes, trailing men on technically more difficult Ama Dablam, but doing slightly better than men on the higher Cho Oyu and Everest. The overall ascent rate for all the commercial routes is nearly even for men and women (43.0% to 42.3%).

Chart A-31 gives the male to female member ascent ratios, which is another way to compare the ascent rates between men and women. The ascent ratio is defined as the male ascent rate divided by the female ascent rate.

For the 1950-1989 period, the ascent ratios vary from under 1.3 for the 6000ers to over 1.8 for the 8000ers, which is approaching a success rate for men of almost double of that for women for the 8000ers. The chart also shows that the higher the peak, the greater the difference in ascent ratios between men and women.

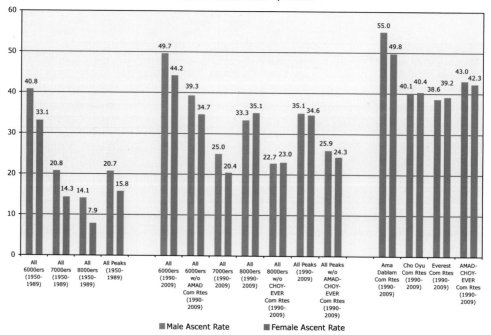

Chart A-30: Member ascent rates by gender from 1950-1989 and 1990-2009

Male/Female Member Ascent Ratios

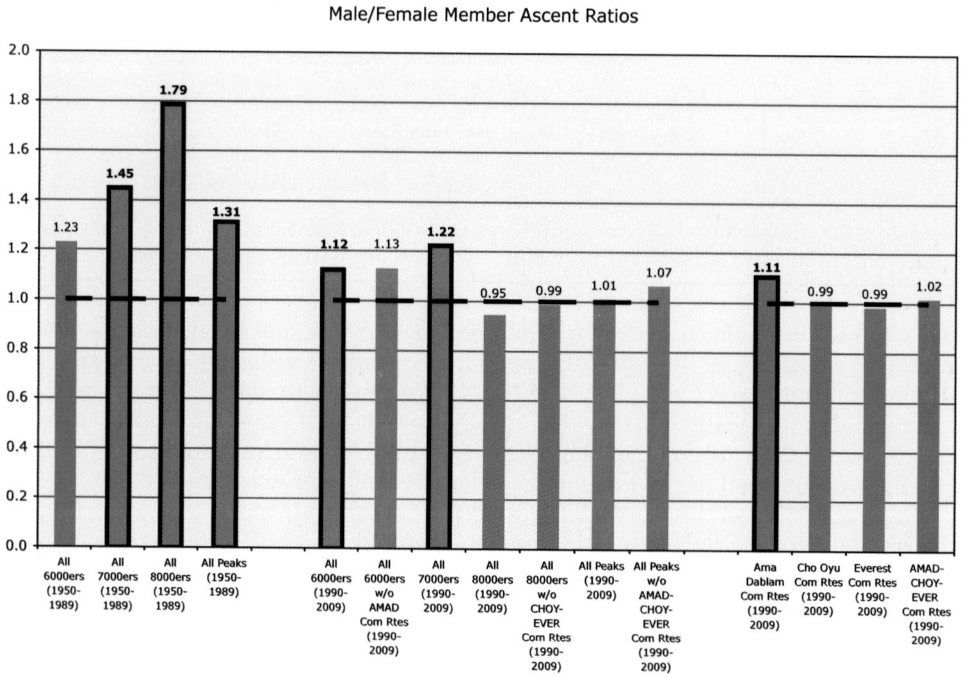

Chart A-31: Male to Female member ascent ratios from 1950-1989 and 1990-2009
(red columns show better rates for men, blue columns show better rates for women)
the columns with statistically significant differences are outlined in black)

96 Ascent Analysis

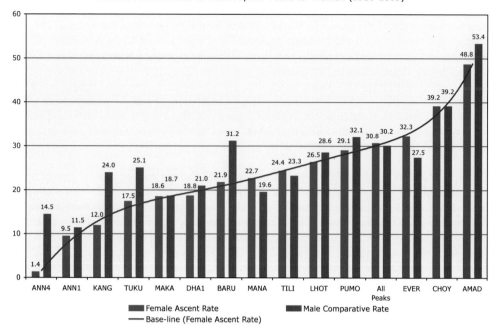

Member Ascent Rates for Most Popular Peaks for Women (1950-2009)

**Chart A-32: Ascent rates for peaks with 40+ women above base camp from 1950-2009
(includes all routes for Ama Dablam, Cho Oyu, Everest, and other peaks)**

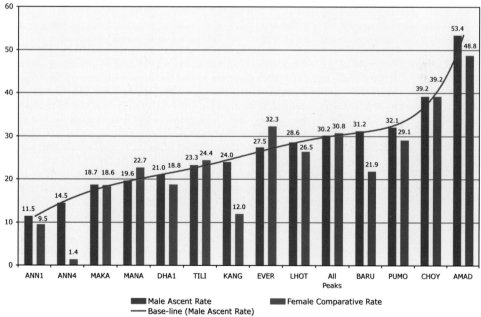

Member Ascent Rates for Most Popular Peaks for Men (1950-2009)

**Chart A-33: Ascent rates for peaks with 400+ men above base camp from 1950-2009
(includes all routes for Ama Dablam, Cho Oyu, Everest, and other peaks)**

For the 1990-2009 period, the ascents ratios are much closer varying from .95 to 1.23. Ascent ratios under 1.0 (shown in **blue**) indicate better ascent rates for women. The increased level of success that women have had on Cho Oyu and Everest combined with the very large numbers of climbers to those peaks has dramatically narrowed the difference of ascent rates between men and women for all the 8000ers and for all peaks. From 1990 to 2007, men had better success rates on the non-commercial 8000ers, but in 2008 and 2009 the successes of a small core of women competing for the 14 8000ers closed the gap to about even with the men. However women still fare worse on expeditions to the 7000ers, which in many cases use less hired support and require heavier load carrying by the climbers themselves.

Chart A-32 shows the female ascent rates along with the male comparative rates for the most popular peaks climbed by women, those peaks with 40 or more women above base camp. The female rates in general are comparable to the male rates except for Annapurna IV, Kangchenjunga, Tukuche, and Baruntse. The women slightly exceled on Everest when considering all climbing routes (because men had lower success rates on the non-commercial routes that were less frequently attempted by women). Chart A-33 shows male ascent rates along with female comparative rates for the most popular peaks climbed by men, those peaks with 400 or more men above base camp. The female rates in general are comparable to the male rates except for Annapurna IV, Kangchenjunga, and Baruntse.

An "Unsupported" Ascent of Everest

From *The Seasonal Stories* of Elizabeth Hawley – Spring 1995

Alison Hargreaves, Britain's best woman climber, reached the top of Everest via the North Col-northeast ridge on 13 May 1995 at 12:08 p.m., shortly after two Italians, who had camped very near her last camp at 8300m. She was the first woman to make an unsupported ascent of Everest, and she accomplished this without the use of any supplemental oxygen.

Hargreaves does not claim to have made a solo ascent as some of the British press trumpeted – how could she when there were 182 other climbers including the two Italians on the same route and 33 more on the Japanese route that joins hers very high up? Nor does she claim to have been the first woman to summit without using any bottled oxygen. That distinction belongs to a New Zealander, Lydia Bradey. But Hargreaves is the first British woman to have done so. And other climbers on her route concur that she can rightfully claim to have made the first unsupported ascent by any woman. By "unsupported" she means that she was an entirely self-contained unit above advance base camp, that she carried all her own supplies of tents, gear and food up the mountain, slept in her own tents rather than in camps pitched by or with others, ate her own high-altitude food which she cooked herself, and did not climb in the company of anyone else. The other climbers noted that she had refused invitations to come into their tents for a chat or a cup of their tea; she stayed outside to visit with them, and she drank her own brews.

According to her account, Hargreaves carried her loads of supplies in three trips to the North Col (7000m), where the north ridge begins, slept there the third time, then down to advance base; went up to 7000m, pitched a tent and slept one night there, then again down to advance base. Finally she started her summit push on 11 May, went up to the Col, picked up gear including a tent and went to her other tent at 7700m where she slept that night. On the 12th she climbed to 8300m and pitched there the tent she had brought from the Col; she had a hard time making her own platform for this tent, having to move a lot of stones to do so, and she spent the night melting snow and drinking liquids, occasionally falling into a light sleep. She had no sleeping bag with her at 8300m because she had lightened her final load as much as she possibly could.

At 4:40 on the morning of the 13th (Nepalese time) she left the tent for the top of the world in very clear weather with no wind, but "it was incredibly cold." She took with her a water bottle, a small camera, a walkie-talkie radio and spare batteries for her foot-warmers (she had suffered frostbitten toes on earlier climbs and did not want frozen feet again). Climbing not far behind the two Italian summiters, Marco Bianchi and Christian Kuntner, she joined them on the summit at 12:08 p.m. and left them after 40 minutes. She had noticed a single set of footprints coming up to the top from the Nepalese side, prints that she learned later would have been made on 7 May by Lobsang Jangbu Sherpa of a commercial team from Nepal. She took photos and sent a message by walkie-talkie: "to Tom and Kate, my two children, I'm on top of the world and I love them dearly." Then down she went.

At 4:00 p.m. she packed up her tent at 8300m, chatted with some Sherpas, and set off down to 7700m, where she arrived at 7:00 p.m. in fading daylight and stayed the night. (The Italians, she said, descended only as far as 8300m, and the leader of another expedition reported that she descended "in good order," whereas the Italians were quite sick). On the next day, the 14th, she continued down alone to 6500m, where an American and a New Zealander came up to meet her, and the three went down together to advance base, where she arrived at perhaps 2:00 p.m. "very, very tired."

Throughout this final day's descent, all of the 20 or more Sherpas she met wanted to shake her hand and hug her, and the dozen foreigners along the route congratulated her and gave her hand a shake. "At this point, I realized that I had done something people thought was quite special. I still find it hard to believe [in a posh Kathmandu hotel a week later] that I actually climbed Mount Everest."

Commented Bianchi when he too had returned to Kathmandu: "She is a new star of the Himalaya – of women for sure, but also of men. She climbs like a man. She is very strong. And very kind." Her future climbing plans were immediate: she would go next to the world's second highest mountain, K2 in Pakistan's Karakoram range, a month or so later and to the third highest, Kangchenjunga, in the autumn or next spring.

Note: Reinhold Messner is the only climber that has truly soloed Everest, during the summer of 1980 when he was entirely alone on the mountain. Alison Hargreaves died on K2 in the summer of 1995, trapped near the summit in a severe storm.

Ascents by Citizenship

Table A-34 shows *member* ascent rates by citizenship for all peaks and Everest for those nationalities that had a substantial number of members above base camp (60 or more for all peaks and 20 or more for Everest). Citizens from countries that had fewer than the 60- or 20-member cutoff points are grouped into the "**All Others**" category.

Citizens of Nepal and China are split into two groups: Sherpas/non-Sherpas and Tibetans/non-Tibetans, respectively, in order to differentiate the higher-altitude from the lower-altitude residents. Also for Nepalese Sherpas and Chinese Tibetans, the numbers above base camp include only those who were actual members of an expedition, not those who were hired as high-altitude assistants. For all peaks and Everest, the Sherpas and Tibetans performed much better than their countrymen as full members of expeditions, but the actual ascent rates of Tibetans may be somewhat suspect due to the lack of reliable information regarding whether they were actually full members or hired personnel because the climbing permits issued in China do not

All Peaks				Everest			
Citizenship	Above BC	Ascent Cnt	Ascent Rate	Citizenship	Above BC	Ascent Cnt	Ascent Rate
Kazakhstan	115	69	60.0	Mexico	61	35	57.4
USSR	239	140	58.6	USSR	62	31	50.0
China (Tibetan)	323	177	54.8	Malaysia	29	14	48.3
Ukraine	195	95	48.7	China (Tibetan)	211	100	47.4
Iran	143	69	48.3	Kazakhstan	35	16	45.7
Russia	728	338	46.4	Slovenia	22	10	45.5
Nepal (Sherpa)	235	109	46.4	**All others**	284	123	43.3
All others	775	333	43.0	Russia	230	95	41.3
Mexico	162	69	42.6	Iran	37	15	40.5
Singapore	60	25	41.7	New Zealand	159	63	39.6
Finland	87	36	41.4	Nepal (Sherpa)	137	53	38.7
New Zealand	493	204	41.4	Ukraine	34	13	38.2
China (non-Tibetan)	368	148	40.2	S Africa	56	21	37.5
S Africa	83	32	38.6	Singapore	24	9	37.5
Norway	287	106	36.9	Finland	27	10	37.0
Denmark	137	49	35.8	Greece	25	9	36.0
Switzerland	1620	566	34.9	Australia	163	56	34.4
Australia	759	258	34.0	USA	1412	477	33.8
Germany	1564	527	33.7	Denmark	36	12	33.3
USA	4037	1355	33.6	Ireland	51	17	33.3
Ireland	120	40	33.3	Norway	84	28	33.3
Chile	104	33	31.7	Canada	234	75	32.1
W Germany	680	214	31.5	India	447	142	31.8
Romania	61	19	31.1	W Germany	45	14	31.1
Slovenia	348	106	30.5	Bulgaria	42	12	28.6
Japan	4806	1456	30.3	Poland	96	27	28.1
Canada	690	206	29.9	UK	853	236	27.7
UK	3064	899	29.3	Colombia	33	9	27.3
France	3208	930	29.0	China (non-Tibetan)	250	66	26.4
Colombia	72	20	27.8	Chile	54	13	24.1
Austria	1390	383	27.6	Japan	717	165	23.0
Nepal (non-Sherpa)	368	97	26.4	Switzerland	221	48	21.7
Poland	955	249	26.1	Austria	141	30	21.3
Greece	120	31	25.8	Germany	133	27	20.3
India	1085	279	25.7	Nepal (non-Sherpa)	129	26	20.2
Belgium	300	76	25.3	France	451	90	20.0
Brazil	87	22	25.3	Sweden	81	16	19.8
Hungary	87	22	25.3	Belgium	67	13	19.4
Italy	2008	499	24.9	Brazil	47	9	19.1
Sweden	234	58	24.8	Italy	326	62	19.0
Czech Republic	373	91	24.4	Netherlands	85	16	18.8
Spain	2541	584	23.0	Taiwan	48	9	18.8
Netherlands	463	102	22.0	Croatia	22	4	18.2
S Korea	2217	468	21.1	S Korea	600	109	18.2
Taiwan	73	15	20.5	Spain	531	87	16.4
Yugoslavia	432	86	19.9	Argentina	29	4	13.8
Bulgaria	184	36	19.6	Yugoslavia	82	11	13.4
Croatia	80	15	18.8	Czech Republic	62	8	12.9
Slovakia	123	23	18.7	Indonesia	24	2	8.3
Argentina	131	20	15.3	Hungary	42	3	7.1
Czechoslovakia	312	46	14.7	Czechoslovakia	60	4	6.7
Mean Ascent Rate			**30.2**	**Mean Ascent Rate**			**27.9**

Table A-34 Member ascents by citizenship from 1950-2009
(minimum 60 Above BC for all peaks, minimum 20 Above BC for Everest)
(blue rows are above the mean ascent rate, black rows are below the mean ascent rate)

make this distinction. *The Himalayan Database* reasonably differentiates between members and hired personnel for foreign expeditions, but the data for the larger Chinese national expeditions are only estimates.

Several countries listed in Table A-34 were transformed by internal political events with the result that many climbers were reclassified with new citizenships:

Autumn 1990 - W Germany & E Germany unified into Germany
Spring 1992   - Slovenia & Croatia seceded from Yugoslavia
Autumn 1992 - USSR split into Russia, Kazakhstan, Ukraine, Georgia, etc.
Spring 1995   - Czechoslovakia split into Czech Republic and Slovakia

The seasons listed above are when climbers first began travelling to Nepal with their new citizenships and passports. Even though the Soviet Union collapsed in late 1991, Soviet climbers continued to use USSR passports during the spring 1992 season.

The climbers from the Soviet-bloc countries (e.g., USSR, Russia, Kazakhstan, Ukraine, Georgia) have done remarkably well because many expeditions from those countries have attempted only the 8000m peaks or difficult routes on the 7000m peaks; fewer have ventured to the 6000m peaks, most likely due to funding constraints that limited training expeditions to the Pamir and Caucasus mountain ranges in Russia. The Japanese, who do very well at the older ages as shown in the earlier section, are much closer to the average when all ages are considered.

Ascents by Team Composition

Expedition team size can also play a role in the ascent rates for climbers. In this section, we look at two factors:

(1)   the number of members above base camp per expedition, and
(2)   the number of hired personnel for each team member above base camp per expedition expressed as the ratio of the number of hired to the number of members above base camp.

Charts A-35a-b show member ascent rates by the numbers above base camp and the hired to member ratios for the Cho Oyu northwest ridge commercial route, the Everest South Col and North Col commercial routes, and the remainder of the 8000ers without these commercial routes from 1950 to 2009. For these higher peaks, team composition plays an important role in expedition success.

Teams with fewer members (3 and under) did better than larger teams, especially single climbers on the 8000m non-commercial routes. Many of these were alpine-style ascents by highly skilled and experienced Himalayan veterans. For the Cho Oyu and Everest commercial routes, the results were much more even regarding overall team size as the composition of commercial teams varied widely from operator-to-operator and year-to-year. The spike in ascent rates for teams of 26-35 members in Chart A-35a was due in part to a 32-member USSR Kangchenjunga traverse in 1989 (27 members summited).

The ratio of hired to members above base camp was more critical for the Cho Oyu and Everest commercial routes as teams with .50 to 2.99 hired per member fared the best

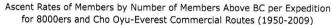

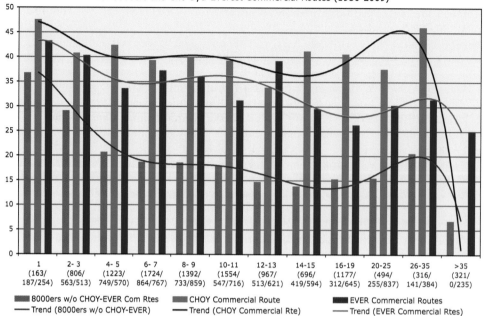

Chart A-35a: Member ascent rates by number of members above base camp per expedition for 8000ers and the Cho Oyu and Everest commercial routes from 1950-2009

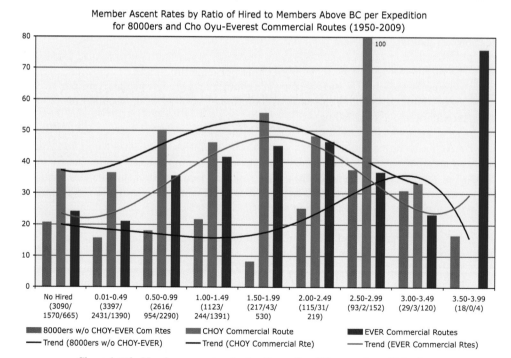

Chart A-35b: Member ascent rates by the ratio of the number of hired to number of members above base camp per expedition for 8000ers and the Cho Oyu and Everest commercial routes from 1950-2009

with 1.50-2.49 being the optimal ratios for success. Everest and Cho Oyu teams with no hired personnel or with very low ratios (<.50) did worse on average than teams with higher ratios. Very few expeditions had ratios higher than 3.0 and for those that did, the results were erratic and unpredictable.

Charts A-36a-b show member ascent rates by the numbers above base camp and the hired to member ratios for the Everest commercial and non-commercial routes from 1990 to 2009. Small teams fared relatively well especially on the non-commercial routes, but the few very large commercial route teams also did exceptionally well (some of those were Indian military and Chinese national expeditions plus a couple of large commercial expeditions). Everest teams with few or no hired personnel had lower ascent rates indicating that too little assistance may have posed difficulties or the teams were opting for the increased challenge.

Chart A-36b shows that for all peaks a hired/members ratio from 3:1 to 4:1 to be the optimum for success. However, it will be shown later in the death analysis chapter that a lower ratio of 1:1 to 2:1 is safer in terms of death risk. Many Everest commercial expeditions currently use a ratio of about 1:1 to 1:2 (one Sherpa or Tibetan assistant for each potential summit climber, plus additional personnel for rope fixing and establishing high camps).

Charts A-37a-b show member ascent rates by the numbers above base camp and the hired to member ratios for all of the 7000ers from 1950 to 2009.

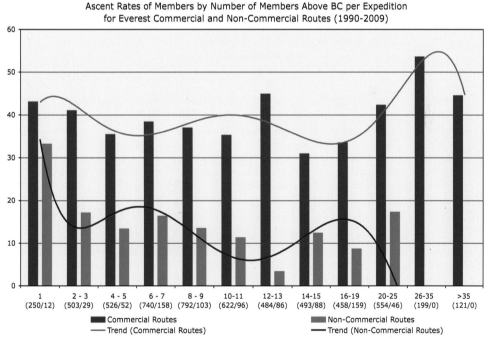

Chart A-36a: Member ascent rates by number of members above base camp
per expedition for the Everest commercial and non-commercial routes from 1990-2009

The numbers in parentheses along the horizontal axes in Charts A-34a through A-38b indicate the number of members above base camp.

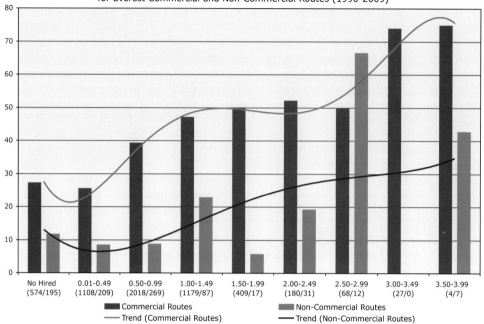

Member Ascent Rates by Ratio of Hired to Members Above BC per Expedition
for Everest Commercial and Non-Commercial Routes (1990-2009)

Commercial Routes
Non-Commercial Routes
Trend (Commercial Routes)
Trend (Non-Commercial Routes)

Chart A-36b: Member ascent rates by the number of hired to number of members above base camp per expedition for the Everest commercial and non-commercial routes from 1990-2009

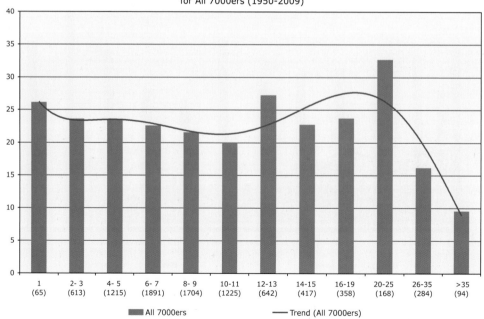

Ascent Rates of Members by Number of Members Above BC per Expedition
for All 7000ers (1950-2009)

All 7000ers
Trend (All 7000ers)

Chart A-37a: Member ascent rates by number of members above base camp per expedition for all 7000ers from 1950-2009

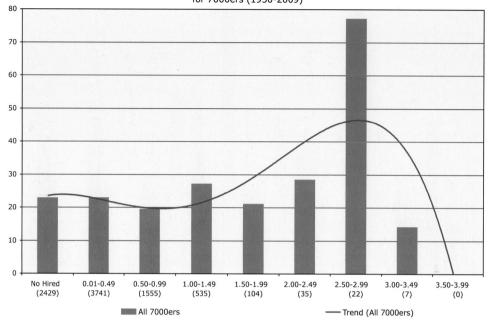

Chart A-37b: Member ascent rates by the ratio of the number of hired to number of members above base camp per expedition for all 7000ers from 1950-2009

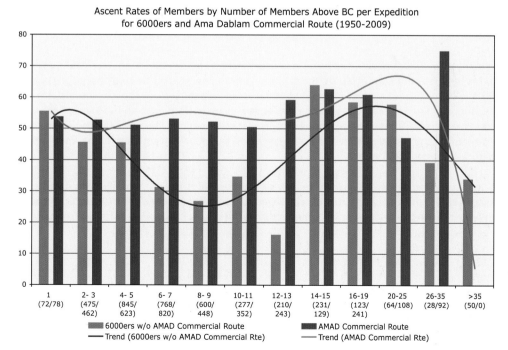

Chart A-38a: Member ascent rates by number of members above base camp per expedition for 6000ers and the Ama Dablam commercial route from 1950-2009

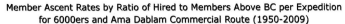

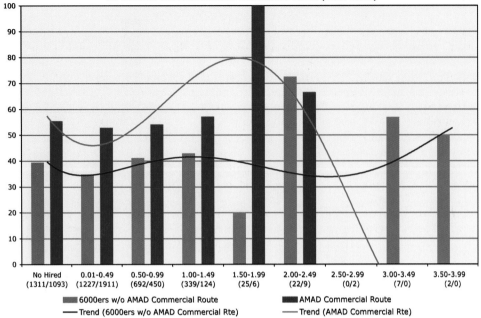

**Chart A-38b: Member ascent rates by the ratio of the number of hired to
number of members above base camp per expedition for 6000ers
and the Ama Dablam commercial route from 1950-2009**

Charts A-38a-b show member ascent rates by the numbers above base camp and the
hired to member ratios for the Ama Dablam southwest ridge commercial route and the
remainder of the 6000ers without the commercial route from 1950 to 2009.

For the sub-8000m peaks, the results are less clear. The optimal team size and number
of hired personnel employed are most likely very dependent on the particular peak. But
for the lower peaks, a point is reached when sheer expedition size becomes counter-
productive. The spike in the ascent rate for teams of 26-35 members in Chart A-38b
was due to two 30-member commercial Ama Dablam expeditions in 2004 and a large
34-member commercial Ama Dablam expedition in 2007. These three teams had very
high ascent rates (63 to 96%).

For all peaks very large teams or teams with excessive hired support had declining
ascent rates indicating that too much assistance may have posed difficulties. It would
appear that teams with over 35 members or hired above base camp suffered from the
sheer size of the expedition and the accompanying logistical problems.

Ascent Rates from High Camp

Up to this point, we have been basing ascent rates on the number of members that
climbed above base camp. But how much are summit chances improved if a climber has
reached the highest camp and is actually proceeding towards the summit?

Charts A-39a-d show the ascent rates from 1990 to 2009 for members dependent on
how far the climber progressed towards the summit: climbing above *base* camp and

climbing above *high* camp on a summit bid (*The Himalayan Database* has the most complete data for this period).

Charts A-40a-d show similar ascent rates from base camp and high camp from 1990 to 2009 for members on the commercial routes of Ama Dablam, Cho Oyu, and Everest.

For Ama Dablam through 2006 many expeditions placed their high camp at 6400m on a small snowfield that was just below the giant ice serac that forms the dablam, which allowed for a reasonably short 400m climb to the summit. But a fatal avalanche in November 2006 destroyed this site killing 6 climbers (see the inset box below, *2006 Ama Dablam Serac Avalanche*). Since that accident, the 6400m site is seldom used with most expeditions camping much lower to avoid the danger of further avalanching from the dablam, which still appears to be quite unstable. Consequently summit day climbers have a 600-800m climb that is much more difficult and exhausting.

For Cho Oyu, high camp on the northwest ridge normally is from 7100m to 7400m on a snowfield below the yellow band. Most climbers reach the summit plateau at 8000m in 4-8 hours and then proceed on to the true summit in 1-2 hours.

For Everest, the high camp is generally at 7900m at the South Col or at 8300m below the First Step on the north side. From high camp, most climbers reach the summit in 8-12 hours including a potential wait at the Hillary Step or the Second Step ladder due to summit day conjestion. Because of the closure of Tibet to foreign expeditions in 2008 and 2009 due to the Chinese Olympic Torch expedition and civil unrest in Tibet, Chart A-40d shows results only through the 2007 season.

Table A-41 summarizes the ascent rates for members that went above base camp and went above high camp. The anomalous high ascent rate for members above base camp in winter for Cho Oyu (61.1%) is based on only 18 members above base camp.

Charts A-42a-b compare the reasons for termination for unsuccessful members below and above high camp on the Ama Dablam commercial route during the spring and autumn seasons from 1990 to 2009. For the spring season, the overwhelming reasons

---

2006 Ama Dablam Serac Avalanche

From *The Seasonal Stories* of Elizabeth Hawley – Autumn 2006

Ama Dablam climbers Duncan Williams from England, and Swedes Mikael Forsberg and Daniel Carlsson, plus their three Sherpas, were asleep in their third and last high camp at 6400m at about 5:00 a.m. on 13 November 2006, just before they were due to crawl out of their tents and go for their summit. They probably never knew what hit them. It was a huge mass of ice that broke away from "the dablam" above, swept them hundreds of meters down the mountainside and buried them in a big mound of avalanche debris. One of Williams' teammates reached the camp's site later that day and found only one metal spoon and two pieces of rope that had been fixed, but were pulled out by the avalanche.

Before that autumn a total of only 11 climbers had perished on Ama Dablam since the first attempts in the late 1950s. Now half that number died on a single day. This was the first fatal avalanche ever to strike the standard southwest ridge route. Thousands of men and women had safely ascended the this ridge; seven had died while climbing it, but six of those had fallen and the other one had succumbed to acute altitude sickness.

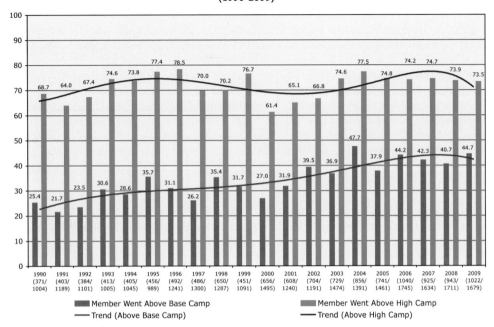

Chart A-39a: High camp success rates for all peaks and all routes from 1990-2009 (the numbers of members above base camp and high camp are given below each year for this and the following charts)

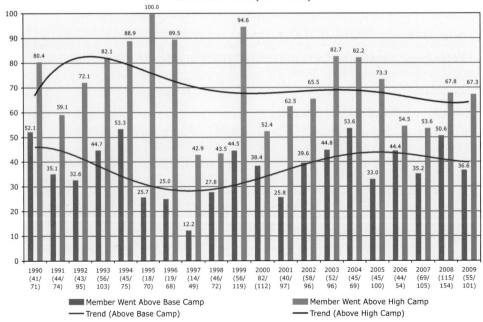

Chart A-39b: High camp success rates for all 6000ers without the Ama Dablam commercial route from 1990-2009

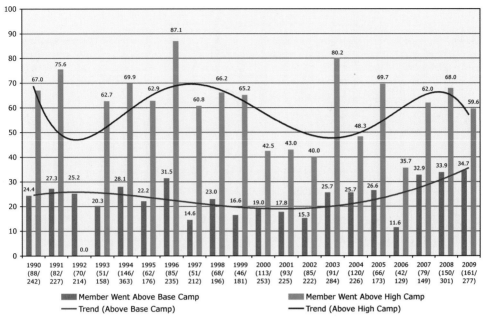

Chart A-39c: High camp success rates for all 7000ers from 1990-2009

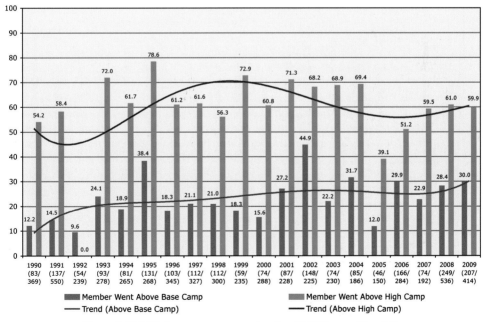

Chart A-39d: High camp success rates for all 8000ers without the Cho Oyu and Everest commercial routes from 1990-2009

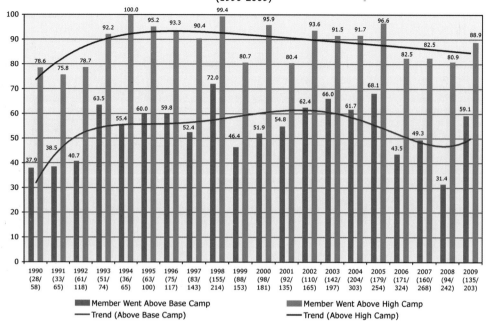

Chart A-40a: High camp success rates for the Ama Dablam SW Ridge commercial route from 1990-2009

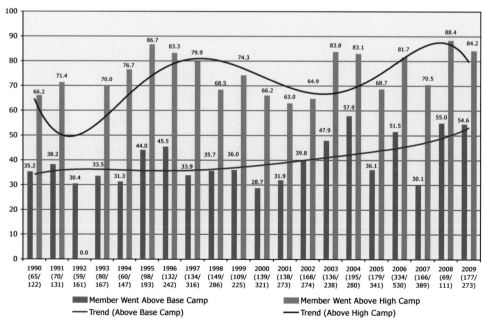

Chart A-40b: High camp success rates for the Cho Oyu NW Ridge commercial route from 1990-2009

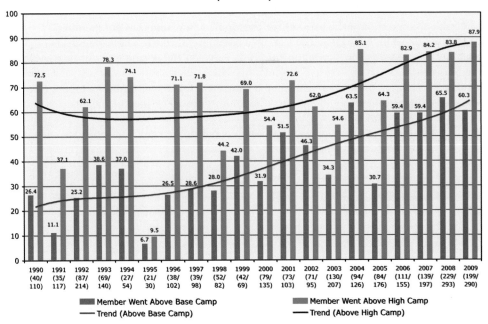

Chart A-40c: High camp success rates for the Everest S Col-SE Ridge commercial route from 1990-2009

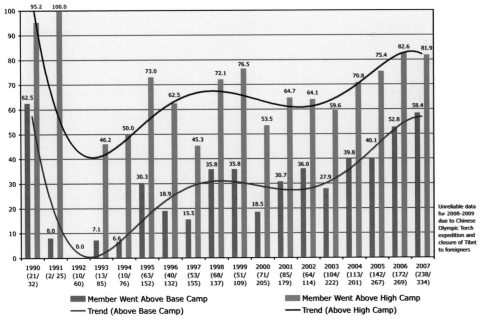

Chart A-40d: High camp success rates for the Everest N Col-NE Ridge commercial route from 1990-2007

are bad weather and bad conditions, whereas for the autumn season, there is a broader range of reasons indicating that more climbing has been attempted than in spring.

Charts A-43a-b compare the reasons for termination for unsuccessful members below and above high camp on the Cho Oyu commercial route. The distribution of terminations reasons shows a similar pattern between the spring and autumn seasons.

Charts A-44a-d compare the reasons for termination for unsuccessful members below and above high camp on the Everest commercial routes. For the autumn season, the overwhelming reason is bad weather for both sides. For the spring season, bad weather is still the dominate reason for termination, but not to the same extent as for autumn.

	Above Base Camp			Above High Camp		
	Spring	Autumn	Winter	Spring	Autumn	Winter
All Peaks	35.1	35.3	27.9	69.8	74.6	71.1
6000ers w/o Com Rte	39.5	37.8	25.8	71.6	67.5	66.7
Ama Dablam Com Rte	26.7	60.3	44.0	71.9	92.0	79.1
7000ers	24.9	24.6	16.0	64.3	61.7	55.2
8000ers w/o Com Rtes	28.0	16.8	9.5	63.8	58.8	50.0
Cho Oyu Com Rte	34.0	44.0	61.1	70.2	79.0	78.6
Everest South Com Rte	47.8	18.9	0.0	74.1	55.0	0.0
Everest North Com Rte	38.6	1.7	0.0	72.4	13.5	0.0

Table A-41: Ascent rates for members that went above base camp and went above high camp from 1990-2009

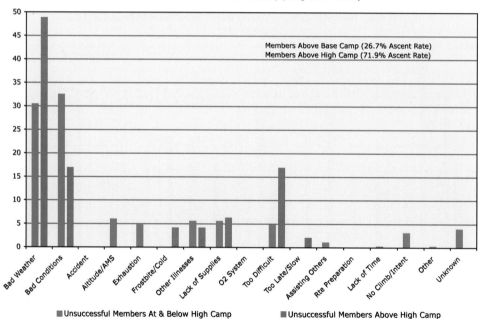

Chart A-42a: Termination percentages for unsuccessful members below and above high camp on the Ama Dablam commercial route during the spring season from 1990-2009

The termination percentages are adjusted in this and following charts so that their sums equal 100% in order to facilitate a more accurate comparison between the two groups.

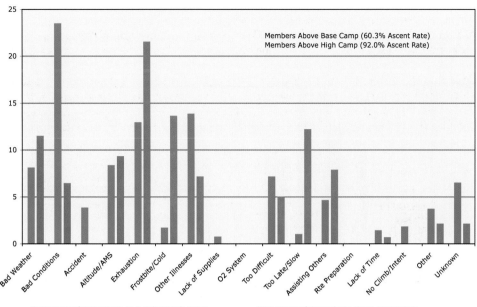

Chart A-42b: Termination percentages for unsuccessful members below and above high camp on the Ama Dablam commercial route during the autumn season from 1990-2009

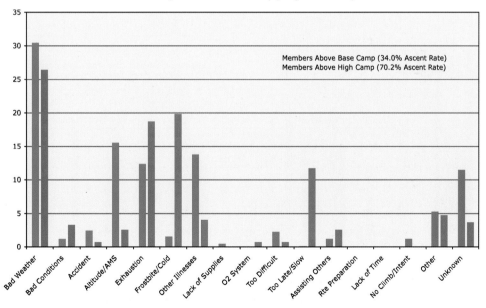

Chart A-43a: Termination percentages for unsuccessful members below and above high camp on the Cho Oyu commercial route during the spring season from 1990-2009

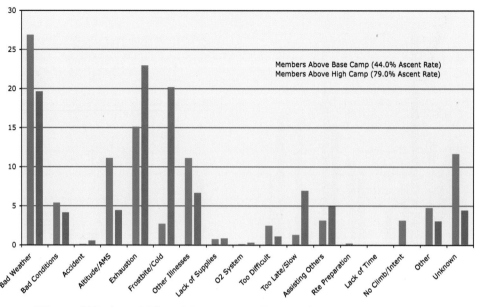

Chart A-43b: Termination percentages for unsuccessful members below and above high camp on the Cho Oyu commercial route during the autumn season from 1990-2009

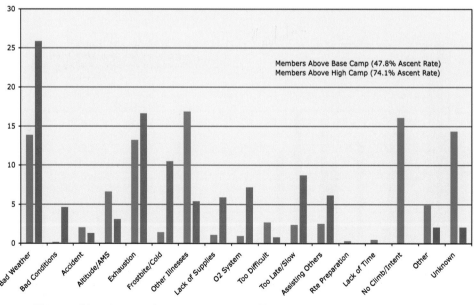

Chart A-44a: Termination percentages for unsuccessful members below and above high camp on the Everest south commercial route during the spring season from 1990-2009

114 Ascent Analysis

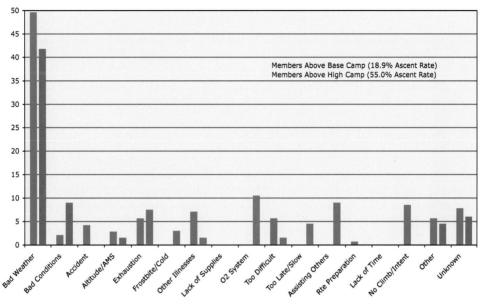

Chart A-44b: Termination percentages for unsuccessful members below and above high camp on the Everest south commercial route during the autumn season from 1990-2009

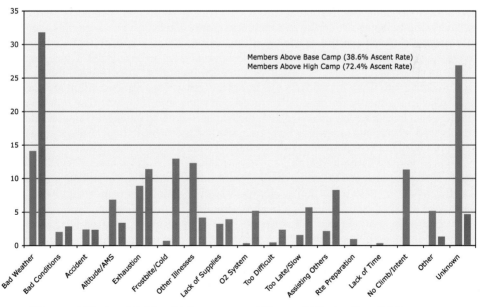

Chart A-44c: Termination percentages for unsuccessful members below and above high camp on the Everest north commercial route during the spring season from 1990-2009

Ascent Analysis 115

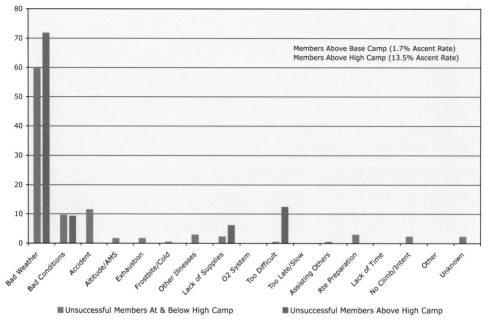

Chart A-44d: Termination percentages for unsuccessful members below and above high camp on the Everest north commercial route during the autumn season from 1990-2009

Average Expedition Duration and Days to Summit

Charts A-45a-g show the average duration (the time from arrival of the first members at base camp to departure of the last members from base camp) for successful expeditions (the blue lines in the charts) and the average number of days taken to reach the team's first summit (the red lines) for the period from 1970 to 2009. These charts show the times for all peaks, the 6000ers, the 7000ers, the 8000ers, Ama Dablam, Cho Oyu, and Everest. They may be used as indicator of how long an expedition should plan to be on the mountain in order to succeed in their summit quest. The quickest and longest times for each peak are given in Table A-47. The quickest times should not be confused with speed ascents, which are usually done several days or weeks after arrival at base camp and after proper acclimatization has been completed.

Chart A-46 compares the duration of all expeditions to that of successful expeditions for all peaks from 1970 to 2009. The closeness of the two lines indicates that most unsuccessful expeditions do make a serious attempt at summiting before abandoning their climbs. Expeditions that did not reach base camp or made no attempt to climb are in not included in the data because many of these had no intention of summiting, for example, those expeditions getting climbing permits for trekking purposes, holding multiple permits and using only some of them, or arriving at base camp and discovering conditions unsuitable for climbing.

Table A-47 shows climbing activity for popular peaks in Nepal (50 or more members above base camp), and for successful expeditions shows the average duration and number of days to summit, and the shortest and longest times to summit.

Average Number of Days for Successful Expeditions and Summits
for All Peaks (1970-2009)

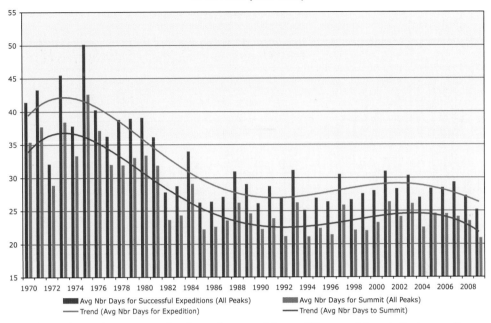

Chart A-45a: Average number days of successful expeditions and days to first summit for all peaks from 1970-2009

Average Number of Days for Successful Expeditions and Summits
for 6000ers (1970-2009)

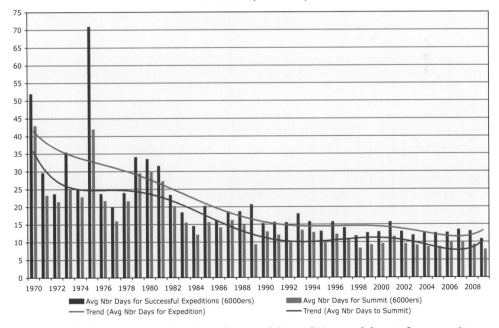

Chart A-45b: Average number days of successful expeditions and days to first summit for all 6000ers from 1970-2009

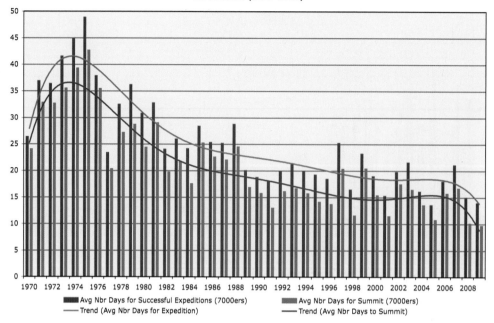

Average Number of Days for Successful Expeditions and Summits
for 7000ers (1970-2009)

**Chart A-45c: Average number days of successful expeditions and days to first summit
for all 7000ers from 1970-2009**

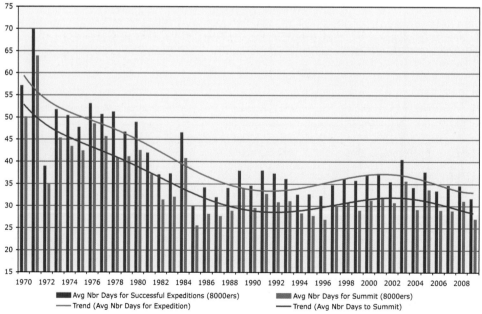

Average Number of Days for Successful Expeditions and Summits
for 8000ers (1970-2009)

**Chart A-45d: Average number days of successful expeditions and days to first summit
for all 8000ers from 1970-2009**

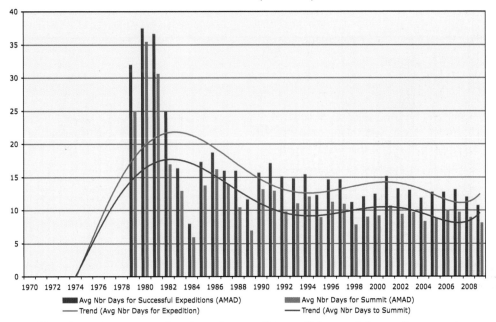

**Chart A-45e: Average number days of successful expeditions and days to first summit
for Ama Dablam from 1970-2009**

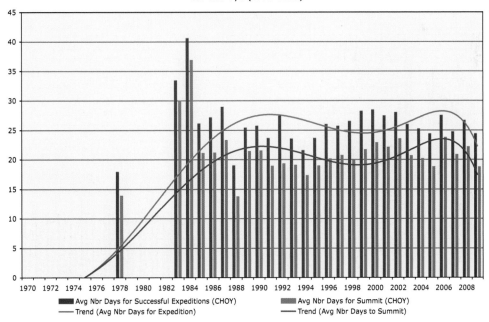

**Chart A-45f: Average number days of successful expeditions and days to first summit
for Cho Oyu from 1970-2009**

Average Number of Days for Successful Expeditions and Summits
for Everest (1970-2009)

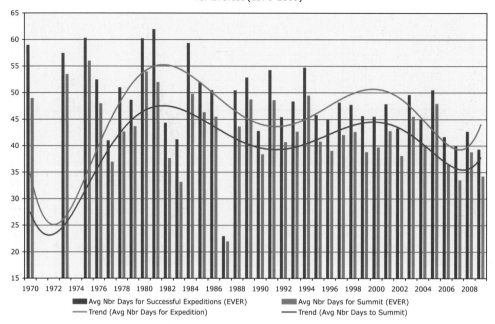

Chart A-45g: Average number days of successful expeditions and days to first summit for Everest from 1970-2009

Average Number of Days for All Expeditions and
Successful Expeditions for All Peaks (1970-2009)

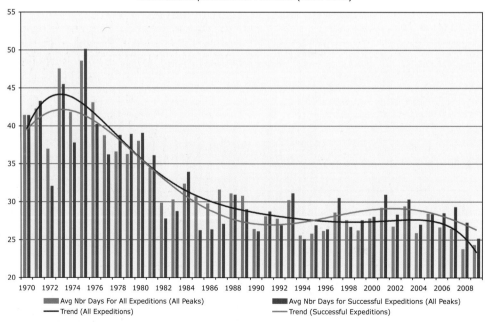

Chart A-46: Average number days of all expeditions and successful expeditions for all peaks from 1970-2009

120 Ascent Analysis

Peak ID	Peak Name	Height	Region	Exp Cnt	Mbrs Abv BC	Avg Exp Days	Avg Suc Exp Days	Avg Smt Days	Min Smt Days	Max Smt Days
AMAD	Ama Dablam	6814	2	742	3963	13.2	13.4	10.0	1	38
ANN1	Annapurna I	8091	5	169	1111	29.9	31.4	28.1	3	62
ANN2	Annapurna II	7937	5	30	182	34.0	44.3	40.2	19	63
ANN3	Annapurna III	7555	5	31	213	28.2	30.2	26.2	16	46
ANN4	Annapurna IV	7525	5	75	581	20.5	24.7	21.1	8	64
ANNS	Annapurna South	7219	5	32	194	27.4	34.6	28.3	19	38
APIM	Api Main	7132	7	12	83	26.3	23.0	17.7	14	19
BARU	Baruntse	7152	2	198	1137	12.9	14.8	10.3	1	33
BHRI	Bhrikuti	6476	5	10	70	5.8	5.6	3.9	1	8
CHAM	Chamlang	7321	2	10	65	23.0	25.4	21.4	15	28
CHOL	Cholatse	6423	2	14	69	19.3	19.4	13.1	2	23
CHOY	Cho Oyu	8188	2	1019	5638	25.6	26.0	21.0	1	52
CHRE	Churen Himal East	7371	6	7	55	34.0	28.5	25.5	10	41
CHRW	Churen Himal West	7371	6	12	80	29.2	28.3	24.5	4	39
DHA1	Dhaulagiri I	8167	6	288	1698	30.4	31.7	26.9	3	118
DHA2	Dhaulagiri II	7751	6	15	99	33.6	39.3	32.0	28	36
DHA4	Dhaulagiri IV	7661	6	11	108	52.0	53.0	47.0	46	48
DHAM	Dhampus	6012	6	14	91	12.7	12.7	3.6	1	13
DORJ	Dorje Lhakpa	6966	3	27	150	19.7	20.9	17.3	7	36
EVER	Everest	8850	2	1274	9131	44.8	45.5	40.4	7	75
FANG	Fang	7647	5	9	79	39.3	59.5	40.5	35	46
GAN1	Ganesh I	7422	4	8	51	25.6	41.0	34.0	34	34
GAN2	Ganesh II	7118	4	9	57	35.7	31.0	28.0	27	29
GAN4	Ganesh IV	7104	4	9	65	24.1	27.0	24.0	16	40
GANC	Ganchempo	6387	3	14	53	17.2	19.3	16.0	6	28
GANG	Gangapurna	7455	5	23	149	27.2	37.4	30.6	19	44
GAUR	Gaurishankar	7135	2	23	155	27.2	34.0	31.7	30	34
GIMM	Gimmigela Chuli	7350	1	6	64	31.5	36.7	29.7	26	37
GLAC	Glacier Dome	7193	5	25	177	21.3	23.3	19.9	7	53
GURJ	Gurja Himal	7193	6	8	66	23.6	24.9	20.7	9	28
GYAC	Gyachung Kang	7952	2	12	90	31.2	31.0	25.0	21	32
GYAJ	Gyajikang	7074	5	9	68	12.0	15.2	10.4	5	18
HIME	Himalchuli East	7893	4	24	194	40.8	44.0	38.6	28	49
HIML	Himlung Himal	7126	5	42	268	14.6	16.0	10.7	4	26
JANU	Jannu	7711	1	47	271	32.5	36.5	33.2	6	60
JONG	Jongsang	7462	1	5	65	29.0	0.0	0.0	0	0
KABS	Kabru South	7318	1	2	52	22.0	0.0	0.0	0	0
KANB	Kangbachen	7902	1	5	53	35.3	39.5	30.5	21	40
KANC	Kangchenjunga Cntrl	8482	1	7	50	39.5	47.8	42.0	19	71
KANG	Kangchenjunga	8586	1	108	833	40.7	42.3	36.8	12	71
KGUR	Kang Guru	6981	5	31	180	15.4	16.9	13.7	7	36
KIRA	Kirat Chuli	7362	1	7	58	22.4	0.0	0.0	0	0
KOTA	Kotang	6148	1	12	85	12.5	13.0	9.5	6	13
KTEG	Kangtega	6783	2	23	112	17.7	18.3	15.3	3	27
LAMJ	Lamjung Himal	6983	5	8	60	31.6	31.2	28.7	19	38
LANG	Langtang Lirung	7227	3	42	265	26.1	33.2	29.8	12	58
LEON	Leonpo Gang	6979	3	7	50	34.9	38.7	32.7	24	40
LHOT	Lhotse	8516	2	192	1071	38.2	37.2	32.0	4	58
LSHR	Lhotse Shar	8382	2	32	250	44.8	51.6	43.3	31	63
LSIS	Langshisa Ri	6412	3	11	60	15.0	13.7	10.7	5	21
MAK2	Makalu II	7678	2	45	242	26.0	30.7	24.0	12	52
MAKA	Makalu	8485	2	223	1411	36.4	36.6	31.8	5	65
MANA	Manaslu	8163	4	275	1624	29.6	31.0	27.2	6	63
MANN	Manaslu North	6994	4	9	69	19.4	24.3	20.8	8	28
NEPA	Nepal Peak	7177	1	5	57	22.8	19.0	17.0	17	17
NILN	Nilgiri North	7061	5	13	78	22.5	26.2	21.6	13	32
NUMB	Numbur	6958	2	15	91	18.7	20.6	18.3	12	28
NUPT	Nuptse	7864	2	38	174	26.0	43.2	33.4	20	46
PK29	Peak 29	7871	4	8	87	37.7	35.0	32.0	32	32
PUMO	Pumori	7165	2	226	1296	15.9	18.1	14.6	2	45

Peak ID	Peak Name	Height	Region	Exp Cnt	Mbrs Abv BC	Avg Exp Days	Avg Suc Exp Days	Avg Smt Days	Min Smt Days	Max Smt Days
PUTH	Putha Hiunchuli	7246	6	39	291	15.1	15.6	12.1	6	36
RATC	Ratna Chuli	7035	5	8	71	16.0	19.8	13.8	8	24
RATH	Rathong	6682	1	4	62	9.0	9.0	7.0	6	8
ROCN	Roc Noir	7485	5	8	66	32.6	42.4	33.8	19	44
SAIP	Saipal	7030	7	11	63	26.2	30.0	25.8	19	37
SARI	Saribung	6328	5	12	74	6.2	6.2	4.5	2	11
TAWO	Tawoche	6495	2	20	78	16.6	15.0	11.6	2	21
THAM	Thamserku	6618	2	13	56	19.0	19.5	17.5	2	33
TILI	Tilicho	7134	5	65	453	13.2	14.6	11.0	3	23
TKPO	Tengkangpoche	6487	2	14	57	17.7	26.0	21.0	18	24
TUKU	Tukuche	6920	6	45	303	12.6	13.2	10.9	4	20
YALU	Yalung Kang	8505	1	18	170	40.8	40.3	34.4	23	54

Geographical Region Codes:

1 = Kangchenjunga-Janak
2 = Khumbu-Makalu-Rolwaling
3 = Langtang-Jugal
4 = Manaslu-Ganesh

5 = Annapurna-Damodar-Peri
6 = Dhaulagiri-Mukut
7 = Kanjiroba-Far West

Table A-47: Average duration and days to first summit for successful expeditions

A Contrast of Styles

From *The Seasonal Stories* of Elizabeth Hawley – Spring 1988

The contrast was startling. A massive expedition went to Mount Everest in the spring of 1988 with 252 members and a budget of probably $7 million to spend on climbing and live television coverage. At the very same time there was another team of just four men whose funds probably totaled no more than two or three percent of that amount. Both succeeded.

The little one, composed of two Americans, one Briton and a Canadian, put the British climber, Stephen Venables, on the top the world by a new route up the vast east face of the mountain, a face which had been scaled successfully only once before. The huge expedition of Japanese, Chinese and Nepalese sent 14 members to the summit by the two easiest routes on Everest that had been conquered before them by a total of nearly 150 men and women. The big party got the television coverage and a series of gala victory celebrations in three nations' capitals while the little group quietly went their separate ways home.

The four-man team who made the remarkable oxygenless ascent of Everest's east face from Tibet could well have been the subject of such a debate themselves, but all of them survived. They were able to find a line up a previously unclimbed buttress, which they have called the Neverest (Everest/Never-rest) Buttress, that provided a direct route to the South Col, and here they came to the normal route from the south side up the southeast ridge. They reached the Col on May 10 and pitched their small tent there at nearly 8000m.

One of the four, the Canadian, Paul Teare, realized he was developing altitude sickness, and next morning he descended the whole east face entirely alone. He reached their advance base camp safely in seven hours and recovered swiftly. Meanwhile the other three spent the day at the Col waiting for the winds to lessen and were finally able to set out for the summit at 11:00 that night.

In the lead was Stephen Venables, 34-year-old mountaineering writer and lecturer from London, who plodded on and on up the southeast ridge and finally found himself at the highest summit in the world at 3:40 the following afternoon. His two friends, expedition leader Robert Anderson, an American who lives in New Zealand, and the team's other American, Edward Webster, from Colorado, had turned back in the deteriorating weather, and they took refuge that night of May 12/13 in a tent that the tri-national team had left at 8300m. Venables had to spend the night out without shelter when he could not find the way back to the South Col in the misty weather; he made his unprepared bivouac at a point that was about 200 meters above the tent his friends were in.

On the 13th Venables caught up with the other two and all three reached their tent at the Col, where they rested for the remainder of the day and the night before beginning their very slow descent of the face. It was not until the 17th and 18th that they separately managed at last to get down to advance base camp, delayed by new snowfall and their own exhaustion, starved for food and liquids and frostbitten.

Venables had realized when he set out from the Col for the summit that he was beginning to have no feeling in his toes. He took the conscious decision to carry on anyway; he may lose the tips of five frostbitten toes. Webster, a professional photographer, had taken great pains to get his shots just right, and he will probably lose the ends of five fingers. Anderson suffered milder frostbite. But all of them did manage to get down alive.

There could be no debate over anyone being left anywhere on their mountain by the Chinese-Japanese-Nepalese Everest team, for there were too many camps, climbers, walkie-talkie radios, oxygen bottles and support staff at the two base camps, one on the north side and the other on the south, for that. In addition with three nations' governments and climbing establishments involved in their climb, detailed planning had been done months in advance – the Japanese climber who would make the first north-south traverse had already been chosen well before departure from Japan – and the expedition's tri-national commanders, sitting in Peking, could radio instructions to their climbing leaders on the scene. In fact, with an elaborate command structure, a small village of support personnel (cooks, doctors, interpreters, radio operators) plus television and newspaper journalists and technicians at each base camp and 176 people climbing above their bases, it is a wonder that the whole enterprise did not collapse of its own weight before the mountain could be climbed.

But collapse it did not, and no doubt a large amount of credit goes to the two Japanese climbing leaders, Tsuneo Shigehiro on the north side in Tibet in charge of progress via the North Col and the northeast ridge, the classical route of the first British efforts in the 1920s and 1930s, and Gota Isono managing the climb from Nepal in the south via the South Col and the southeast ridge, the route pioneered 35 years ago by Hillary and Tenzing. Fourteen men succeeded in gaining the summit, nine from the north and five from the south, on May 5 and 10. Six of them descended the opposite sides from which they had come up.

First on the top on May 5 were the north-south traverse team of one man from each of the three nations, Noboru Yamada from Japan in his third Everest ascent, Lhakpa Nuru Sherpa (also known as Ang Lhakpa) of Nepal, and a Tibetan, Cering Doji, representing China. They waited an hour on the summit, but when neither the south-north traverse party nor the television crew for live telecasting from the top of the world had appeared, they began their descent of the southern route, the first people ever to cross Mount Everest from one side of the Sino-Nepalese border to the other by way of the summit.

As they were about to make their way down the southeast ridge, the first member of their so-called support team, meant to be bringing them fresh supplies of oxygen, arrived at the summit; these three men later descended the route they had climbed. The Chinese in this support party, Li Zhixin, the only non-Tibetan amongst the four Chinese citizens to make it to the top, had not actually carried out his support role, for he had brought oxygen only for himself. Apparently it was politically necessary for at least one Han Chinese (an ethnic Chinese, not of a minority race like the Tibetans) to stand on the summit, and to ensure this, Li had not burdened himself with an extra bottle for anyone else.

Last to arrive at the top from the north side were the three-man Japanese television crew whose live telecast from the highest point on earth, the first ever achieved in Everest climbing history, was the reason Nippon Television Networks Corporation had put up millions of dollars worth of financing for this expedition. The arrangements for the television coverage were most elaborate with tons of costly sophisticated equipment including a satellite dish at the northern base camp and a specially devised climber's helmet with a very light camera attached. Unfortunately the summiting cameraman forgot to bring along the helmet: the camera actually used on the summit was a conventional hand-held unit.

The day's last arrivals at the summit were the south-north traverse team of two Tibetan Chinese and a Nepalese Sherpa, and when they reached the top the cameraman was able to show to the watching world their last slow, tired steps as they made their way with considerable effort through deep snow on the southeast ridge.

After May 5's major successes from the expedition's commanders' point of view, the double traverse of the mountain and the first live television pictures from the summit, the leadership decided that the men poised for subsequent ascents should be instructed that the climb was over. The leadership wanted to call a halt while the safety record was so good – no accidents, no frostbite and no serious illness except for the fatal heart attack of a base-camp doctor whose death was not related to the climb. But this decision was greeted with dismay by Japanese climbers, who had paid to come on the expedition and were ambitious for their own summit successes, and by Nepalese Sherpas keen to set more records for the number of times they had been to the top of the world. The Japanese climbing leadership on the spot managed to keep discipline amongst their compatriots, but six Nepalese on the south side rebelled – it was their country after all – and made their own summit bid on May 10. Two men succeeded; one of them was Sungdare Sherpa, who became the first person ever to conquer Everest five times.

The summiters and their leaders were showered with congratulations, awards and victory celebrations in Kathmandu, Peking and Tokyo. King Birendra of Nepal bestowed high decorations on them, Chinese premier Li Peng and the prime minister of Japan, Keizo Obuchi, received them at gala functions. Their success had been a great historic mountaineering achievement, it was said, and a glorious contribution to international friendship. "It is an historic feat and an example of human success in conquering nature," said Mr. Obuchi. A Nepalese minister noted that "the feat coincidentally marks the 35th anniversary of the first ascent of Sagarmatha. If in 1953 with the success of human beings on Sagarmatha, mountaineering history was written, today the joint expedition has added yet another chapter by achieving the unique feat of traversing the peak simultaneously from the southern and northern sides. ... The success of this expedition is the tale of the indomitable human spirit and the coordinated work of all the members from China, Japan and Nepal."

But was it really a magnificent accomplishment? Sir Edmund Hillary seems to dissent. While the expedition was getting underway in March, he expressed a strong lack of enthusiasm for its goal: "A double traverse is not very impressive. ... I think it's a massive undertaking and I personally think a singularly unattractive one. You've got hundreds of people milling around on the mountain, and it's not all that big a deal climbing the easiest two routes and descending the easiest routes already prepared. They're spending more money on the expedition than anyone has ever spent before. Maybe that's the most unusual aspect of it."

"Mountaineering traverses are certainly highly regarded only when a party climbs up one route and descends a side of the mountain they don't have a prepared route down. ... I find it extremely difficult to get the least bit excited about this massive traverse, and I think this would be the attitude of most climbers throughout the world. We all know the Nepalese climbers can climb it, and all they have to do is trundle down the other side. ... I think mountaineering is at its best when the people involved have raised the money themselves, planned it themselves, and climbed it themselves. I find the whole project basically unattractive. I'm just glad we climbed Everest 35 years ago when we didn't have all this hullabaloo going on."

Death Analysis

This chapter analyzes deaths on the principle peaks in the Nepal Himalaya, those peaks officially open for mountaineering and a few additional peaks with significant activity. Border peaks such as Everest, Cho Oyu, and Kangchenjunga are included for expeditions from the Nepalese, Chinese, and Indian sides of the border. The tables and charts cover the period from 1950 through 2009 unless specified otherwise.

Deaths for members and hired personnel are analyzed by several different categories: peak altitude, geographical region, climbing season, causes of death, time of day, age, historically over time, citizenship, and gender. Death rates are given for the most popular peaks. Deaths are also analyzed by team composition, that is, the number of members and hired personnel on an expedition and the ratio between the two. Particular attention is given to avalanches, falls, and physiological factors, the leading causes of death in the Himalaya.

Deaths by Peak Altitude Ranges

Table D-1 shows death counts and rates for members and hired personnel for all peaks from 6000m to 8850m pooled in 500m increments from 1950 to 1989 and 1990 to 2009.

Peak Altitude Range	Members			Hired		
1950-1989	Above BC	Death Cnt	Death Rate	Above BC	Death Cnt	Death Rate
6000-6499m	573	5	0.87	223	0	0.00
6500-6999m	1607	17	1.06	586	4	0.68
7000-7499m	2429	66	2.72	883	14	1.59
7500-7999m	1804	60	3.33	865	18	2.08
8000-8499m	3052	104	3.41	1441	40	2.78
8500-8850m	3388	75	2.21	2719	48	1.77
Totals	12853	327	2.54	6717	124	1.85
1990-2009						
6000-6499m	690	0	0.00	214	0	0.00
6500-6999m	4469	24	0.54	1162	17	1.46
7000-7499m	3654	34	0.93	934	18	1.93
7500-7999m	789	11	1.39	241	1	0.42
8000-8499m	8854	107	1.21	2711	31	1.14
8500-8850m	7817	105	1.34	5738	33	0.58
Totals	26273	281	1.07	11000	100	0.91

Table D-1: Member and hired deaths for peak altitude ranges
(6000-8850m) from 1950-1989 and 1990-2009

This table includes the effect of the catastrophic accident on Kang Guru (6981m) in 2005 that claimed the lives of 7 members and 11 hired (65% of the hired death count in the 6500-6999m range for the 1990-2009 period), which greatly affects hired death rates as illustrated in the charts that follow (see the inset box, *Worst Disaster in Nepalese Himalaya Wipes Out French Team*, on pg. 128).

Chart D-1a shows member and hired death rates from 1950 to 1989. The member death rates topped out in the 7500-7999m range at 3.33% and in the 8000-8499m range at 3.41% and then declined at the highest altitudes, whereas the hired death rates topped out at 2.78% in the 8000-8499m range, suggesting that the 8000-8499m peaks were the deadliest for both members and hired personnel during this period. Hired personnel also fared better than members in all altitude ranges.

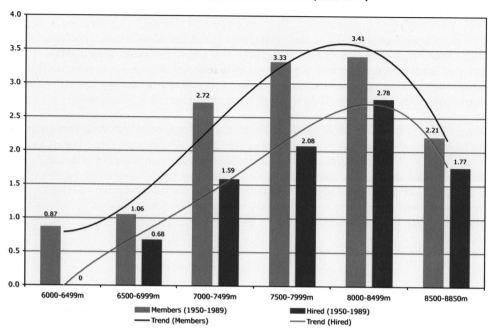

Chart D-1a: Member and hired death rates for all peaks from 1950-1989

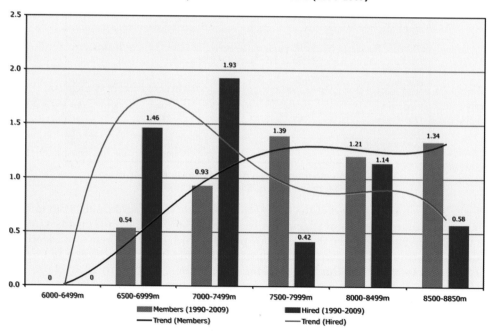

Chart D-1b: Member and hired death rates for all peaks from 1990-2009

The death rates in the above and subsequent charts in this chapter represent the percentage of climbers that died for each category in the chart.

Chart D-1b shows member and hired death rates from 1990 to 2009, showing the death rates when the 2005 Kang Guru accident is included. Death rates for members have decreased in all groups when compared to the 1950-1989 period. Death rates for hired generally have decreased from those of the 1950-1989 period except in the 6500-6999m range and in the 7000-7499m range. But in the 7500-7999m range, the hired death rate has dropped to 0.42% most likely due to the fewer hired personnel used above base camp for ferrying loads through the dangerous avalanche zones by more recent expeditions attempting the 7000ers in alpine style.

The early 1990s coincide with the increase in popularity of commercial climbing, which has contributed significantly to the numbers of climbers going above base camp (almost 54% of all climbers above base camp were on the commercial routes of one of these three peaks after 1990).

1990-2009	Members			Hired		
	Above BC	Death Cnt	Death Rate	Above BC	Death Cnt	Death Rate
6000-6499m	690	0	0.00	214	0	0.00
6500-6999m w/o KGUR & AMAD Com Rte	1083	7	0.65	294	2	0.68
7000-7499m	3654	34	0.93	934	18	1.93
7500-7999m	789	11	1.39	241	1	0.42
8000-8499m w/o Cho Oyu Com Rte	3834	81	2.11	1207	28	2.32
8500-8850m w/o Everest Com Rtes	2075	33	1.59	1160	8	0.69
Totals w/o ACE Commercial Routes	**12132**	**173**	**1.43**	**4061**	**68**	**1.67**
2005 Kang Guru Accident	7	7	1.00	11	11	1.00
Ama Dablam Commercial Route	3379	10	0.30	857	4	0.47
Cho Oyu Commercial Route	5020	26	0.52	1504	3	0.20
Everest Commercial Routes	5742	72	1.25	4578	25	0.55
ACE Commercial Route Totals	**14141**	**108**	**0.82**	**6939**	**32**	**0.46**

Table D-2: Deaths for peak altitude ranges (6000-8850m) from 1990-2009 excluding the 2005 Kang Guru accident and for the Ama Dablam, Cho Oyu, and Everest commercial routes

When the 2005 Kang Guru accident and the commercial routes for Ama Dablam, Cho Oyu, and Everest are excluded in the 1990-2009 period, a different picture emerges as shown in Table and Chart D-2.

Comparing Charts D-1b and D-2, one can see that the 8000m+ death rates are higher when the Cho Oyu and Everest commercial routes are removed and more closely resemble what one would expect for non-commercial Himalayan climbing.

In Chart D-2 the death rate continues to climb into the 8000m-8499m range topping out at 2.11% for members and 2.32% for hired, then declines for the very highest peaks.

The three most dangerous peaks, Annapurna I, Manaslu, and Dhaulagiri I (see Table D-3) are in the 8000m-8499m range and their death rates are strongly affected by avalanches (see the later section *Avalanche Deaths* in this chapter).

The death rates for Ama Dablam, Cho Oyu, and Everest are lower than the other peaks in their respective altitude ranges suggesting that they are relatively safer. But this appearance of safety may be due to the fact that the vast majority of the climbers are on the easiest and safest routes with extensive fixed ropes and in many cases under the direct supervision of experienced commercial guides or Sherpa and Tibetan assistants.

During the 1950-1989 period before commercial climbing become common and when other more challenging routes were being attempted in higher proportions, the death rates on Ama Dablam, Cho Oyu, and Everest were much higher.

Worst Disaster in Nepalese Himalaya Wipes Out French Team

From *The Seasonal Stories* of Elizabeth Hawley – Autumn 2005

The worst disaster ever to befall an expedition in the Nepalese Himalaya struck a seven-member French team on Mt. Kang Guru. The only previous death on the mountain was that of a West German named Bernd Arenz, who died in a fall on 24 October 1985. Now twenty years later almost to the day, on 20 October, all the French, led by Daniel Stolzenberg and including his wife, and 11 of their Nepalese employees who were in their base camp tents after the members' late afternoon tea, when they were swept by avalanching into a deep gorge below.

All 18 people perished. Several other porters were outside their tents and managed to survive and to trek to the nearest village, Meta, where they met a French-Israeli expedition planning to climb another mountain in the area, Ratna Chuli. This team immediately informed the French embassy in Kathmandu of the disaster.

Early rescue attempts to retrieve the climbers' bodies were mostly ineffective. One, that of Bruno Chardin, a ski resort manager, was found before they suspended their search because of continued avalanching. In the meantime French specialists in post-avalanche searches with special equipment and two sniffer dogs arrived from France. By mid-November, when they too called off their work until early next year, the bodies of another member, Jean-Francois Jube, an advisor to the French Ministry of Youth and Sports, and a low-altitude porter, Mani Lal Gurung, had been discovered.

The previous record death toll on a single expedition in Nepal had been set by a South Korean team on Manaslu. In April 1972 15 men—10 Nepalese, four Koreans and one Japanese cameraman—were killed when a big avalanche struck their tents at 3:15 a.m. But most of the Koreans were inexperienced in the Nepalese Himalaya, whereas at least two of the Frenchmen had been to Nepalese or Pakistani 8000m mountains, and all of them lived in mountainous parts of France. Stolzenberg, for example, who came from Chamonix, was a professional guide and had been a professor at the prestigious ENSA (National School of Skiing and Alpinism). And they had an experienced sirdar (leader of the Nepalese staff) named Iman Gurung, who had summited Everest twice, most recently in May this year, as well as Cho Oyu twice.

It is easy to be wise after the event, and some people questioned the wisdom of the base camp's location. It was surrounded by 35-40 degree slopes. One porter reportedly suggested that the camp be moved to what he considered a safer location downhill, but his proposal was not acted upon.

A noted French climbing instructor, Jean Coudray, who came to Kathmandu after he had discussed this subject with previous Kang Guru leaders, noted that the team had placed their base camp at the normal site. "In this area, there is no place for base camp that is completely safe; there is no safer site for it" than the one everyone has used. In any case, "the cost of mountaineering is a little risk."

Furthermore, he pointed out, there was continuous heavy snowfall for many hours. The resulting avalanching was made of powder snow, the worst kind of avalanche because it travels down a slope of 30 degrees or more very fast—200 or more kilometers per hour—and its "target" is impossible to predict: it can shift direction often. In this case, the avalanching happened to target base camp.

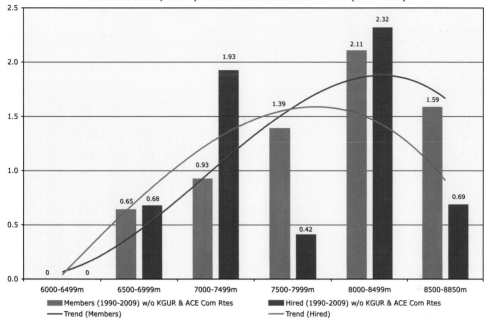

Death Rates by Peak Altitude for All Peaks without 2005 Kang Guru Accident
and Ama Dablam, Cho Oyu and Everest Commercial Routes (1990-2009)

Members (1990-2009) w/o KGUR & ACE Com Rtes
Hired (1990-2009) w/o KGUR & ACE Com Rtes
Trend (Members)
Trend (Hired)

Chart D-2: Member and hired death rates for all peaks from 1990-2009 excluding the 2005 Kang Guru accident and the Ama Dablam, Cho Oyu, and Everest commercial routes

Deaths on Popular Peaks

Table and Chart D-3 give the death rates for the most popular peaks in Nepal, those peaks with more than 750 members above base camp (roughly equivalent to 75 or more expeditions).

	Exped Cnt	Members			Hired			Total		
		Above BC	Death Cnt	Death Rate	Above BC	Death Cnt	Death Rate	Above BC	Death Cnt	Death Rate
BARU (7152m)	198	1137	4	0.35	352	6	1.70	1489	10	0.67
AMAD (6814m)	742	3963	17	0.43	963	4	0.42	4926	21	0.43
All 6000ers	1395	7339	46	0.63	2185	21	0.96	9524	67	0.70
CHOY (8188m)	1019	5638	36	0.64	1716	9	0.52	7354	45	0.61
LHOT (8516m)	192	1071	11	1.03	668	1	0.15	1739	12	0.69
EVER (8850m)	1274	9131	139	1.52	7303	71	0.97	16434	210	1.28
All Peaks	6358	39126	608	1.55	17717	224	1.26	56843	832	1.46
MAKA (8485m)	223	1411	23	1.63	589	14	2.38	2000	37	1.85
All 8000ers	3627	23111	391	1.69	12609	152	1.21	35720	543	1.52
All 7000ers	1336	8676	171	1.97	2923	51	1.74	11599	222	1.91
PUMO (7165m)	226	1296	32	2.47	278	9	3.24	1574	41	2.60
MANA (8163m)	275	1624	45	2.77	684	14	2.05	2308	59	2.56
DHA1 (8167m)	288	1698	50	2.94	574	15	2.61	2272	65	2.86
KANG (8586m)	108	833	25	3.00	388	7	1.80	1221	32	2.62
ANN1 (8091m)	169	1111	45	4.05	413	17	4.12	1524	62	4.07

Table D-3: Deaths for peaks with more than 750 members above base camp from 1950-2009 ordered by increasing member death rate

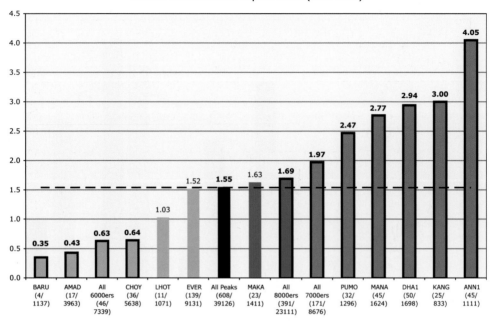

Member Death Rates for Popular Peaks (1950-2009)

| | BARU (4/ 1137) | AMAD (17/ 3963) | All 6000ers (46/ 7339) | CHOY (36/ 5638) | LHOT (11/ 1071) | EVER (139/ 9131) | All Peaks (608/ 39126) | MAKA (23/ 1411) | All 8000ers (391/ 23111) | All 7000ers (171/ 8676) | PUMO (32/ 1296) | MANA (45/ 1624) | DHA1 (50/ 1698) | KANG (25/ 833) | ANN1 (45/ 1111) |

Death rates by peak: BARU 0.35, AMAD 0.43, All 6000ers 0.63, CHOY 0.64, LHOT 1.03, EVER 1.52, All Peaks 1.55, MAKA 1.63, All 8000ers 1.69, All 7000ers 1.97, PUMO 2.47, MANA 2.77, DHA1 2.94, KANG 3.00, ANN1 4.05

**Chart D-3: Member death rates for popular peaks from 1950-2009
with more than 750 members above base camp
(the death rate is above the column bar; the death and above BC counts are below)
(see Appendix A for the definitions of the peak symbols in this and subsequent charts)**

> The columns outlined in black in the above chart and in the six charts that follow for the deadliest 6000ers, 7000ers, and 8000ers for members and hired represent peaks or groups of peaks that statistically have either significantly higher (in red) or lower (in blue) death rates than the mean death rate for all peaks (in black). Statistical significance means that there is less than a 5% probability that the result occurred by chance. For the non-outlined peaks, the death rates can be considered as only anecdotal evidence of higher or lower death rates than the mean rate for all peaks.

Ama Dablam and Cho Oyu are significantly safer for members than the mean (average) of 1.55% for all peaks (in black), whereas Everest is very close to the mean for all peaks (in part because it contributes so much to the overall rate). For two other peaks that often are climbed commercially, Baruntse is very safe at 0.35% whereas Pumori is much more dangerous at 2.47%.

Deadliest Peaks for Members

The next group of charts shows member death rates for the deadliest peaks in Nepal, those peaks with member death rates above average and with some significant amount of climbing activity.

Chart D-4 shows the 6000m peaks with member death rates above average for peaks with 25 or more members above base camp. All of these peaks have death rates higher than the mean death rate of 0.63% for all 6000ers. But it should also be noted that many 6000m peaks only have one or two member deaths, which means that a single

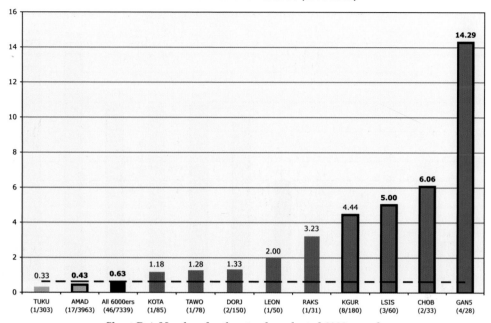

**Chart D-4: Member death rates for selected 6000m peaks
with 25+ members above base camp from 1950-2009
(the death rate is above the column bar; the death and above BC counts are below)**

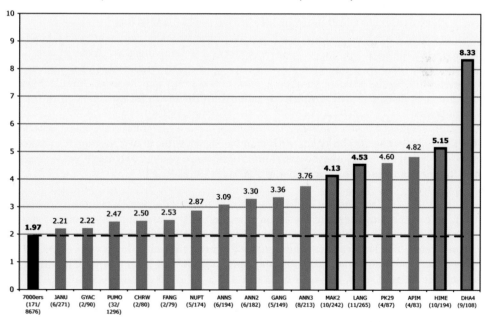

**Chart D-5: Member death rates for selected 7000m peaks
with 75+ members above base camp from 1950-2009
(the death rate is above the column bar; the death and above BC counts are below)**

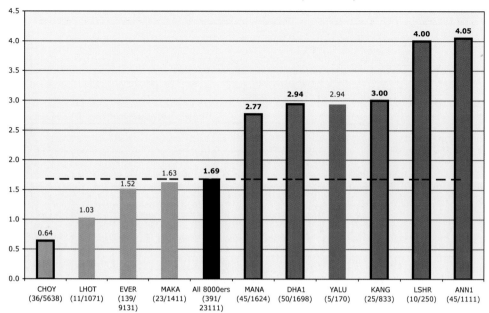

**Chart D-6a: Member death rates for 8000m peaks
with 150+ members above base camp from 1950-2009
(the death rate is above the column bar; the death and above BC counts are below)**

accident can easily alter the results. Only Ama Dablam with 17 deaths, Kang Guru with 8 deaths (7 of which occurred in 2005), Ganesh V with 4 French deaths (all the result of one avalanche), and Langshisa Ri with three Japanese deaths (again the result of a single avalanche) have more fatalities; the two Austrian deaths on Chobuje also were the result of a single avalanche. Kang Guru, Langshisa Ri, Chobuje, and Ganesh V are the only peaks with statistically significantly higher death rates given the number of deaths and the numbers of climbers attempting the peak. Ama Dablam with the most deaths is still significantly safer than the mean for members on the other 6000m peaks.

Chart D-5 shows the 7000m peaks with member death rates above average for peaks with 75 or more members above base camp. All of these peaks have death rates equal to or higher than the mean death rate of 1.97% for all 7000ers.

Dhaulagiri IV (7661m) has the highest death rate for members with over four times the mean. Five of the nine member deaths on Dhaulagiri IV occurred in one accident when five Austrians and their Sherpa disappeared on a summit bid in 1969 along a heavily corniced ridge. The last walkie-talkie contact with the summit team was at 6 p.m. on 9 November, the night before their planned summit bid. But after 7 days of no further contact, the summit team was presumed lost and a helicopter search was requested. Bad weather delayed the search until 21 November. Their bodies were never found and were presumed lost in an avalanche or a fall from the ridge.

However, the deaths rates for each of the 7000ers are only statistically significant for Dhaulagiri IV, Himalchuli East, Langtang Lirung, and Makalu II. The death rates for

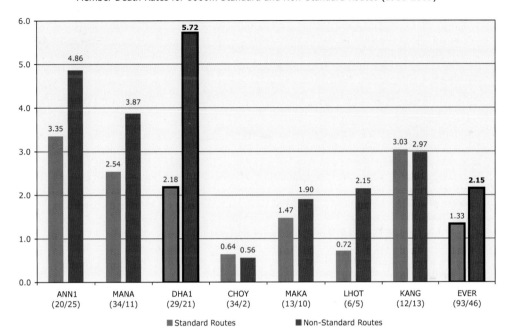

Member Death Rates for 8000m Standard and Non-Standard Routes (1950-2009)

Chart D-6b: Member death rates for 8000m standard and non-standard routes from 1950-2009
(the death rates are above the column bars; the death counts are below)
(column pairs outlined in black indicate statistically significant differences
in death rates between the standard and non-standard routes)

8000m Standard Routes:		
ANN1 – N Face	CHOY – NW Ridge	KANG – W Face
MANA – NE Face	MAKA – Makalu La-NW Ridge	EVER – S Col-SE Ridge,
DHA1 – NE Ridge	LHOT – W Face	N Col-NE Ridge

two other peaks, Pumori and Annapurna III, are close to the limits of being significant due to their higher above base camp counts.

Chart D-6a shows member death rates for the 8000m peaks with 150 or more members above base camp. The most deadly 8000m peaks are Annapurna I, Lhotse Shar, Manaslu, Kangchenjunga, and Dhaulagiri I, all with death rates significantly higher than the mean death rate of 1.69% for all 8000ers, and all are avalanche prone and technically demanding. Only Cho Oyu has a death rate significantly lower than the mean at 0.64%.

The death rates for Everest and Makalu, despite their high above base camp counts, are too close to the death rate for all 8000ers to be significantly lower than the mean. The above base camp count for Yalung Kang is too small to be significant.

Chart D-6b shows member death rates for the standard and non-standard routes on the eight major 8000m peaks in Nepal. The non-standard routes are significantly more dangerous only on Dhaulagiri I and Everest. For Dhaulagiri I, the north face and southeast ridge have had numerous member fatalities; for Everest the north and southwest faces have been the most dangerous.

The Death of Dawa Wangchu on Cheo Himal

From the Elizabeth Hawley notes of an interview with Alan Burgess - 6 Nov 1990

On the 29th of October Alan Burgess and Dawa Wangchu went on recce to see if it was feasible to climb the southeast ridge; they decided it was and then returned to C1. On the 30th the team set out for the ridge (and the summit if possible, but this was "a long shot"). Burgess, Mathew Golden, John Whiteley, Derek Nobles, and Dawa Wangchu left C1 at 4 a.m. Nobles turned back after an hour (trouble with his crampons and he was not entirely well) while the other four continued on. At 11 a.m. they were about 200 ft below the southeast ridge with Whiteley and Golden 300 ft behind Burgess and Dawa Wangchu. Dawa Wangchu was now leading and he put in an ice stake and Burgess climbed up to him and from there Dawa was to go on up and put in another ice stake that would be better anchored. Dawa anchored the rope and came down his fixed line and tied on another rope to the fixed rope but became disconnected from the fixed rope (probably the rope broke after he had untied a knot that Burgess had put there to tie off a flaw in the rope). Dawa fell 800 vertical feet (1000 ft in distance) but he was still alive after landing in deep snow at the bottom of a section of very dangerous ice cliffs. Burgess reached him in 30 minutes: he had massive head injuries (a fractured skull) and was bleeding from his skull profusely and coughing blood. Burgess stayed with him 3 hours, and finally got him standing. Dawa could see but could not speak. Burgess tried to pull him down a steep snow slope and got him down 60 ft, but then Dawa disconnected his harness and took off his gloves and turned away from Burgess and lay down signaling Burgess to go on alone. Regretfully Burgess left him. Now the ice and ice cliffs will soon take him all the way down (he probably would have died in next half hour).

Deadliest Peaks for Hired Personnel

The next group of charts show death rates for hired personnel for the most dangerous peaks in Nepal, those peaks with death rates above average and with a significant number of hired personnel that went above base camp.

Chart D-7 shows the 6000m peaks with hired death rates above average for peaks with 10 or more hired above base camp. All of these peaks have death rates higher than the mean death rate of 0.96% for all 6000ers.

Only five peaks have hired death rates higher than the mean rate illustrating how relatively safe the 6000ers have been for hired personnel. Note from the Chart D-7, the five peaks with death rates higher than the mean had only a total of 16 deaths: one on Kantega, two on Leonpo Gang, one on Cheo Himal, one on Raksa Urai, and eleven on Kang Guru, indicating the low numbers of hired personnel used on the 6000m peaks (see Table D-1). Only on Kang Guru is the hired death rate statistically significant. Ama Dablam at 0.42% is significantly safer than the mean for hired personnel.

Chart D-8 shows the 7000m peaks with hired death rates above average for peaks with 25 or more hired above base camp. All of these peaks have death rates equal to or higher than the mean death rate of 1.74% for all 7000ers. Dhaulagiri IV and Gangapurna have been extremely dangerous for hired with deaths rates approaching five times the average. Only these two peaks have statistically significantly higher death rates than the mean death rate for all 7000ers.

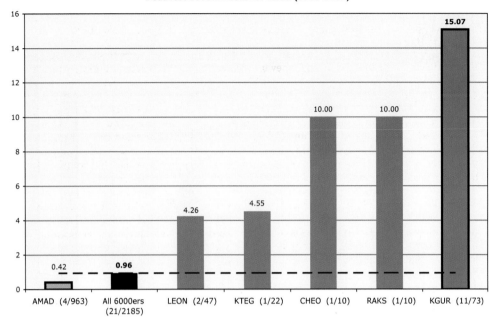

Deadliest 6000m Peaks for Hired (1950-2009)

Chart D-7: Hired death rates for selected 6000m peaks
with 10+ hired above base camp from 1950-2009
(the death rate is above the column bar; the death and above BC counts are below)

Combined with the very high death rates for members, *Dhaulagiri IV is the most dangerous peak* for all climbers in the Nepal Himalaya. Out of eleven expeditions (mostly Japanese to Dhaulagiri IV from 1969 to 1975), five ended with fatalities (four deaths by avalanches, three by falls, one by AMS, and six by disappearance of the team on their summit bid). After the Japanese summited Dhaulagiri IV on three successive days in 1975 (the first verified ascents of the peak), the peak has never been attempted again, perhaps not surprisingly!

Chart D-9a shows hired death rates for the 8000m peaks with 75 or more hired above base camp. The most deadly 8000m peaks are Annapurna I, Dhaulagiri I, and Makalu with death rates significantly higher than the mean death rate of 1.21% for all 8000ers. Everest, Cho Oyu, and Lhotse have death rates significantly lower than the mean. The hired death rate of 0.0% Lhotse Shar is particularly striking because the member death rate of 4.00% is one of the highest for the 8000ers (see Chart D-6a). Lhotse Shar is more demanding technically, so expeditions tend not to use as many hired personnel at the higher altitudes where the danger of falls and avalanches is greater; but due to the few hired used, the low death rate is also not statistically significant.

The mean death rates for hired personnel are almost identical for both the 7000m and 8000m peaks. The reason for this will become more apparent in the discussion of avalanche deaths later in this chapter.

Chart D-9b shows hired death rates for the standard and non-standard routes on the eight major 8000m peaks in Nepal. The non-standard routes are significantly more

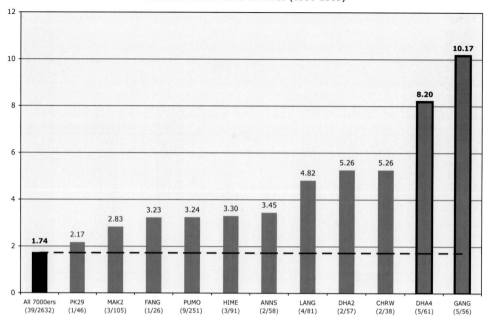

Deadliest 7000m Peaks for Hired (1950-2009)

**Chart D-8: Hired death rates for selected 7000m peaks
with 25+ hired above base camp from 1950-2009
(the death rate is above the column bar; the death and above BC counts are below)**

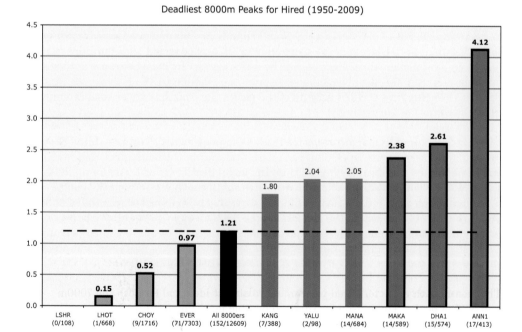

Deadliest 8000m Peaks for Hired (1950-2009)

**Chart D-9a: Hired death rates for 8000m peaks
with 75+ hired above base camp from 1950-2009
(the death rate is above the column bar; the death and above BC counts are below)**

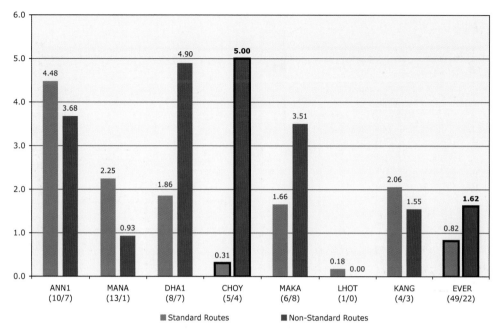

**Chart D-9b: Hired death rates for 8000m standard and non-standard routes from 1950-2009
(the death rates are above the column bars; the death counts are below)
(column pairs outlined in black indicate statistically significant differences
in death rates between the standard and non-standard routes)**

dangerous only on Everest and Cho Oyu. For Everest the southwest face has been the most dangerous; for Cho Oyu, three of the hired deaths were in a single avalanche at 6000m on the southeast face route (and the total number of deaths is low).

Deaths by Geographical Regions

Charts D-10a-b show death rates by geographical region for members and hired personnel. Regions with columns that exceed the death rates for all peaks (indicated by the dashed lines) have higher deaths rates than normal, whereas regions with columns that are lower have lower death rates.

The most dangerous regions for members are in central Nepal from Langtang-Jugal to Dhaulagiri-Mukut, which is more prone to avalanching. The Manaslu-Ganesh region has nearly three times the member death rate as the Khumbu-Makalu-Rolwaling region.

In general, death rates for hired follow a similar pattern for members except for the Kangchenjunga-Janak, Manaslu-Ganesh, and Kanjiroba-Far West regions where hired death rates are substantially lower than member death rates.

The Khumbu-Makalu-Rolwaling region where the most climbing activity has taken place is also the safest for both members and hired, in part due to the extensive and relatively safe commercial climbing done on Ama Dablam, Cho Oyu, and Everest.

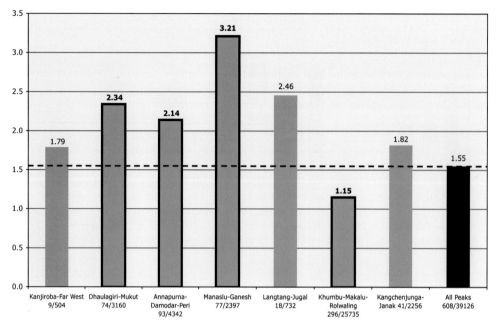

Member Death Rates by Geographical Region (1950-2009)

Chart D-10a: Member death rates by geographical region for all peaks from 1950-2009 (the death rate is above the column bar; the death and above BC counts are below)

The columns outlined in black in the above and following charts represent regions that statistically have significantly higher or lower death rates than the death rates for all peaks (the dashed line).

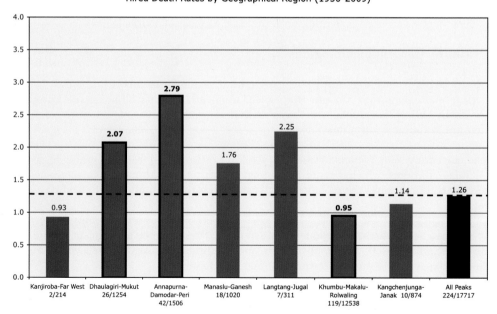

Hired Death Rates by Geographical Region (1950-2009)

Chart D-10b: Hired death rates by geographical region for all peaks from 1950-2009 (the death rate is above the column bar; the death and above BC counts are below)

138 Death Analysis

Deaths by Climbing Season

Chart D-11 shows death rates for members and hired personnel by climbing season for all peaks.

The differences in *member* death rates between seasons are statistically insignificant, even though the summer and winter seasons are considerably lower and higher, respectively, than the mean death rate for all seasons.

The hired death rates for the autumn season of 1.64% and the spring season of 0.96% statistically are significantly higher and lower, respectively, than the mean ascent rate of 1.26% for all seasons. The hired winter death rate of 2.14% is nearly significant, but the lower death and above base camp counts keep it from being as significant as the spring and autumn seasons.

Whether significant or not, death rates are the highest in the winter season for both members and hired as would be expected given the more difficult climbing conditions; but considering that only the more skilled climbers are likely to attempt winter expeditions, the winter season is probably even more dangerous than what is shown.

Tables D-12 and D-13 show death counts and rates for members and hired personnel for selected peaks for the spring, autumn, and winter climbing seasons. The summer season is excluded due to the low number of expeditions during the monsoon season.

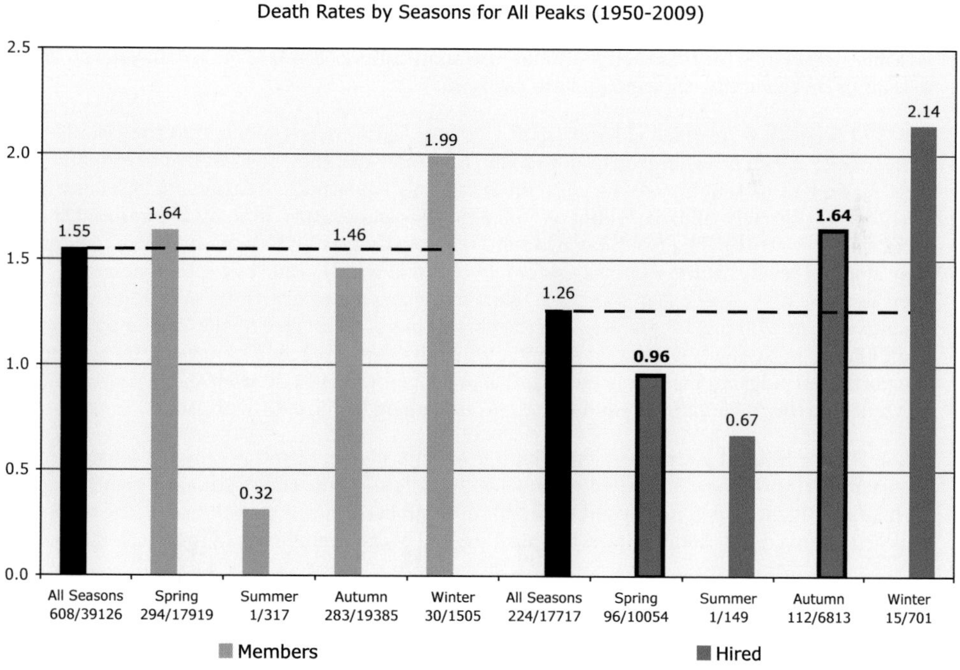

Death Rates by Seasons for All Peaks (1950-2009)

	All Seasons 608/39126	Spring 294/17919	Summer 1/317	Autumn 283/19385	Winter 30/1505	All Seasons 224/17717	Spring 96/10054	Summer 1/149	Autumn 112/6813	Winter 15/701
	1.55	1.64	0.32	1.46	1.99	1.26	0.96	0.67	1.64	2.14

■ Members   ■ Hired

Chart D-11: Member and hired death rates by climbing season for all peaks from 1950-2009 (the death rate is above the column bar; the death and above BC counts are below)

The columns outlined in black in the above chart represent seasons that statistically have either significantly higher or lower death rates than the mean death rate for all seasons.

Death and Survival on Nuptse

From *The Seasonal Stories* of Elizabeth Hawley – Autumn 1997

Slovenians have become noted for their technical skills and their readiness to attempt climbs others consider as impossible and unacceptably dangerous. "Impossible" has been the description given to Nuptse's west face by the few mountaineers who are aware of its existence, tucked as it is in between the northwest and west ridges; it is dramatically steep and threatened by hanging seracs.

Tomaz Humar and his friend, Janez Jeglic, whom Humar rated as Europe's best ice climber in terms of both speed and technical ability, needed three bivouacs for their alpine-style ascent in which they soloed with no belays and no fixed ropes. Belaying would have made their climb too slow, Humar explained; it is essential to move quickly on a 2000m wall that frequently avalanches.

Their climb began from a glacier camp at 5200m, and their first challenge, according to Humar's account after his return to Kathmandu, was the "awful glacier" of crevasses and hanging seracs where they had to spend four hours to actually reach the foot of their precipitous wall of rock and very hard ice that was mostly 50-60 degrees and occasionally 80 degrees steep. Their first bivouac was made on 27 October on a snow shelf at 5900m.

They continued their climb the next day despite strong wind and fog (a low cloud enveloped them) and snow avalanches that passed over them. They gained only 400 vertical meters that day, bivouacked in an overhanging crevasse that did little to protect them from the wind buffeting their small tent, letting them have almost no sleep. On the 29th they ascended another 400 vertical meters over mixed rock and ice and through small couloirs, dodging falling rocks and blocks of thin ice, and they had another night of terrible weather with winds tearing their tent and new snow falling. The fourth day they devoted to cooking and mending their badly battered tent.

On 31 October they resumed their climb at 4:00 a.m. with an agreement that they would turn back at 2:00 p.m. wherever they were at that time, and they now carried extremely light loads with no tent or cooking equipment but only something to drink and chocolate to eat. It was terribly cold: at 7100m at 8:00 a.m. the temperature was -30 Celsius and the wind was very strong. The two Slovenes were last together at 11:30 a.m. at 7500m, where they stopped briefly, but it was still extremely cold and windy, and they soon resumed their ascent singly, Jeglic going up first. "Now there was a storm with terrible wind," but despite this, at 2:00 p.m. Jeglic stood at the very summit of the face at the 7742m pointed peak known as Nuptse's northwest summit, which has been reached by several teams via the northwest ridge and which is perhaps 300m as a crow would fly from the main summit but much farther as a man would have to traverse along a sharp difficult ridge.

When Humar himself got to the peak 15 minutes after Jeglic, he found only his team-mate's footprints in very bad powder snow leading slightly onto the south side; apparently by mistake, Jeglic had gone beyond their summit and been blown off balance by the wind to plunge to his death 2500m down the hard ice and overhanging rock of the south face.

Humar left their summit at 3:00 p.m. and slowly descended the west face totally alone and without fixed ropes. But he did have two ice axes, and he moved with great care and concentration. "If you are pushed and you want to survive, everything is possible," he says. He was at 7100m when night began to fall; his battery was almost dead, but he had to keep moving, to reach shelter in their small tent; he lost his way; but finally about midnight he managed to find the tent.

Two hours later, a candle Humar had lighted caused his fuel supply to explode, but he was unharmed and he remained there until just after noon on the 1st of November, when he resumed his descent. Some falling ice seracs struck his head and slightly wounded him – he wore no helmet in order to save weight – but he kept going down until darkness fell when he was at 540m, and here he stopped, not wanting to risk another descent in the dark. By now he had four frostbitten toes. Marjan Kovac, a teammate who had been at base camp, joined him at 1:00 a.m. on the 2nd and helped him to reach the glacier, from where porters carried him to base camp.

	Spring			Autumn			Winter		
	Above BC	Death Cnt	Death Rate	Above BC	Death Cnt	Death Rate	Above BC	Death Cnt	Death Rate
All Peaks	17919	294	1.64	19385	283	1.46	1505	30	1.99
6000ers	1725	11	0.64	4993	32	0.64	502	3	0.60
7000ers	2779	60	2.16	5630	104	1.85	255	7	2.75
8000ers	13415	223	1.66	8762	147	1.68	748	20	2.67
KANG	673	14	2.08	133	8	6.02	27	3	11.11
MAKA	805	13	1.62	544	9	1.65	62	1	1.61
LHOT	724	6	0.83	315	5	1.59	32	0	0.00
EVER	6720	100	1.49	1985	35	1.76	275	3	1.09
CHOY	2164	18	0.83	3390	15	0.44	56	3.00	5.36
MANA	723	26	3.60	819	17	2.08	82	2	2.44
ANN1	455	15	3.30	512	25	4.88	139	5	3.60
DHA1	788	27	3.43	846	21	2.48	62	2	3.23
AMAD	621	5	0.81	2989	11	0.37	353	1	0.28
BARU	295	3	1.02	832	1	0.12	10	0	0.00
PUMO	392	9	2.30	848	19	2.24	56	4	7.14

Table D-12: Member deaths by season for selected peaks from 1950-2009

	Spring			Autumn			Winter		
	Above BC	Death Cnt	Death Rate	Above BC	Death Cnt	Death Rate	Above BC	Death Cnt	Death Rate
All Peaks	10054	96	0.96	6813	112	1.64	701	15	2.14
6000ers	576	2	0.35	1395	19	1.36	146	0	0.00
7000ers	1122	18	1.60	1696	30	1.77	97	3	3.09
8000ers	8356	76	0.91	3722	63	1.69	458	12	2.62
KANG	323	4	1.24	55	2	3.64	10	1	10.00
MAKA	403	10	2.48	175	4	2.29	11	0	0.00
LHOT	442	1	0.23	164	0	0.00	62	0	0.00
EVER	5662	31	0.55	1365	36	2.64	224	4	1.79
CHOY	541	1	0.19	1143	6	0.53	19	1	5.26
MANA	322	13	4.04	336	1	0.30	26	0	0.00
ANN1	179	7	3.91	165	10	6.06	67	0	0.00
DHA1	284	9	3.17	257	4	1.56	27	2	7.41
AMAD	134	0	0.00	735	4	0.54	94	0	0.00
BARU	119	1	0.84	226	5	2.21	7	0	0.00
PUMO	90	3	3.33	165	5	3.03	23	1	4.35

Table D-13: Hired deaths by season for selected peaks from 1950-2009

Charts D-12 and D-13 show death rates for members and hired personnel for selected peaks and peaks ranges for the spring and autumn climbing seasons. The winter and summer seasons are excluded due to the significantly lower climbing activity during those periods.

Overall, the spring death rates are similar to the autumn death rates, except for higher autumn death rates on Kangchenjunga and Annapurna I for both members and hired, and higher spring death rates on Manaslu and Dhaulagiri I for members and hired.

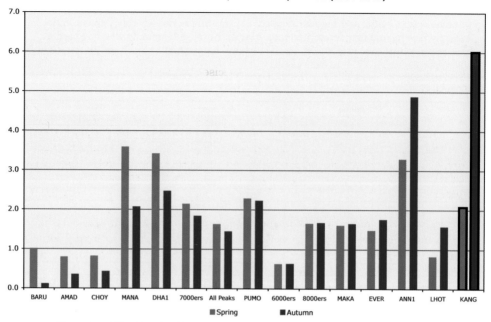

Chart D-12: Member death rates for selected peaks by season from 1950-2009
(ranked from left to right by difference in risk of death from spring to autumn)

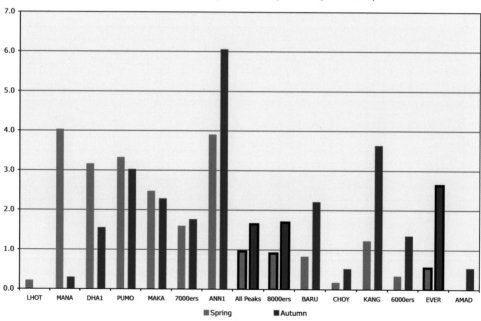

Chart D-13: Hired death rates for selected peaks by season from 1950-2009
(ranked from left to right by difference in risk of death from spring to autumn)

The columns outlined in black in the above charts represent peaks that have statistically significant differences in the death rates between the spring and autumn seasons.

Altitudes of Death

Chart D-14 gives the death counts for altitudes of death for all climbers (members and hired personnel) for all peaks. Death counts are used instead of death rates in the charts below because it is not always known how high each climber went above base camp (*The Himalayan Database* more precisely tracks the altitudes of those who summited or reached the expedition high point).

Altitudes of death for avalanches and falls are added to Chart D-14. The red trend line for avalanche deaths mirrors the shape of the total death blue trend line illustrating the strong impact that avalanches have on overall deaths. The red columns top out at the intermediate altitudes (6500m-6900m) where the snow accumulations are the greatest, and then taper off more rapidly because avalanches are fewer where snow accumulations are less.

The green trend line for falls generally increases illustrating the danger of falling as one gets higher on the mountain and becomes more fatigued. The flattening out of the fall trend line is due in part to the fewer number of climbers reaching altitudes above 7500m (the majority of the peaks are lower than 7500m).

Chart D-15 give the altitudes of death for all climbers for the 8000ers. When considering only the 8000m peaks, the green trend line for falls continues to rise as altitude increases better illustrating the danger of falling at the very high altitudes.

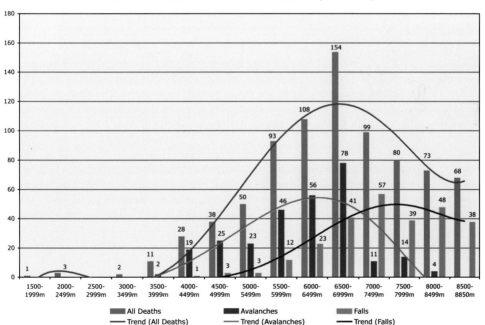

Chart D-14: Altitudes of death for all peaks from 1950-2009

> The altitudes of death given in Charts D-14 and D-15 represent the altitude of the incident that led to the eventual death; for example, if a climber sustained fatal injuries from a fall at 7500m, but died later at base camp, the altitude of death would be recorded as 7500m.

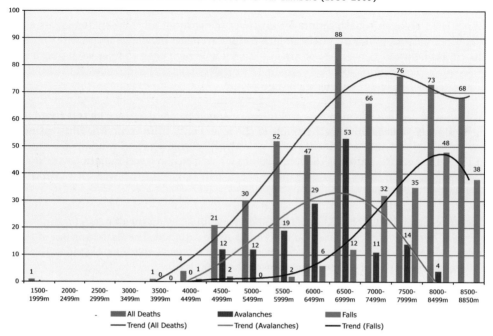

Chart D-15: Altitudes of death for all 8000ers from 1950-2009

Causes of Death

Table D-16 gives the causes of death for members and hired personnel for all peaks from 6000m to 8850m. The last two rows of the table indicate the number of deaths where acute mountain sickness (AMS) or major storms were either the primary cause or a contributing factor. For example, the primary cause of death for Scott Fischer on Everest was exposure/frostbite with the contributing factors of AMS and the disastrous storm of May 1996.

For both members and hired personnel, the majority of the deaths are due to falls or avalanches. For members, falling was the leading cause of death (39.0%), whereas for hired avalanches were the leading cause (46.4%), most likely because hired spent much of their time and energy establishing and supplying camps located in avalanche-prone zones.

Somewhat surprisingly, AMS did not figure as prominently as might be expected. AMS may be a hidden factor that was not known or accurately reported; for example, AMS may well have caused a few falls during descents from summit bids of the 8000m peaks, even though it went unreported.

Table D-16 includes deaths that occurred on expedition approach or return marches or at base camp as a result of non-climbing events. These deaths often were the results of trail accidents, illnesses, heart attacks, etc. For example, two leaders of an autumn 1992 Makalu II expedition were killed in the PIA air crash while flying into Kathmandu to join their team (taking the concept of approach march to the extreme).

144 Death Analysis

Cause of Death	Members		Hired		Total	
	Cnt	Pct	Cnt	Pct	Cnt	Pct
AMS	46	7.6	20	8.9	66	7.9
Exhaustion	18	3.0	2	0.9	20	2.4
Exposure/Frostbite	35	5.8	1	0.4	36	4.3
Fall	237	39.0	31	13.8	268	32.2
Crevasse	15	2.5	5	2.2	20	2.4
Icefall Collapse	2	0.3	15	6.7	17	2.0
Avalanche	175	28.8	104	46.4	279	33.5
Falling Rock/Ice	14	2.3	9	4.0	23	2.8
Disappearance	26	4.3	2	0.9	28	3.4
Illness (non-AMS)	26	4.3	15	6.7	41	4.9
Other	12	2.0	12	5.4	24	2.9
Unknown	2	0.3	8	3.6	10	1.2
Totals	608	100.0	224	100.0	832	100.0
AMS-related	67	11.0	18	8.0	74	8.9
Weather/Storm-related	44	7.2	6	2.7	50	6.0

**Table D-16: Causes of death for all deaths for all peaks
from 1950-2009**

Death Classification for All Deaths	Members		Hired		Total	
	Cnt	Pct	Cnt	Pct	Cnt	Pct
Death enroute to/from BC	19	3.1	35	15.6	54	6.5
Death at BC	21	3.5	33	14.7	54	6.5
Route preparation	270	44.4	122	54.5	392	47.1
Ascending in Smt Bid	72	11.8	6	2.7	78	9.4
Descending from Smt Bid	194	31.9	22	9.8	216	26.0
Expedition evacuation	32	5.3	6	2.7	38	4.6
Other/Unknown	0	0.0	0	0.0	0	0.0
Totals	608	100.0	224	100.0	832	100.0

**Table D-17: Death classification for all deaths for all peaks
from 1950-2009**

Table D-17 classifies deaths based on the phase of the expedition at which the deaths occurred. Ascending and descending deaths on summit bids are recorded regardless of whether the actual summit was attained.

Route preparation, the phase when lower camps are established and stocked and the summit teams position themselves at their highest camp in anticipation of a summit bid, was the most dangerous phase of an expedition for both members and hired. The second most dangerous phase for members was descents from summit bids. But if danger is viewed on a per-day basis, then for the larger peaks summit day would be the most dangerous day because the number of summit days is far less that the number of route preparation days for most expeditions.

For hired, the second most dangerous phase was the approach or return march often because lowland porters were unable to adapt to the higher, colder climates due to inferior clothing and equipment or undetected illnesses (five died from AMS and seven died from other illnesses). In addition, six died from avalanches below base camp, and six staff members of a spring 2002 Spanish Makalu expedition were lost in a helicopter disappearance (probable crash) while returning to Kathmandu from their expedition.

Table D-18 shows causes of death during route preparation. For members, avalanches followed by falls were the most prevalent. For hired, only avalanching posed much of a problem; icefall collapse was a distant second with the majority of those icefall

Cause of Death Route Preparation	Members		Hired		Total	
	Cnt	Pct	Cnt	Pct	Cnt	Pct
AMS	13	4.8	4	3.3	17	4.3
Exhaustion	3	1.1	0	0.0	3	0.8
Exposure/Frostbite	15	5.6	0	0.0	15	3.8
Fall	71	26.3	5	4.1	76	19.4
Crevasse	7	2.6	4	3.3	11	2.8
Icefall Collapse	2	0.7	15	12.3	17	4.3
Avalanche	137	50.7	81	66.4	218	55.6
Falling Rock/Ice	9	3.3	7	5.7	16	4.1
Disappearance	4	1.5	0	0.0	4	1.0
Illness (non-AMS)	8	3.0	3	2.5	11	2.8
Other	0	0.0	3	2.5	3	0.8
Unknown	1	0.4	0	0.0	1	0.3
Totals	270	100.0	122	100.0	392	100.0

Table D-18: Causes of death during route preparation for all peaks
from 1950-2009

Cause of Death Ascending in Smt Bid	Members		Hired		Total	
	Cnt	Pct	Cnt	Pct	Cnt	Pct
AMS	0	0.0	0	0.0	0	0.0
Exhaustion	2	2.8	0	0.0	2	2.6
Exposure/Frostbite	0	0.0	0	0.0	0	0.0
Fall	39	54.2	5	83.3	44	56.4
Crevasse	2	2.8	0	0.0	2	2.6
Icefall Collapse	0	0.0	0	0.0	0	0.0
Avalanche	13	18.1	0	0.0	13	16.7
Falling Rock/Ice	0	0.0	0	0.0	0	0.0
Disappearance	14	19.4	1	16.7	15	19.2
Illness (non-AMS)	2	2.8	0	0.0	2	2.6
Other	0	0.0	0	0.0	0	0.0
Unknown	0	0.0	0	0.0	0	0.0
Totals	72	100.0	6	100.0	78	100.0

Table D-19: Causes of death during summit bid ascents for all peaks
from 1950-2009

collapses being in the Khumbu Icefall on Everest (six Sherpas died in one accident in 1970). The 1970 serac collapse as well as other accidents in the Khumbu Icefall during the 1960-1980s gave it the reputation of being most dangerous part of Everest; but since 1986, only two fatal accidents have occurred: three Sherpas died in 2006 due to a serac collapse and one more in 2009 due to an ice avalanche off the West Shoulder.

Table D-19 shows causes of death while *ascending* during a summit bid. For members, falls followed by unexplained disappearances (probable falls) were by far the most prevalent. For hired, minimal (only 6) deaths occurred during summit bid ascents.

Table D-20 shows causes of death while *descending* from a summit bid (includes both those who summited and those who did not summit). For members, falls were the major cause of death, followed by exposure/frostbite, AMS, and exhaustion. This supports the general consensus that descending from the summit late in the day when cold and exhausted is a particularly perilous time of a climb. For hired, falls were the primary cause of death during descent from a summit bid.

Table D-21 gives the causes of death for members on summit day (while ascending or descending in a summit bid). Across all altitudes, falls are by far and away the leading of cause of death, from 63.3% for the 7000ers down to 44.0% for Everest. In general as

Cause of Death Descending in Smt Bid	Members		Hired		Total	
	Cnt	Pct	Cnt	Pct	Cnt	Pct
AMS	20	10.3	1	4.5	21	9.7
Exhaustion	12	6.2	0	0.0	12	5.6
Exposure/Frostbite	20	10.3	0	0.0	20	9.3
Fall	114	58.8	19	86.4	133	61.6
Crevasse	3	1.5	0	0.0	3	1.4
Icefall Collapse	0	0.0	0	0.0	0	0.0
Avalanche	4	2.1	2	9.1	6	2.8
Falling Rock/Ice	3	1.5	0	0.0	3	1.4
Disappearance	8	4.1	0	0.0	8	3.7
Illness (non-AMS)	6	3.1	0	0.0	6	2.8
Other	3	1.5	0	0.0	3	1.4
Unknown	1	0.5	0	0.0	1	0.5
Totals	194	100.0	22	100.0	216	100.0

Table D-20: Causes of death during summit bid descents for all peaks from 1950-2009

Cause of Death During Summit Bids	All Peaks		6000ers		7000ers		8000ers		Everest	
	Cnt	Pct	Cnt	Pct	Cnt	Pct	Cnt	Pct	Cnt	Pct
AMS	20	7.5	0	0.0	1	1.7	19	9.9	8	9.5
Exhaustion	14	5.3	0	0.0	0	0.0	14	7.3	12	14.3
Exposure/Frostbite	20	7.5	0	0.0	2	3.3	18	9.4	15	17.9
Fall	153	57.5	8	57.1	38	63.3	107	55.7	37	44.0
Crevasse	5	1.9	1	7.1	2	3.3	2	1.0	0	0.0
Icefall Collapse	0	0.0	0	0.0	0	0.0	0	0.0	0	0.0
Avalanche	17	6.4	5	35.7	7	11.7	5	2.6	0	0.0
Falling Rock/Ice	3	1.1	0	0.0	2	3.3	1	0.5	0	0.0
Disappearance (Unexplained)	22	8.3	0	0.0	8	13.3	14	7.3	6	7.1
Illness (non-AMS)	8	3.0	0	0.0	0	0.0	8	4.2	5	6.0
Other	3	1.1	0	0.0	0	0.0	3	1.6	0	0.0
Unknown	1	0.4	0	0.0	0	0.0	1	0.5	1	1.2
Totals	266	100.0	14	100.0	60	100.0	192	100.0	84	100.0
Ascending in summit bid	72	27.1	7	50.0	21	35.0	44	22.9	17	20.2
Descending from summit bid	194	72.9	7	50.0	39	65.0	148	77.1	67	79.8
AMS-related	33		0		2		31		16	
Weather/Storm-related	24		0		5		19		13	

Table D-21: Causes of death for members while ascending or descending in summit bids from 1950-2009

peaks become higher, other factors come into play. For the 6000-7000ers, avalanches are more frequent and for the 8000ers, the physiological factors (AMS, exhaustion, and exposure-frostbite) become more important. Unexplained disappearances are also a factor, but many of those are likely due to falls. And across all altitudes, falls during descent are much more prevalent (two to three times the rate of falling during ascent).

Charts D-21a-b show altitudes of death on summit day for the commercial routes on Everest. For the south side, falls are the leading cause (12) followed closely by physiological causes (9) with most of the deaths occurring above the Balcony (17 of 22 deaths). For the north side, the reverse is true: physiological causes (23) outstrip falls (10) with most of the deaths occurring at or above the First Step (31 of 41 deaths). The four disappearances most likely are from falls or physiological causes leading to falls. The preponderance of physiological deaths on the north side may be due to climbers spending more time above 8000m because their highest camp is normally at 8300m, 400m higher than the high camp at 7900m on the South Col.

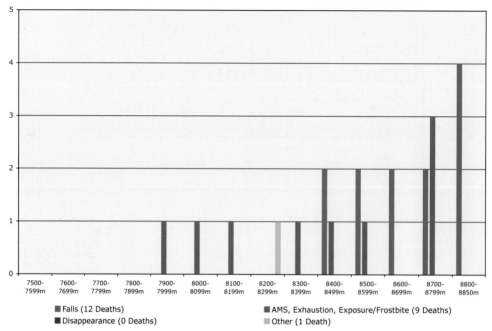

Chart D-21a: Causes of death for members while ascending or descending in summit bids on Everest South Col-SE Ridge commercial route from 1950-2009
(S Col=7900m, Balcony=8400m, S Summit=8750m, Hillary Step=8800m)

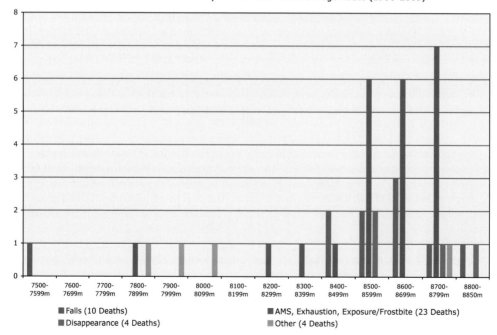

Chart D-21b: Causes of death for members while ascending or descending in summit bids on Everest North Col-NE Ridge commercial route from 1950-2009
(Normal high-camp=8300m, 1st Step=8450m, 2nd Step=8680m, 3rd Step=8700m)

A Deadly Bolt From the Sky

From *The Seasonal Stories* of Elizabeth Hawley – Spring 1991

Hans Kammerlander, Friedl Mutschlechner, and Karl Grossrubatscher planned an alpine-style ascent of the normal northeast-face route on Manaslu from a camp at 6000m near the base of their 8163m mountain.

But their program did not work out in several ways. They climbed without any Nepalese Sherpas or artificial oxygen, as planned, but unfavorable weather with frequent heavy snowfall caused them to set up three successively higher camps in the course of their ascent.

After nearly three weeks of climbing, they decided that bad weather and lack of time was forcing them to give up hope of reaching the summit, but early in the morning of 10 May three of them started up from camp 3 at 6900m. They could see that the weather would not remain good long enough for them to make a summit bid, but the morning was fine and they would climb upwards for a while.

After half an hour's climb, at about 7000m, Mutschlechner's fingers were becoming numb from the extremely cold wind, and having suffered from frostbitten fingers before, he did not want another episode of that, and he turned back to camp 3. When the two others had reached about 7200m, Grossrubatscher had to stop climbing up; he had not brought his ice ax with him that morning, and now the terrain required one. So he, too, returned to camp 3 and was seen moving around its tent by teammates watching from base camp until clouds moved across and the camp was no longer visible from below. Kammerlander continued alone to 7500m and then finally he also abandoned the climb.

When Kammerlander arrived back at camp 3, Mutschlechner asked him, "Where is Karl?" Near the tent they discovered his ice ax with a glove in its strap. A bit farther away, perhaps 100m, they found his body. His neck was broken. How this had happened is a mystery: his legs, arms and head were not badly broken; the slope where camp 3 was located was gentle with snow in good condition; if he had climbed up to a nearby serac and fallen from it, there was no trace of his fall in the snow; he was a healthy, strong professional mountaineer.

The two survivors placed their friend's body atop a closed crevasse that in warmer weather will open and receive it. They then took down the tent, descended to camp 2 at 6200m, packed up that tent and, roped together and on skis, they continued down the snow-covered slopes. But now fog or wisps of cloud were passing over them and visibility was poor; finally, about 100m above camp 1 at 5600m, they were enveloped in such thick cloud that Mutschlechner suggested they wait for the mists to clear a bit. They could hear continuous soft thunder, their hair was full of electricity and their ice axes were humming from it, but they saw no lightning in their dense fog. But suddenly Kammerlander had a sharp popping sound in his ear, which felt as though it had been bitten. He dropped to the snow and tugged on the rope between him and Mutschlechner; there was no answering tug, and when he went to Mutschlechner later, Kammerlander saw that he was dead with three burn marks on his head and his cap. Mutschlechner had been only eight meters away from his colleague and a mere two vertical meters above him at the highest point of a small snow-covered hill. It was about 4:00 p.m. and snow was falling. Mutschlechner is believed to have been the first mountaineer ever killed by lightning in Nepal.

Avalanche Deaths

Avalanches have always been a major concern to Himalayan climbers. They can strike at anytime without warning, wreak havoc on camps, and have snuffed out the lives of some of the world's most elite climbers: Claude Kogan on Cho Oyu in 1959 from a high-camp avalanche that killed two climbers and two Sherpas; Reinhard Karl on Cho Oyu in 1982 from an ice-block avalanche that smashed into tents nested in a bergschrund; and Anatoli Boukreev on Annapurna I on Christmas Day of 1997 from an avalanche triggered by an ice cornice that fell from a ridge above.

Hired personnel in particular have born the brunt of some of the deadliest avalanche accidents: eleven on Kang Guru in 2005, ten on Manaslu in 1972, and six on Everest in 1970 as noted earlier, and seven on Everest in 1922 in an accident below the North Col that included George Mallory who narrowly escaped with his own life.

Chart D-22 shows avalanche death rates for members and hired personnel by climbing season for all peaks and illustrates the increased avalanche frequency that occurs during the autumn season due to the build up of snow during the summer monsoons.

Chart D-23 shows avalanche deaths as a percentage of total deaths for members and hired personnel by climbing season for all peaks. This chart illustrates in a different manner the increased avalanche risk during the autumn season, that is, the percentage of all deaths due to avalanching increases during that time. The summer season is omitted from the chart because only two deaths have occurred during the summer season as very few climbers are willing to attempt expeditions during the heavy monsoon rains and snows.

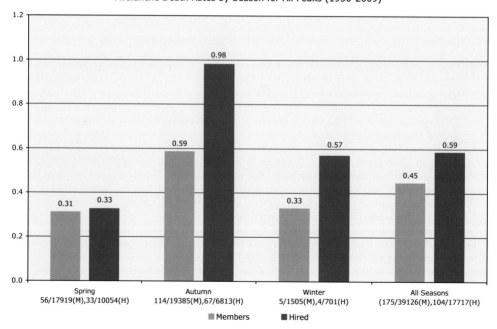

Chart D-22: Avalanche death rates by season for members and hired personnel for all peaks (the death rate is above the column bar; the death and above BC counts are below)

150 Death Analysis

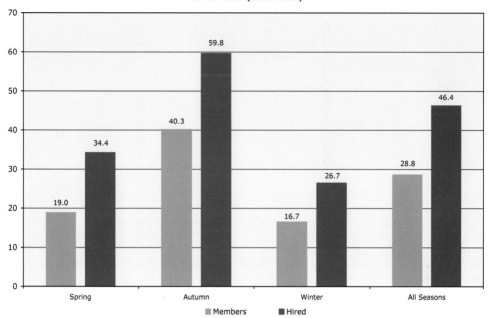

Chart D-23: Avalanche deaths as a percentage of total deaths by season for all peaks

Members	Spring			Autumn			Winter		
	Above BC	Death Cnt	Death Rate	Above BC	Death Cnt	Death Rate	Above BC	Death Cnt	Death Rate
All Peaks	17919	56	0.31	19385	114	0.59	1505	5	0.33
6000ers	1725	2	0.12	4993	20	0.40	502	0	0.00
7000ers	2779	14	0.50	5630	46	0.82	255	1	0.39
8000ers	13415	40	0.30	8762	48	0.55	748	4	0.54
KANG	673	0	0.00	133	5	3.76	27	0	0.00
MAKA	805	0	0.00	544	2	0.37	62	0	0.00
LHOT	724	0	0.00	315	2	0.64	32	0	0.00
EVER	6720	9	0.13	1985	8	0.40	275	0	0.00
CHOY	2164	1	0.05	3390	2	0.06	56	0	0.00
MANA	723	12	1.66	819	3	0.37	82	0	0.00
ANN1	455	8	1.76	512	14	2.73	139	2	1.44
DHA1	788	10	1.27	846	6	0.71	62	2	3.23
AMAD	621	0	0.00	2989	4	0.13	353	0	0.00
BARU	295	0	0.00	832	0	0.00	10	0	0.00
PUMO	392	3	0.77	848	10	1.18	56	0	0.00

Table D-24: Member avalanche deaths by season from 1950-2009

Tables and Charts D-24 and D-25 show avalanche death rates for members and hired personnel for selected peaks and peaks ranges for the spring, autumn, and winter climbing seasons. For these charts, the winter season is excluded due to the low number of expeditions during that period.

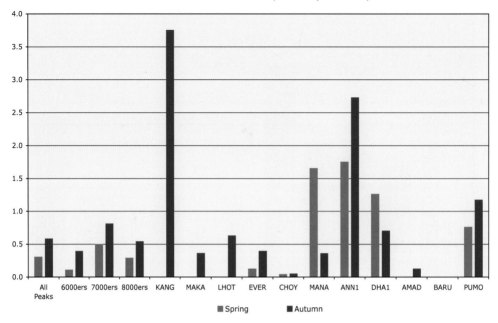

Member Avalanche Death Rates by Season (1950-2009)

Chart D-24: Member avalanche death rates for selected peaks by season from 1950-2009

Hired	Spring			Autumn			Winter		
	Above BC	Death Cnt	Death Rate	Above BC	Death Cnt	Death Rate	Above BC	Death Cnt	Death Rate
All Peaks	10054	33	0.33	6813	67	0.98	701	4	0.57
6000ers	576	2	0.35	1395	15	1.08	146	0	0.00
7000ers	1122	9	0.80	1696	13	0.77	97	2	2.06
8000ers	8356	22	0.26	3722	39	1.05	458	2	0.44
KANG	323	0	0.00	55	0	0.00	10	0	0.00
MAKA	403	0	0.00	175	0	0.00	11	0	0.00
LHOT	442	1	0.23	164	0	0.00	62	0	0.00
EVER	5662	1	0.02	1365	21	1.54	224	0	0.00
CHOY	541	0	0.00	1143	5	0.44	19	0	0.00
MANA	322	11	3.42	336	1	0.30	26	0	0.00
ANN1	179	2	1.12	165	8	4.85	67	0	0.00
DHA1	284	7	2.47	257	4	1.56	27	2	7.41
AMAD	134	0	0.00	735	3	0.41	94	0	0.00
BARU	119	0	0.00	226	0	0.00	7	0	0.00
PUMO	90	1	1.11	165	5	3.03	23	0	0.00

Table D-25: Hired avalanche deaths by season from 1950-2009

Tables D-26 and Charts D-26a-b show avalanche death rates and avalanche death to total death percentages for members by geographic regions for the spring and autumn climbing seasons.

Tables D-27 and Charts D-27a-b show avalanche death rates and avalanche death to total death percentages for hired personnel by geographic regions for the spring and autumn climbing seasons.

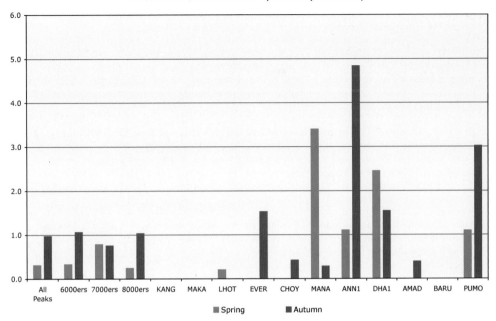

Chart D-25: Hired avalanche death rates for selected peaks by season from 1950-2009

	Spring				Autumn			
	Members Above BC	Aval Death Cnt	Aval Death Rate	Pct Aval of Total Deaths	Members Above BC	Aval Death Cnt	Aval Death Rate	Pct Aval of Total Deaths
All Peaks	17919	56	0.31	19.0	19385	114	0.59	40.3
Kangchenjunga-Janak	1412	0	0	0	781	7	0.90	38.9
Khumbu-Makalu-Rolwaling	12475	13	0.10	8.0	12112	37	0.31	31.1
Langtang-Jugal	284	6	2.11	100.0	372	6	1.61	60.0
Manaslu-Ganesh	1056	14	1.33	41.2	1243	19	1.53	47.5
Annapurna-Damodar-Peri	1309	12	0.92	46.2	2739	34	1.24	54.8
Dhaulagiri-Mukut	1231	10	0.81	25.0	1842	11	0.60	34.4
Kanjiroba-Far West	152	1	0.66	16.7	296	0	0	0

Table D-26: Member avalanche deaths for regions by season from 1950-2009

	Spring				Autumn			
	Hired Above BC	Aval Death Cnt	Aval Death Rate	Pct Aval of Total Deaths	Hired Above BC	Aval Death Cnt	Aval Death Rate	Pct Aval of Total Deaths
All Peaks	10054	33	0.33	34.4	6813	67	0.98	59.8
Kangchenjunga-Janak	632	0	0	0	219	0	0	0
Khumbu-Makalu-Rolwaling	7677	3	0.04	6.4	4311	35	0.81	53.8
Langtang-Jugal	155	3	1.94	100.0	125	1	0.80	50.0
Manaslu-Ganesh	500	11	2.20	68.8	489	1	0.20	50.0
Annapurna-Damodar-Peri	519	4	0.77	40.0	849	24	2.83	80.0
Dhaulagiri-Mukut	494	12	2.43	80.0	716	6	0.84	66.7
Kanjiroba-Far West	77	0	0	0	104	0	0	0

Table D-27: Hired avalanche deaths for regions by season from 1950-2009

Death Analysis 153

Double Trouble on Gangapurna

From *The Himalayan Database* notes of Elizabeth Hawley – October 1971

On October 15, Kiyoshi Shimizu, Takeshi Akahane, and Girme Dorje reached the summit of Gangapurna from C4 at 2:15 p.m. and then returned to C4 at 7 p.m. where a second summit team of four was waiting. They planned continue down to C3 that day where three teammates were waiting in support of the two summit teams, but heavy snows pinned all seven of them down at C4.

At 6 p.m. on October 16, the two higher camps failed to make radio contact with three more Japanese climbers and three Sherpas waiting for them down at C2. The next day Girme Dorje and Pemba Norbu went down to C2 from C4 to investigate. The following morning of October 18 at 8 a.m. Girme reported by radio to C3 from the C2 site that the camp had completely disappeared, presumably swept away by an avalanche on the afternoon of October 16 killing all six occupants.

After reporting this, Girme said that he and Pemba would return back up to C3, but the Japanese in C3 advised against this since the route between the two camps was avalanche prone. Girme and Pemba were not seen or heard from again. It is presumed that they were swept away by an avalanche or fell into a crevasse.

Icefall and serac collapses, a related form of avalanching, but not included in the data above, have been largely confined to the Khumbu Icefall on Everest. The worst icefall collapse was on the 1970 Japanese Everest ski expedition led by Yuichiro Miura when six Sherpas were killed by an early morning serac collapse at 5700m. This was the fourth deadliest accident for Sherpas, the worst being the 2005 Kang Guru avalanche

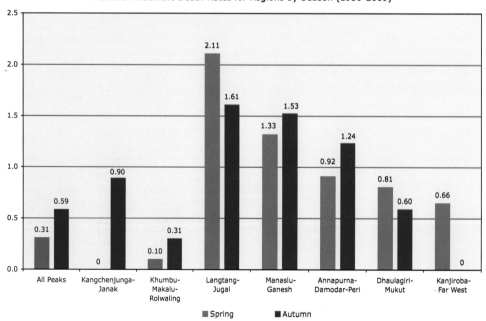

Chart D-26a: Member avalanche death rates for regions by season from 1950-2009

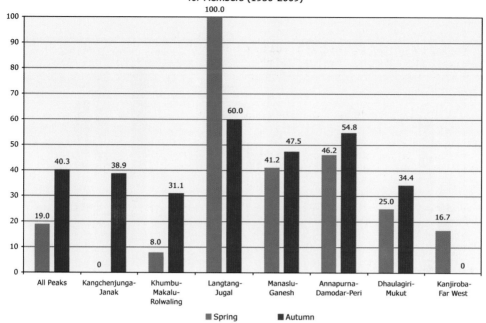

Chart D-26b: Percentages of avalanches deaths to total deaths for regions by season for members from 1950-2009

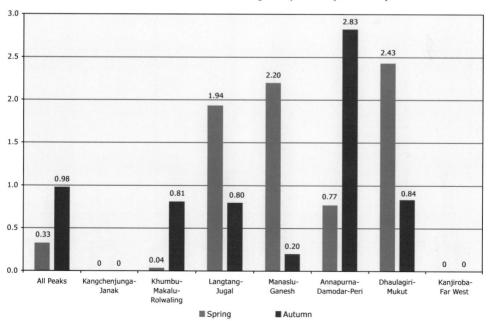

Chart D-27a: Hired avalanche death rates for regions by season from 1950-2009

Percentages for Avalanche Deaths to Total Deaths for Regions by Season
for Hired (1950-2009)

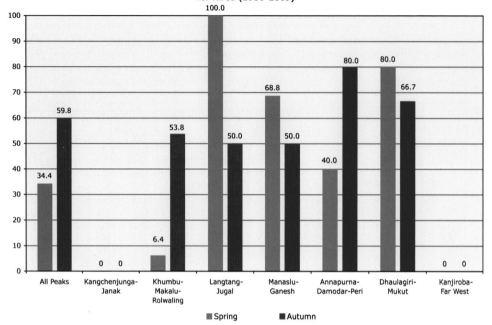

**Chart D-27b: Percentages of avalanche deaths to total deaths for regions
by season for hired from 1950-2009**

Total Deaths by Avalanche by Time of Day (1950-2009)

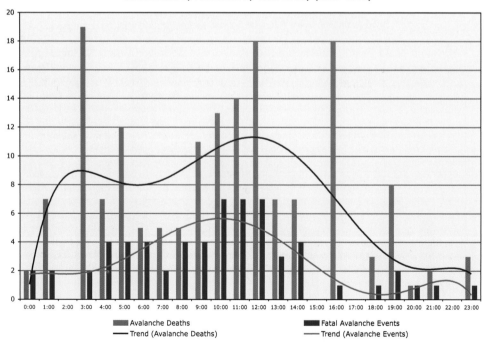

**Chart D-28: Avalanche deaths and fatal avalanche events by time of day
for members and hired personal from 1950-2009**

156 Death Analysis

that killed eleven Sherpas, the 1972 Manaslu avalanche that killed ten Sherpas, and a 1922 Everest expedition avalanche below the North Col that killed seven Sherpas.

Chart D-28 shows by time of day the number of fatal avalanche events and total deaths for both members and hired personnel (a fatal avalanche event is an avalanche that kills one or more climbers). As shown, the majority of the fatal avalanches occur in the very early morning hours when temperatures are the lowest or during the late morning hours after the sun has warmed up the snow pack. But two of the worst avalanches occurred at 3:15 a.m. (15 killed on Manaslu in 1972) and 4:00 p.m. (18 killed on Kang Guru in 2005), both outside of the primary avalanche times, illustrating that no time of day is completely safe (see the inset boxes, *Double Trouble on Gangapurna*, on pg. 154, and *One of Nepal's Deadliest Avalanches Hits Manaslu*, below).

One of Nepal's Deadliest Avalanches Hits Manaslu

From a *Reuter's News* Dispatch by Elizabeth Hawley – April 14, 1972

One Korean Kim Yae-Sup and two Sherpas survived a huge avalanche that completely destroyed the Koreans' C3 (6500m) on Manaslu early in the morning of April 10.

Kim who actually survived five avalanches and gale force winds that terrible morning briefly recounted his horror to Reuter's this morning in Shanta Bhawan Hospital while nurses gently bathed his badly frostbitten feet in warm water. He was brought to Kathmandu ex-basecamp by helicopter this morning with the expedition leader's eldest brother Kim Jung-Sup and the expedition's reporter Yun Byung-Hae who were not at C3.

The avalanche took the lives of four Koreans, one Japanese and ten Sherpas. One Korean dead was the climbing leader Kim Ho-Sup, who had vowed to conquer Manaslu this time and recover the body of another brother Kim Ki-Sup, who died last spring at 7600m on the same side of Manaslu from fierce winds that swept him off his feet. Other dead are Oh Sae-Keun, Song Joon-Haeng, Park Chang-Hee, Japanese photographer Kazunari Yasuhisha, nine high-altitude Sherpa porters and one Sherpa cook.

Kim Yae-Sup said he woke about midnight of that fatal night to make some hot water and to prepare for an early climbing start. Two Sherpas commented to him that there had been too much snowfall. They were worried about the snow conditions on the mountainside. At about 3:15 a.m., Kim heard the terrible noise of the huge avalanche and woke two members, Park and Yasuhisha, in the same tent. They tried to get outside, but the avalanche struck first and they were carried 800m downwards from C3 (at 6500m) with three shattering bounces before on the 4th bound they stopped moving.

Both Kim's companions were still alive and spoke to him: Park said the whole midsection of his torso was crushed and his spine was broken; Yasuhisha told Kim his left rib and right shoulder were broken.

Then another avalanche struck them, fatally burying Kim's two friends and carrying him 300m further downwards. Three more avalanches hit Kim, but he survived with frostbitten feet and fingers; possible internal injuries are not yet known. "I think I am a very lucky boy and God is with me," Kim said this morning in his hospital bed. Kim's family are Christians.

There were four other tents in C3. In one were three Koreans, Kim Ho-Sup, Oh Sae-Keun, and Song Joon-Haeng and two other tents held ten Sherpas. All perished in this disaster. The expedition is not continuing. Four surviving Koreans are still in the mountains and will return with recoverable baggage.

Deaths by Falling

Whereas avalanches are the leading cause of death for hired personnel, falls are the leading cause of death for members. Some of the world's best ended their careers with fatal falls: Jerzy Kukuczka fell off the south face of Lhotse at 8350m in 1989 while going for the summit alone, and Pierre Beghin fell to his death on Annapurna I at 7100m in 1992 while climbing with Jean-Christophe Lafaille (who subsequently disappeared on Makalu in January 2006 perhaps also due to a fall).

Death Classification Deaths by Falling	Members		Hired		Total	
	Cnt	Pct	Cnt	Pct	Cnt	Pct
Death enroute BC	3	1.3	1	3.2	4	1.5
Death at BC	0	0.0	0	0.0	0	0.0
Route preparation	71	30.0	5	16.1	76	28.4
Ascending in Smt Bid	39	16.5	5	16.1	44	16.4
Descending from Smt Bid	114	48.1	19	61.3	133	49.6
Expedition evacuation	10	4.2	1	3.2	11	4.1
Other/Unknown	0	0.0	0	0.0	0	0.0
Totals	237	100.0	31	100.0	268	100.0
AMS-related	10	4.2	1	3.2	11	4.1
Weather/Storm-related	15	6.3	2	6.5	17	6.3

Table D-29: Death classification for deaths by falling for all peaks from 1950-2009

As shown in Table D-29 above, the majority of fatal falls occur on summit day, ascending or descending in a summit bid (64.6% for members and 77.4% for hired personnel). The most critical phase, descending from a summit bid, is where most of the fatal falls occur (48.1% for members and 61.3% for hired).

Charts D-30a–d show altitudes of falls for all peaks and for peaks in the 7500-7999m, 8000-8499m, and 8500-8850m ranges, the groups in which the majority of falls occur.

The spike in deaths in the 7000-7249m range of Chart D-30a is due in part to three multiple-fatality falls during route preparation: three Japanese deaths at 7000m on Dhaulagiri V (1971) when one climber slipped and pulled his two rope-mates with him, two Swiss deaths at 7100m on Lhotse Shar (1981) when two climbers disappeared and were later found dead at 6000m, and three Russian deaths at 7200m on Manaslu (1990). In addition, three multiple-fatality falls occurred on summit day: two deaths each at 7000m on Tilicho (1988) and Annapurna I (1989) and two deaths at 7200m on Nuptse (1975). These six accidents account for 14 of the 35 deaths by falling at 7000-7249m. Taking away these 14 deaths would still leave a spike at 7000-7249m, but a much smaller one.

Chart D-31 shows for all peaks the location of fatal falls as measured by the vertical distance from the summit. This chart suggests that most falls occur on summit day and within 500m of the summit. At the higher altitudes (the left side of the chart), those descending from a successful summit bid in general have the most fatalities, most likely because they are exhausted from climbing the farthest and for the longest time.

The spikes in deaths in the 500-599m and 600-699m ranges are due in part to four multiple-fatality falls on summit day: three Slovakian deaths at 6650m on Pumori (1997) during ascent to the summit, four Czech deaths at 8300m on Everest (1988)

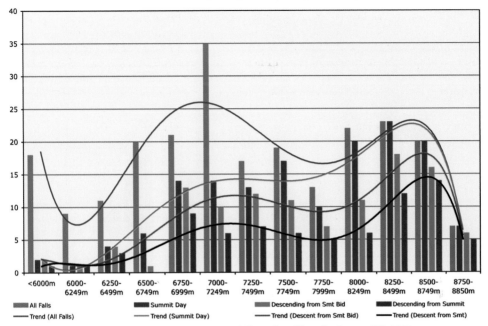

Chart D-30a: Member deaths by falling for all peaks from 1950-2009
(measured as altitude of fall)

Blue trend line – all deaths by falling.
Red trend line – all deaths on summit day (ascending or descending).
Green trend line – all deaths descending from all summit bids.
Black trend line – all deaths descending from a successful summit bid.

Under the **black** line represents all deaths descending from the summit.
Between the green and **black** lines are all deaths descending from a failed summit bid.
Between the red and green lines are all deaths while ascending in a summit bid.
Between the blue and red lines are all deaths during route preparation or evacuation.

during descent from the summit, two Yugoslav deaths at 8000m on Kangchenjunga (1991) after turning back from a summit bid, and two British deaths at 7200m on Nuptse (1975). Also one accident occurred during route preparation: the three Japanese deaths at 7000m on Dhaulagiri V (1971) mentioned above. These five accidents account for 14 of the 45 deaths by falling at a distance of 500 to 699m from the summit. Taking away these 14 deaths will still leave spikes at 500-599m and 600-699m, but much smaller ones.

Table D-32 and Charts D-32a-b show the time of day for all deaths by falling and deaths by falling while descending from a summit bid. There are two particularly dangerous times, mid-morning from about 9 to 11 a.m. and late afternoon from 3 to 6 p.m. But for falls while descending from a summit bid, only the afternoon period is particularly dangerous, probably because those still descending late in the afternoon have been climbing for more hours, are on longer summit-day routes, or are slower due to age or lack of climbing skills.

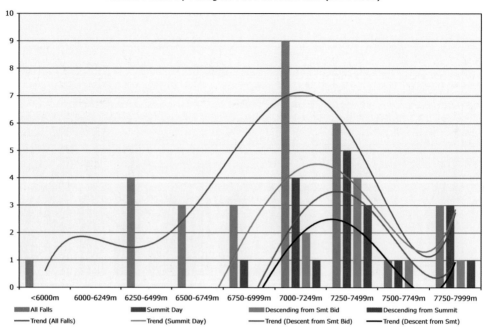

Chart D-30b: Member deaths by falling for 7500-7999m peaks from 1950-2009 (measured as altitude of fall)

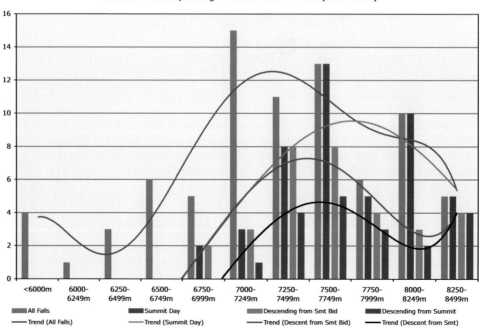

Chart D-30c: Member deaths by falling for 8000-8499m peaks from 1950-2009 (measured as altitude of fall)

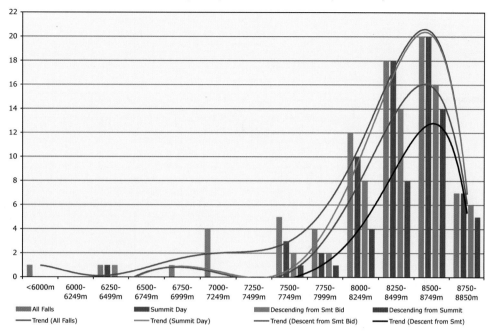

Chart D-30d: Member deaths by falling for 8500-8850m peaks from 1950-2009 (measured as altitude of fall)

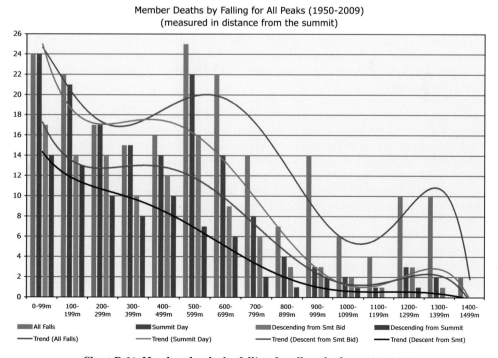

Chart D-31: Member deaths by falling for all peaks from 1950-2009 (measured as distance from summit in vertical meters)

Time of Day	All Falls					Falls Descending from Smt Bids				
	All Peaks	6000ers	7000ers	8000ers	EVER	All Peaks	6000ers	7000ers	8000ers	EVER
Unknown	96	5	21	70	20	45	0	10	35	11
00:00-00:59	1	0	0	1	0	1	0	0	1	0
01:00-01:59	0	0	0	0	0	0	0	0	0	0
02:00-02:59	0	0	0	0	0	0	0	0	0	0
03:00-03:59	1	0	0	1	0	1	0	0	1	0
04:00-04:59	1	0	1	0	0	0	0	0	0	0
05:00-05:59	1	1	0	0	0	1	1	0	0	0
06:00-06:59	6	1	0	5	4	1	0	0	1	1
07:00-07:59	3	0	2	1	1	2	0	2	0	0
08:00-08:59	6	2	0	4	2	0	0	0	0	0
09:00-09:59	10	2	2	6	1	4	1	0	3	1
10:00-10:59	13	0	5	8	3	3	0	0	3	1
11:00-11:59	5	1	1	3	1	1	0	0	1	1
12:00-12:59	6	0	3	3	0	1	0	0	1	0
13:00-13:59	10	1	3	6	2	7	1	1	5	2
14:00-14:59	10	2	4	4	3	2	0	1	1	1
15:00-15:59	10	0	8	2	1	8	0	6	2	1
16:00-16:59	17	1	6	10	0	9	0	1	8	0
17:00-17:59	13	0	1	12	7	8	0	1	7	5
18:00-18:59	8	1	0	7	2	4	1	0	3	2
19:00-19:59	8	1	4	3	0	7	1	3	3	0
20:00-20:59	10	2	3	5	1	7	0	2	5	1
21:00-21:59	1	0	0	1	0	1	0	0	1	0
22:00-22:59	1	1	0	0	0	1	1	0	0	0
23:00-23:59	0	0	0	0	0	0	0	0	0	0
Totals	237	21	64	152	48	114	6	27	81	27

Table D-32: Deaths by falling by time of day for all peaks from 1950-2009

5 of the 14 deaths in the 10 a.m. bracket were the result of two accidents while ascending in summit bids: Gerry Owens and Richard Summerton (both UK) at 7200m on Nuptse in spring 1975, and Pavol Dzurman, Peter Lenco, and Frantisek Miscak (all Slovaks) at 6550m on Pumori in autumn 1997. The remainder of the accidents in the 9 to 11 a.m. brackets were all single fatalities, one being Pierre Beghin's fall off the south face of Annapurna I.

The other major falling accident was in autumn 1988 when Dusan Becik, Peter Bozik, Jaroslav Jasko, and Jozef Just (all Czechs) fell in descent near 8300m on the southeast ridge of Everest shortly after their last radio contact at 5:30 p.m. Other notable falls include Jerzy Kukuczka falling on the south face of Lhotse at 6 a.m., Marco Siffredi disappearing at 8600m around 3 p.m. while attempting to snowboard down the Great Couloir on north face of Everest, and Benoit Chamoux disappearing down the north face of Kangchenjunga around 5 p.m.

The worst falling accident occurred in November 1994 when three rope teams of nine Germans, one Swiss, and a Sherpa guide plunged off the west ridge of Pisang Peak apparently after becoming entangled when the rope team slipped, perhaps caught in a snowslide while descending from the summit. But this accident is not included in the above Table D-32 above because it occurred on a trekking peak.

The chart pattern for deaths by falling in descent from a successful summit bid are very similar to the above chart pattern for descents for all summit bids.

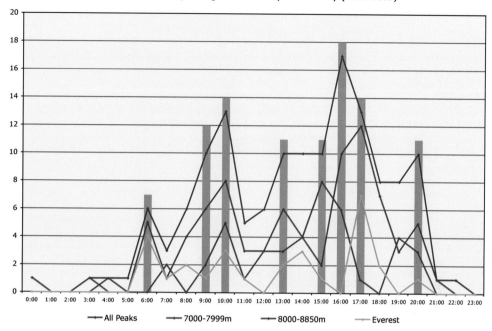

**Chart D-32a: Member deaths by falling for all falls
by time of day from 1950-2009**

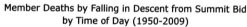

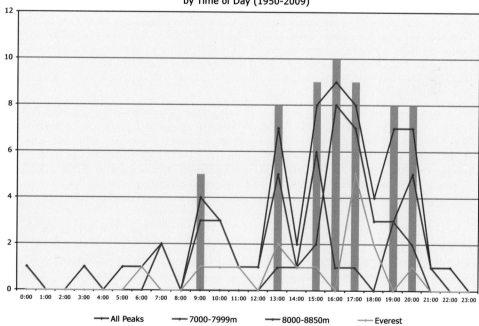

**Chart D-32b: Member deaths by falling in descent from summit bid
by time of day from 1950-2009
(the gray vertical bands in the above charts indicate the most dangerous times)**

Fatal Determination on Kangchenjunga and Dhaulagiri

From *The Seasonal Stories* of Elizabeth Hawley – Spring 1992

The deaths of Mrs. Wanda Rutkiewicz on the north face of Kangchenjunga and of the two Romanians, Mrs. Taina Coliban and Mrs. Sandita Isaila, who climbed together on the normal northeast-ridge route up Dhaulagiri I, were strikingly similar in several ways. All three women from eastern Europe were fiercely determined to reach their summits. But they were over 40 years old, which is approaching old age for Himalayan climbers: Rutkiewicz was 49, Coliban 48 and Isaila 42. Perhaps because of their ages, they were extremely slow climbers. Despite this handicap, they had very few other climbers on their teams and in the end were attempting to reach their towering summits without companions, without artificial oxygen and with a minimum of climbing gear. Alone high on their two mountains with no means of communication, they simply failed to return to those who were waiting for them far below, and their fates are unknown.

Rutkiewicz had eight 8000m summits already to her credit: she was the only woman ever to have conquered more than four of the world's 8000ers; her first was Everest in 1978, when she became the first European woman and the third woman of any nation to conquer it. In recent years she had conceived the ambitious plan to bag all 14 of these giant mountains. Last autumn she hoped to finish them all this year; this spring she hoped to do the job by next spring. She even wanted to attempt a second 8000m peak also this spring, and her name was actually on the membership list of the Romanians' Dhaulagiri I team. This summer she was to be a member of an expedition to Broad Peak in the Karakoram.

Rutkiewicz was last seen alive shortly after 8:00 p.m. on 12 May. She and Carlos Carsolio, the Mexican leader of her Kangchenjunga team, had left their fourth high camp, camp 4 in an ice cave at 7900m on the north face, at 3:30 that morning in good weather. According to Carsolio, she was climbing even more slowly than usual, and he soon went far ahead of her despite the fact that he was having to break trail in deep snow while she could follow in his footsteps. "She was climbing extremely slowly," Carsolio reported later. "Maybe it was because of her age, maybe because of her leg," which she had injured while climbing another 8000er a decade or more ago and which had given her trouble when she conquered Annapurna I last autumn. She had said just before going to Kangchenjunga, "I will not be very quick. I don't want to take risks. I have a lot of respect for Kangchenjunga," which she had attempted before from the southwest side.

Carsolio reached the top alone at 5:00 p.m., the first Latin American ever to gain Kangchenjunga's summit, and during his descent to camp 4, he met Rutkiewicz three hours later at 8250 or 8300m. She was inside a wind hole, a kind of cave carved out of the snow by the wind, where she had stopped to bivouac an hour and a half earlier. "It was good protection for her," said Carsolio. "It was a very cold night but clear and not windy." She told him she was cold, that her old down suit was not warm enough, and she had her bivouac sack around her. She had no sleeping bag, stove, fuel or food, and she had taken from camp 4 that morning only a liter of water. (As Carsolio later pointed out, "without enough to drink, you cannot survive. Also she was very tired.") She did have a headlamp and extra batteries, 20 meters of rope, extra gloves and goggles and perhaps some sweets.

She planned to go for the summit next morning, she told Carsolio, and "she showed in her eyes her determination to reach the summit," he said. "I think she felt this was her last chance to climb Kangchenjunga." He told her he was going to camp 4 for the night and would then descend to camp 2 at 6890m and wait for her there; there was no food or fuel left in camp 4. They were together for perhaps ten minutes, and she was clear mentally.

Then Carsolio went on down, never to see or hear from her again. A member at a lower camp watched the mountain on the 13th, the day she should have gone for the summit, and saw no movement by her. But she could have left her bivouac during the dark early morning hours and would have been out of sight when she reached an altitude of 8400m.

Carsolio left camp 4 at noon on the 13th and spent that night and two more nights at camp 2 waiting for Rutkiewicz. On the 14th the weather turned bad with high winds driving heavy snow. When she had failed to appear at camp 2 by the morning of the 16th, he left for base camp, leaving behind at camp 2 a tent, sleeping bag, walkie-talkie radio (one of only two they had with them, the other was at base), food, gas and a thermos of water. At base camp he and two teammates, who had been unwell and unable to go for the summit, had the other walkie-talkie open all the time, but no sound came from it. The three remaining members finally left base camp in very bad weather on 21 May with no idea as to what had happened to Rutkiewicz.

"It was very difficult for us to leave the mountain," Carsolio said in Kathmandu, "but I am sure that she could have survived because of the bad weather and because she was extremely tired and without drink." These factors he felt counteracted the fact that "she was very good at surviving at high altitudes," had endured the fatal drama on K2 in 1986, and that on Kangchenjunga she had had no problems with altitude sickness, nor had she succumbed to frostbite in April when two Mexican teammates whom she and Carsolio were with did get seriously frostbitten and had to go home for medical treatment.

"I have no idea what happened to her," Carsolio said. "Maybe she reached the summit and then fell. Maybe she died during the night of the 12th and never made it to the summit. Maybe she went to the summit and tried to descend the other side" which she had been on a year ago. And perhaps she simply collapsed somewhere high on this vast mountain, alone, without shelter and without the strength to go one step farther.

"It is a very sad loss for all of us and for the mountaineering world," said Carsolio. "She was a safe climber, but she was extremely slow. But on Kangchenjunga, the wind changes and the snow comes and you have to be fast." She told Carsolio that she was climbing three times more slowly than she had climbed on Everest. And on Everest she had been only 35 years old and using bottled oxygen, whereas now she was 49 and had not been climbing with artificial oxygen for several years. She now remarked to Carsolio that she must finish all the 8000ers quickly before she became even slower.

Was Rutkiewicz's disappearance a tragic case of ambition outstripping physical abilities? And was it the same on Dhaulagiri I for Coliban and Isaila, who also had been climbing extremely slowly, according to others who watched them? The Romanians did not have Rutkiewicz's great experience in the Himalaya. Coliban had climbed in Nepal once, seven years ago, at which time she made a brief attempt on Dhaulagiri I, and both Romanian women had successfully scaled a much lower peak, 6995m Khan Tengri in the Tien Shan range of the Kirgiz-Chinese border area, in 1990. Perhaps they now made some fatal error of judgement during their climb. Or, since their equipment was not the best, according to their Sherpa, he thinks perhaps their inadequate tent pegs could not hold their small tent securely against fierce winds while they were inside it, and it and they were blown off the ridge and down the mountainside.

They had not intended to climb alone, had hoped to add themselves to someone else's expedition to an 8000m mountain (like Rutkiewicz had done) but they had been unable to find a team they could join and so took a permit of their own for Dhaulagiri I, put the names of Rutkiewicz and the young Polish man with her on Kangchenjunga on their membership list and added a Chilean, who started out with them but was able to climb only a short distance above base camp before he became ill, gave up the effort and left their base some days before they went missing.

Coliban and Isaila were last seen at about midday on 11 May. Their Sherpa, Kaji, who had been helping them carry up supplies at the start of their climb, had been asked to stay at base camp while they went for the summit as quickly as possible, and he watched from there as well as he could without binoculars. Every day during this period the mornings were clear while the afternoons brought some clouds and light snowfall. On the 11th he saw them at about 6500m climbing up a snow ridge. Above them at 7000m was their next expected camping site, which was exposed to the wind. The site was visible from base camp, but Kaji never saw their tent there, so he does not know whether they reached it that day or any other day. He scanned the ridge day after day but never again saw any sign of them, and they had no radio communication. Then came a change in the weather with a big snowstorm on the 23rd. He finally struck base camp on 29 May, taking their personal belongings with him back to Kathmandu but leaving some food and fuel just in case they miraculously got down to base.

Deaths by Physiological Causes

Physiological factors (AMS, exhaustion, and exposure-frostbite) are the third leading cause of death for members (over 16% as shown in table D-16). 80 of those 95 deaths have occurred over 6000m (most of the others have occurred at base camp or lower shortly after expedition arrival). Of the 80 deaths above 6000m, more than half have occurred on Everest at high altitudes as shown in Chart D-33.

Closer examination of the Everest deaths in Charts D-34a-b shows that 13 deaths have occurred between the First and Second Steps (8450-8680m) on the NE ridge. These 13 deaths represent about 23% of all the deaths above 6000m and make this portion of the N Col-NE Ridge route on Everest extremely dangerous.

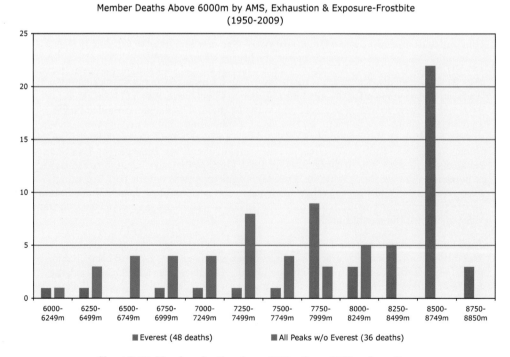

Chart D-33: Member deaths above 6000m from AMS, exhaustion, and exposure-frostbite from 1950-2009

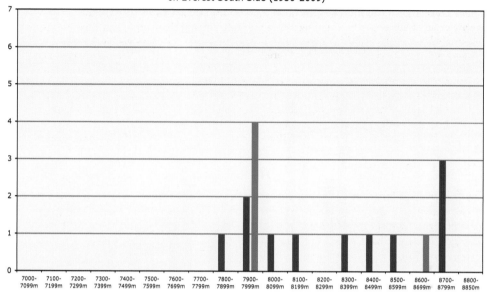

Chart D-34a: Member deaths above 7000m from AMS, exhaustion, and exposure-frostbite on the south side of Everest from 1950-2009

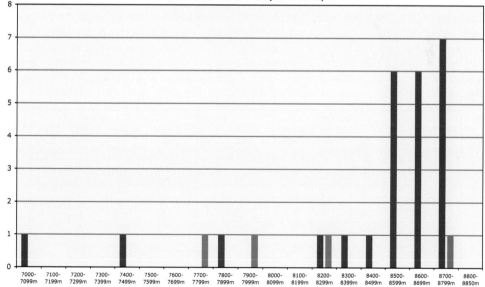

Chart D-34b: Member deaths above 7000m from AMS, exhaustion, and exposure-frostbite on the north side of Everest from 1950-2009

Deaths by Expedition Years

Chart D-35 shows the member and hired personnel death rates by expedition in 5-year steps,

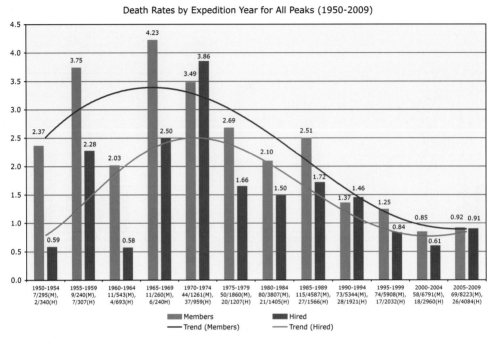

Chart D-35: Member and hired death rates by expedition year for all peaks from 1950-2009

The results from the early years from 1950 to 1970 are more erratic due to the lower numbers of expeditions especially in the late 1960s when Himalayan climbing was suspended in Nepal and before the Chinese side of the border was opened to foreign climbers in 1980. From the 1970s onward, the data in Chart D-35 show more consistent results. The trend lines show a steady decrease in fatalities and death rates starting about 1975 for both members and hired until 2005. The 2005 Kang Guru avalanche

Exp Years	All Peaks			Everest			8000ers		
	Above BC	Death Cnt	Death Rate	Above BC	Death Cnt	Death Rate	Above BC	Death Cnt	Death Rate
1950-1954	295	7	2.37	38	0	0.00	128	1	0.78
1955-1959	240	9	3.75	9	0	0.00	110	4	3.64
1960-1964	543	11	2.03	103	3	2.91	132	5	3.79
1965-1969	260	11	4.23	57	1	1.75	86	6	6.98
1970-1974	1261	44	3.49	270	4	1.48	557	23	4.13
1975-1979	1860	50	2.69	292	6	2.06	836	27	3.23
1980-1984	3807	80	2.10	648	17	2.62	1841	50	2.72
1985-1989	4587	115	2.51	1143	23	2.01	2750	63	2.29
1990-1994	5344	73	1.37	1410	16	1.14	3342	53	1.59
1995-1999	5908	74	1.25	1219	27	2.22	3803	63	1.66
2000-2004	6791	58	0.85	1661	19	1.14	4130	46	1.11
2005-2009	8230	76	0.92	2281	23	1.01	5396	50	0.93
Totals	**39126**	**608**	**1.55**	**9131**	**139**	**1.52**	**23111**	**391**	**1.69**

Table D-36: Member deaths by expedition year for all peaks, Everest, and the 8000ers from 1950-2009

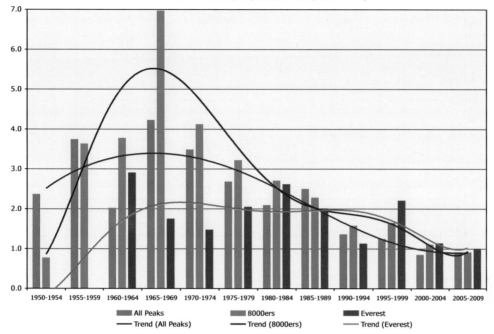

Chart D-36: Member death rates by expedition year from 1950-2009

that killed 7 members and 11 hired personnel, and three separate avalanches on Ama Dablam, Ganesh V, and Pumori in 2006 that killed 14 (7 members and 7 hired) have now reversed the long-term downward trend.

As shown in Table and Chart D-36, the decline of member death rates holds true across the board for all peaks (**blue**), all 8000ers (**green**), and Everest (**red**).

Deaths by Age Groups

Table and Chart D-37 show death counts and rates by age groups in 5-year intervals for members.

The table is divided into three sections: all peaks from 1950 to 2009, all peaks from 1950 to 2009 without the Ama Dablam, Cho Oyu, and Everest commercial routes from 1990 to 2009, and finally the Ama Dablam, Cho Oyu, and Everest commercial routes during the 1990-2009 period.

Chart D-37 shows a striking difference between commercial and non-commercial climbing.

The **blue** trend line for all peaks without the Ama Dablam, Cho Oyu, and Everest commercial routes shows a steady decline in the death rates by age until age 60, indicating that Himalayan climbing becomes relatively safer as one become older (and presumably more skilled, experienced, and perhaps more conservative by sticking to easier peaks or routes, or more willing to turn back without summiting).

Age Groups	All Peaks 1950-2009			All Peaks 1950-2009 without Ama Dablam-Cho Oyu-Everest commercial routes 1990-2009			Ama Dablam-Cho Oyu-Everest commercial routes 1990-2009		
	Above BC	Death Cnt	Death Rate	Above BC	Death Cnt	Death Rate	Above BC	Death Cnt	Death Rate
Unknown	1484	36	2.43	134	0	0.00	1350	36	2.67
10-14	6	0	0.00	4	0	0.00	2	0	0.00
15-19	167	3	1.80	70	0	0.00	97	3	3.09
20-24	2607	56	2.15	614	3	0.49	1993	53	2.66
25-29	7234	125	1.73	1799	13	0.72	5435	112	2.06
30-34	8123	133	1.64	2692	13	0.48	5431	120	2.21
35-39	6935	113	1.63	2773	27	0.97	4162	86	2.07
40-44	5206	57	1.10	2332	16	0.69	2874	41	1.43
45-49	3379	43	1.27	1653	15	0.91	1726	28	1.62
50-54	2034	22	1.08	1066	10	0.94	968	12	1.24
55-59	1113	8	0.72	570	3	0.53	543	5	0.92
60-64	558	9	1.61	295	5	1.70	263	4	1.52
65-69	199	2	1.01	95	2	2.11	104	0	0.00
70-74	69	1	1.45	38	1	2.63	31	0	0.00
75-79	12	0	0.00	6	0	0.00	6	0	0.00

Table D-37: Member deaths by age groups from 1950-2009

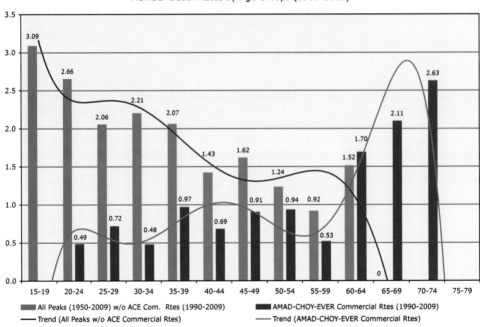

Chart D-37: Member death rates by age groups from 1950-2009 for all peaks
w/o Ama Dablam, Cho Oyu, and Everest commercial routes from 1990-2009 (in blue)
and for Ama Dablam, Cho Oyu, and Everest commercial routes from 1990-2009 (in red)

The red trend line for the Ama Dablam, Cho Oyu, and Everest commercial routes shows a reasonably flat death rate up to about age 60, then a sharp increase due to the much higher death rates for the age 60-74 groups. This may be due to a combination of age and lack of climbing skills and experience for some older commercial climbers.

170 Death Analysis

	Ama Dablam			Cho Oyu			Everest		
	Above BC	Death Cnt	Death Rate	Above BC	Death Cnt	Death Rate	Above BC	Death Cnt	Death Rate
60-64	63	1	1.59	117	1	0.86	115	3	2.61
65-69	24	0	0.00	26	0	0.00	45	2	4.44
70-74	3	0	0.00	17	1	5.88	13	0	0.00
Peak Totals for All Ages	3379	10	0.30	5020	26	0.52	5742	72	1.25

Table D-38: Deaths for members of age 60-74 on ACE commercial routes from 1950-2009

The seven deaths in the 60-74 age groups for Cho Oyu and Everest shown in Table D-38 above are nearly statistically significant (p=0.058) even though the sample size of 333 members above base camp is relatively small (this would become significant if the spring 2010 data that includes the 63-year old Japanese Hiroshi Ogasawara death on Everest were factored in, p=~0.03).

Two deaths on Everest occurred in 2004 when 68-year old Nils Antezana died of exhaustion below the South Summit of Everest at 8500m while descending from the summit and 63-year old Shoka Ota died at 8600m while descending from the summit on the north side. The other deaths occurred on the north side of Everest in 1993 when 66-year old Karl Henize (a former NASA astronaut) died of pulmonary edema during the night at 6000m after being carried down from advanced base camp at 6400m, in 2007 when 63-year old Shinichi Ishii died from AMS on descent from the summit, and on the south side of Everest in 2005 when 63-year old Sean Egan collapsed at Dugla while descending for treatment after suffering cardiac problems when returning to base camp from Camp 1 two days earlier.

On Cho Oyu, 63-year old Fritz Zintl died at base camp from illness (an infection contracted in Tibet), and on Ama Dablam, 60-year old Jean Corniglion died from AMS while being evacuated from base camp after spending one night at Camp 1 at 5800m.

The youngest member death was 18-year-old Brahim Saidi who perished in an avalanche at 6600m on Pumori in 1991 on a commercial expedition.

Because the ages of many hired personnel are not accurately known, their death rates by age groups cannot be accurately calculated. No recorded deaths of hired personnel have occurred above base camp under the age of 20; the oldest hired death recorded was Tenzing Phinzo Sherpa (age 53), who was killed in an icefall collapse in the Khumbu Icefall in 2006.

Deaths by Gender

As shown in Table and Chart D-39, men have a significantly higher death rate than women for all peaks and for the 7000ers. For the other categories, the differences in the death rates are statistically insignificant.

Chart D-40 shows female death rates for the most popular peaks climbed by women, those peaks with 40 or more women above base camp. Four of these peaks (Kangchenjunga, Dhaulagiri I, Annapurna I, and Manaslu) have female death rates much higher than the mean male death rate of 1.61, but none of these is statistically significant when comparing the female death rates to the corresponding male death rates for each of these peaks.

	Total Above BC	Men Above BC	Women Above BC	Total Deaths	Male Deaths	Female Deaths	Total Death Rate	Male Death Rate	Female Death Rate
All Peaks	39126	35668	3458	608	575	33	1.55	1.61	0.95
All 8000ers	23111	21175	1936	391	363	28	1.69	1.71	1.45
All 7000ers	8676	7957	719	171	169	2	1.97	2.12	0.28
All 6000ers	7339	6536	803	46	43	3	0.63	0.66	0.37
Ama Dablam	3963	3508	455	17	15	2	0.43	0.43	0.44
Cho Oyu	5638	5026	612	36	33	3	0.64	0.66	0.49
Everest	9131	8357	774	139	132	7	1.52	1.58	0.90

Table D-39: Member deaths by gender from 1950-2009

Statistical significances of death rates for men (M) and women (W):

All peaks: M (1.61), W (0.95), *p*=.004   Ama Dablam: M (0.43), W (0.44), *p*=.730
8000ers: M (1.71), W (1.45), *p*=.434   Cho Oyu: M (0.66), W (0.49), *p*=.827
7000ers: M (2.12), W (0.28), *p*=.001   Everest: M (1.58), W (0.90), *p*=.189
6000ers: M (0.66), W 0.37), *p*=.467

p-values for statistically significant differences ($p <= .05$) are shown in red above and their columns are outlined in black in Chart D-39. All others are statistically insignificant.

Cause of Death	Women		Men	
	Cnt	Pct	Cnt	Pct
AMS	0	0.0	46	8.0
Exhaustion	2	6.1	16	2.8
Exposure/Frostbite	2	6.1	33	5.7
Fall	14	42.4	223	38.8
Crevasse	1	3.0	14	2.4
Icefall Collapse	0	0.0	2	0.3
Avalanche	9	27.3	166	28.9
Falling Rock/Ice	1	3.0	13	2.3
Disappearance	4	12.1	22	3.8
Illness (non-AMS)	0	0.0	26	4.5
Other	0	0.0	12	2.1
Unknown	0	0.0	2	0.3
Totals	**33**	**100.0**	**575**	**100.0**
AMS-related	3	9.1	64	11.1
Weather/Storm-related	1	3.0	43	7.5

Table D-41: Causes of death for all peaks
from 1950-2009

Death Classification	Women		Men	
	Cnt	Pct	Cnt	Pct
Death enroute BC	0	0.0	19	3.3
Death at BC	1	3.0	20	3.5
Route preparation	15	45.5	255	44.3
Ascending in Smt Bid	5	15.2	67	11.7
Descending from Smt Bid	11	33.3	183	31.8
Expedition evacuation	1	3.0	31	5.4
Other/Unknown	0	0.0	0	0.0
Totals	**33**	**100.0**	**575**	**100.0**

Table D-42: Death classification for all peaks
from 1950-2009

The difference in death rates between men and women for falling is statistically insignificant (*p*=.82); the difference in death rates between men and women for all deaths on summit days is also insignificant (*p*=.70).

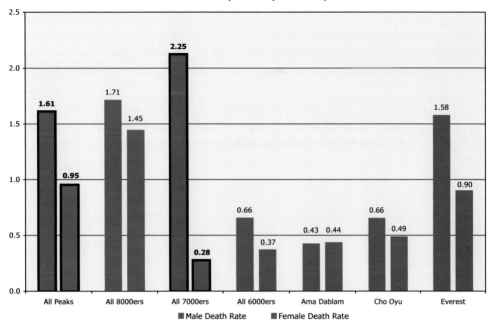

Death Rates by Gender (1950-2009)

Chart D-39: Member death rates by gender from 1950-2009
(the columns outlined in black are statistically significant)

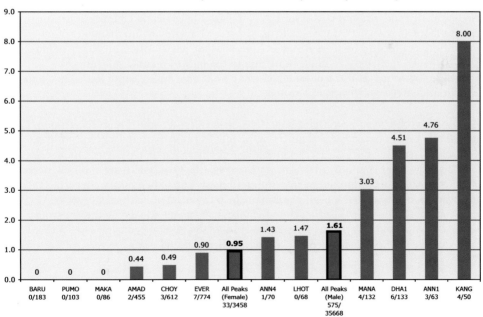

Female Death Rates for Popular Peaks Climbed by Women (1950-2009)

Chart D-40: Female death rates for peaks with 40+ women above base camp from 1950-2009
(the death rate is above the column bar; the death and above BC counts are below)
(the columns outlined in black are statistically significant)

The deaths of some very accomplished women climbers are in this group of peaks: Wanda Rutkiewicz on Kangchenjunga in 1992, and Chantal Mauduit and Ginette Harrison on Dhaulagiri I in 1998 and 1999.

Tables D-41 and D-42 compare the causes of death and death classification rates for women to the rates for men.

The data in the two tables show that for women a slightly higher percentage of deaths occur by falling or disappearance (probable falls) and on summit days, whereas for men a slightly higher percentage occur due to AMS or non-AMS illnesses or enroute to or from base camp or during expedition evacuation. However, these differences are statistically insignificant.

Only two of the women who died were commercial clients: Karine Van Dooren by falling at 6000m on Ama Dablam during route preparation, and Yasuko Namba by exposure at the South Col on Everest during descent from the summit in the tragic storm of May 1996.

Deaths by Citizenship

Table D-43 shows *member* deaths by citizenship for all peaks and Everest for those nationalities that had a substantial number of members above base camp (60 or more for all peaks and 20 or more for Everest). Citizens from countries that had fewer than the 60 or 20 cutoff points are grouped into the "**All Others**" category. Note that no deaths have occurred on Everest for countries that had fewer than 20 members.

The citizens of Nepal and China are split into two groups: Sherpas/non-Sherpas and Tibetans/non-Tibetans, respectively, in order to differentiate the higher-altitude from the lower-altitude residents. Also for the Nepalese Sherpas and Chinese Tibetans, the numbers above base camp include only those who were actual members of an expedition, not those who were hired as high-altitude assistants. The non-Tibetan Chinese death rates may be misleading due to the lack of reliable information regarding the actual number of members that went above base camp for large Chinese expeditions on the north side of Everest.

Many eastern European countries (e.g., Czechoslovakia, Poland, Bulgaria, Hungary) have much higher death rates than the mean death rates, perhaps a result of more climbers attempting difficult routes and fewer climbers participating as commercial clients on the safer commercial routes on Everest, Cho Oyu, and Ama Dablam, or in some cases the use of minimal or inferior equipment due to budgetary concerns (there has been speculation that a used climbing rope purchased in Kathmandu failed to arrest Jerzy Kukuczka's fall from the south face of Lhotse). Most expeditions from eastern Europe and Russia have attempted either the 8000m peaks or more difficult routes on the 7000m peaks such as Jannu and Himalchuli; fewer have ventured to the 6000m peaks.

All Peaks				Everest			
Citizenship	Above BC	Death Cnt	Death Rate	Citizenship	Above BC	Death Cnt	Death Rate
Slovakia	123	7	5.69	Czechoslovakia	60	5	8.33
Romania	61	3	4.92	Poland	96	7	7.29
Hungary	87	4	4.60	Bulgaria	42	3	7.14
Greece	120	5	4.17	Slovenia	22	1	4.55
Bulgaria	184	7	3.80	Taiwan	48	2	4.17
Czechoslovakia	312	11	3.53	Germany	133	5	3.76
Slovenia	348	11	3.16	Czech Republic	62	2	3.23
Argentina	131	4	3.05	India	447	14	3.13
Poland	955	28	2.93	Australia	163	5	3.07
Taiwan	73	2	2.74	Ukraine	34	1	2.94
Kazakhstan	115	3	2.61	China (non-Tibetan)	250	7	2.80
China (non-Tibetan)	368	9	2.45	Denmark	36	1	2.78
Russia	728	16	2.20	Russia	230	6	2.61
Denmark	137	3	2.19	Yugoslavia	82	2	2.44
Japan	4806	105	2.19	Hungary	42	1	2.38
India	1085	23	2.12	Japan	717	16	2.23
Australia	759	16	2.11	W Germany	45	1	2.22
USSR	239	5	2.09	Brazil	47	1	2.13
W Germany	680	13	1.91	New Zealand	159	3	1.89
Yugoslavia	432	8	1.85	Chile	54	1	1.85
S Korea	2217	40	1.80	Nepal (non-Sherpa)	129	2	1.55
Belgium	300	5	1.67	S Korea	600	9	1.50
Ukraine	195	3	1.54	Belgium	67	1	1.49
Austria	1390	21	1.51	Austria	141	2	1.42
France	3208	48	1.50	UK	853	12	1.41
Iran	143	2	1.40	France	451	6	1.33
Colombia	72	1	1.39	Canada	234	3	1.28
Czech Republic	373	5	1.34	Sweden	81	1	1.24
Spain	2541	34	1.34	Italy	326	3	0.92
Netherlands	463	6	1.30	Switzerland	221	2	0.91
Sweden	234	3	1.28	Spain	531	4	0.75
Mexico	162	2	1.24	Nepal (Sherpa)	137	1	0.73
Switzerland	1620	20	1.24	USA	1412	9	0.64
New Zealand	493	6	1.22	Argentina	29	0	0.00
Brazil	87	1	1.15	China (Tibetan)	211	0	0.00
Finland	87	1	1.15	Colombia	33	0	0.00
UK	3064	34	1.11	Croatia	22	0	0.00
Italy	2008	22	1.10	Finland	27	0	0.00
Germany	1564	17	1.09	Greece	25	0	0.00
Chile	104	1	0.96	Indonesia	24	0	0.00
USA	4037	36	0.89	Iran	37	0	0.00
Canada	690	6	0.87	Ireland	51	0	0.00
Nepal (Sherpa)	235	2	0.85	Kazakhstan	35	0	0.00
Nepal (non-Sherpa)	368	3	0.82	Malaysia	29	0	0.00
All others	775	6	0.77	Mexico	61	0	0.00
China (Tibetan)	323	0	0.00	Netherlands	85	0	0.00
Croatia	80	0	0.00	Norway	84	0	0.00
Ireland	120	0	0.00	S Africa	56	0	0.00
Norway	287	0	0.00	Singapore	24	0	0.00
S Africa	83	0	0.00	USSR	62	0	0.00
Singapore	60	0	0.00	**All others**	284	0	0.00
Mean Death Rate			1.58	**Mean Death Rate**			1.64

Table D-43: Member deaths by citizenship from 1950-2009
(minimum 60 Above BC for all peaks, minimum 20 Above BC for Everest)
(blue rows are above the mean death rate, black rows are below the mean death rate)

Deaths by Team Composition

In this section, we look at death rates by expedition team size in the same manner as we did for ascent rates, that is, how do the number of members and hired personnel that went above base camp per expedition and the inter-relationship between the two affect death rates.

Charts D-44a-b show member death rates by the number of members above base camp and the ratio of the number of hired personnel to the number of members above base camp per expedition for all peaks without Everest and for Everest from 1950 to 2009.

Charts D-45a-b compare both member ascent and death rates based on team composition for all peaks excluding Everest. Charts D-46a-b compare both member ascent and death rates based on team composition for Everest.

We saw in the previous chapter that for all peaks including Everest the optimal team size for success was 1-3 members with abundant hired personnel support (a ratio of 1 or more hired per member). But when considering optimal safety (lowest death rates), the picture changes somewhat.

For all peaks excluding Everest, the optimal team size for safety does not vary much until the team sizes become very large (over 24 members) when the results become erratic (Charts D-44a and D-45a). But for Everest, death rates are higher for smaller teams with single climbers faring the worst, then dropping off for mid-sized teams of

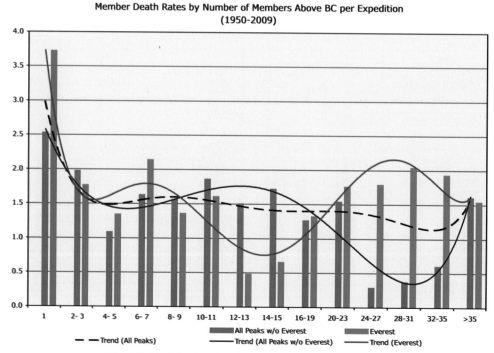

Chart D-44a: Member death rates by number of members
above base camp per expedition from 1950-2009

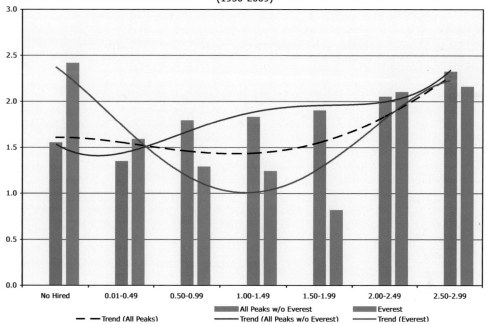

Chart D-44b: Member death rates by the ratio of the number of hired to
number of members above base camp per expedition from 1950-2009

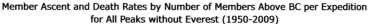

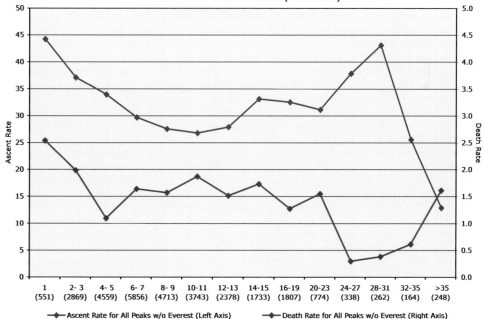

Chart D-45a: Member ascent and death rates by the number of members
above base camp per expedition for all peaks without Everest from 1950-2009
(team counts are given below the team size scale in this and the following charts)

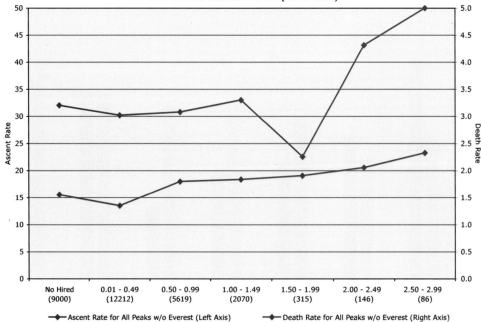

Chart D-45b: Member ascent and death rates by the ratio of hired to members above base camp per expedition for all peaks without Everest from 1950-2009

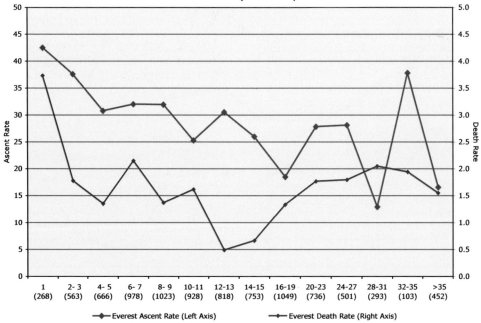

Chart D-46a: Member ascent and death rates by the number of members above base camp per expedition for Everest from 1950-2009

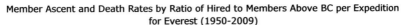

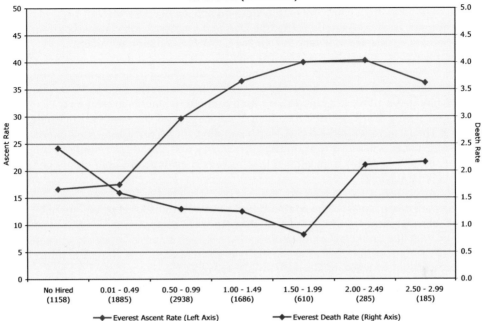

Chart D-46b: Member ascent and death rates by the ratio of hired to members above base camp per expedition for Everest from 1950-2009

12-15 members, before accelerating again for very large teams exceeding 20 members (Charts D-44a and D-46a).

The absolute numbers of hired personnel do not seem to matter as much as the ratio of hired personnel to members. For all peaks excluding Everest, the death rate trends slightly higher as the ratio increases indicating that small fast teams are the safest (Charts D-44b and D-45b). For Everest, the optimal ratio of hired to members for safety is from 1.5 to 1.9 which coincides nicely with the optimal ratio for success being 1.5 or greater (Charts D-44b and D-46b).

Many of the more successful commercial operators for Everest and Cho Oyu usually plan for teams sizes in the 12-15 member range with plenty of Sherpa and Tibetan high-altitude support both for economic and safety reasons.

Death Rates Above and Below High Camp

Chart D-47 shows the death rates for members above high camp and at or below high camp for all peaks from 1990 to 2009. All of the member death rates above high camp (except for the 7000ers and the Everest south commercial route) are statistically significantly either higher or lower (more dangerous or safer) than the mean of 1.23 for all peaks; the death rates for the other two are too close to the mean rate or the death counts are too low to be significant. Member death rates at or below high camp are only significantly higher (more dangerous) for the 8000ers without the Cho Oyu and Everest commercial routes; death rates at or below high camp are only significantly lower (safer) for the Cho Oyu commercial route.

Chart D-48 shows the death rates for hired above and at or below high camp. Hired death counts above high camp are very low and thus not significant. Hired death counts at or below high camp are significant only for the 6000ers without the Ama Dablam commercial route and for the Cho Oyu and Everest north commercial routes, but the death counts are still very low for the latter two commercial routes.

Charts D-49a-b show the death rates for members above and at or below high camp for the standard and non-standard routes on 8000m peaks from 1990 to 2009. The standard route on Kangchenjunga above high camp for members is extremely dangerous with a death rate of 5.51 (about 1 out of every 20 climbers fails to safely return). The Dhaulagiri and Everest North standard routes are also very dangerous above high camp, whereas the Manaslu, Annapurna, and Dhaulagiri standard routes are very dangerous below high camp due to increased avalanching that occurs on the peaks of central Nepal.

The member death rates on the non-standard routes on the 8000m peaks are not statistically significant above or below high camp when compared to the mean rates of 3.41 and 1.29 due to the low number of deaths, but they do provide anecdotal evidence of where the danger zones may be, especially high on Makalu and Kangchenjunga or in the lower avalanche zones of Manaslu and Dhaulagiri.

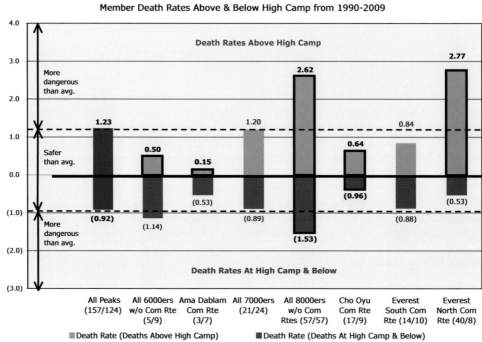

Chart D-47: Member death rates above and below high camp from 1990-2009
(the death counts above and at or below high camp are given below the peak scale
in the above and following charts)

The columns outlined in black in the above and following charts represent seasons that statistically have significantly higher or lower death rates than the average for all peaks.

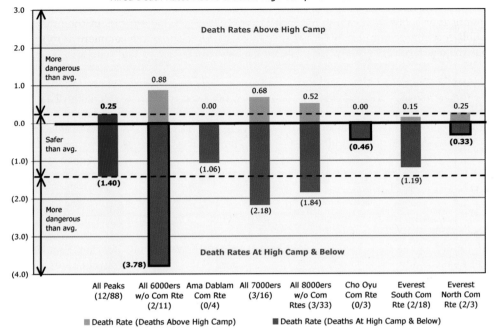

Chart D-48: Hired death rates above and below high camp from 1990-2009

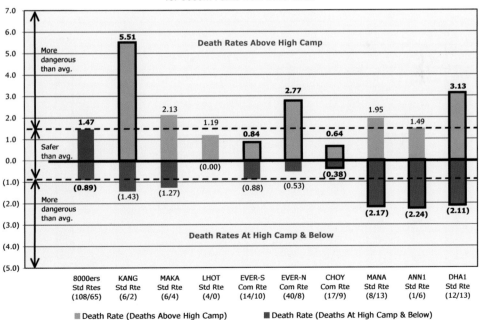

Chart D-49a: Member death rates above and below high camp
on standard routes for 8000m peaks from 1990-2009
(see Chart D-6b for the listing of the 8000m standard routes)

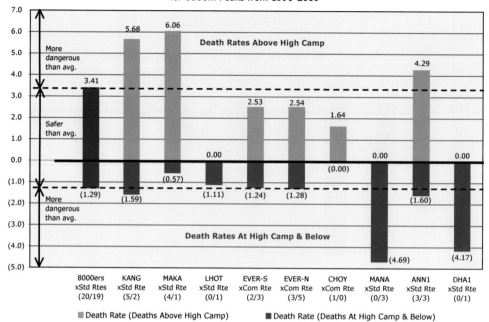

**Chart D-49b: Member death rates above and below high camp
on non-standard routes for 8000m peaks from 1990-2009**

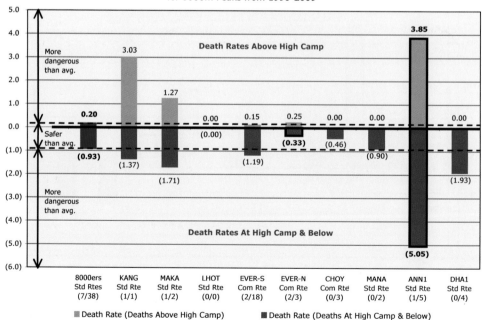

**Chart D-50a: Hired death rates above and below high camp
on standard routes for 8000m peaks from 1990-2009**

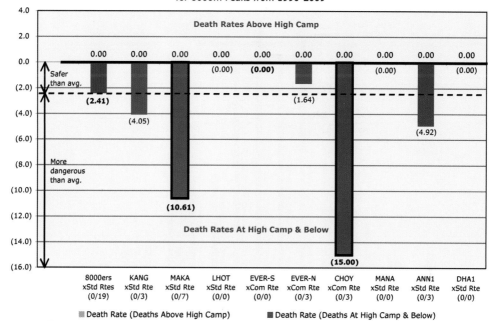

Chart D-50b: Hired death rates above and below high camp
on non-standard routes for 8000m peaks from 1990-2009

Charts D-50a-b show the death rates for hired above and at or below high camp for the standard and non-standard routes on the 8000m peaks from 1990 to 2009. The hired death rates on the standard routes are only significantly higher for Annapurna both above and below high camps. For the non-standard routes, they are only significantly higher below high camp for Makalu and Cho Oyu, but with low death counts. No hired deaths have occurred above high camp on the non-standard routes.

Probability of Death on Everest on Summit Day

Charts D-51a-b show the times of summiting Everest for members and hired personnel survivors and non-survivors on the Everest commercial routes from 1950 to 2009.

For the survivors, the majority summited between 6 a.m. and 1 p.m., whereas for the non-survivors, summit times were on average much later in the afternoon indicating that a late summit time increases the likelihood of trouble on the descent. Both sides of Everest show the same characteristics. The summit times for both sides are based on Nepal Standard Time (converted from Chinese Standard Time when necessary).

Chart D-52 combines the data from the above two charts to give a probability of death based on the time of summiting Everest. For summit times after 3 p.m., the probability of death rises from 10% up to 50% for summit times after 7 p.m. This chart dramatically reinforces the wisdom of commercial leaders setting 2 p.m. or earlier turnaround times for their clients. Some of the deaths during the 1996 Everest disaster might have been avoided if the originally planned 2 p.m. turnaround time had been observed.

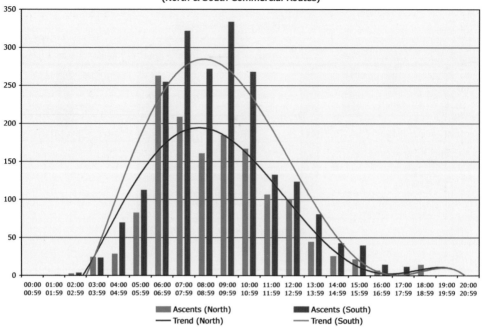

Chart D-51a: Summit times on Everest for members and hired survivors from 1950-2009 (times are given in Nepal Standard Time for this and subsequent charts)

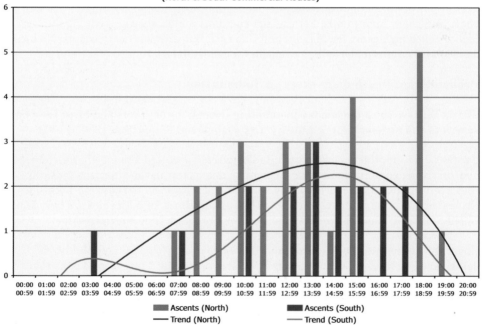

Chart D-51b: Summit times on Everest for members and hired non-survivors from 1950-2009

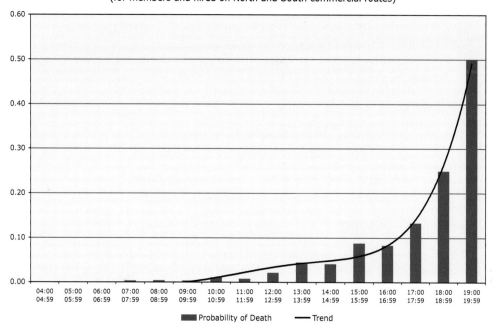

Probability of Death During Descent Based on Times of Summiting Everest (1950-2009)
(for members and hired on North and South commercial routes)

Chart D-52: Probability of death during descent based on Everest summit times for members and hired from 1950-2009

Major Accidents

Table D-53 lists the major accidents where five or more persons were killed in one or more related accidents:

Peak	Season	Nation	Leaders	Mbrs	Hired	Total
Kang Guru	Autumn 2005	France	Daniel Stolzenberg	7	11	18
Manaslu	Spring 1972	S Korea	Kim Jung-Sup	5	10	15
Pisang	Autumn 1994	Germany	Stefan Hasenkopf	10	1	11
Gangapurna	Autumn 1971	Japan	Kiyoshi Shimizu	3	5	8
Everest	Spring 1996		Multiple teams	8	0	8
Everest	Spring 1922	UK	Charles G. Bruce	0	7	7
Dhaulagiri I	Spring 1969	USA	Boyd Nixon Everett Jr.	5	2	7
Dhaulagiri IV	Autumn 1969	Austria	Richard Hoyer	5	1	6
Everest	Spring 1970	Japan	Yuichiro Miura	0	6	6
Everest	Autumn 1974	France	Gerard Devouassoux	1	5	6
Annapurna I	Autumn 1991	S Korea	Ko Yong-Chul	2	4	6
Makalu	Spring 2002	Spain	Juanito Oiarzabal	0	6	6
Ama Dablam	Autumn 2006	Sweden, UK	Two teams	3	3	6
Annapurna I	Spring 1973	Japan	Shigeki Tsukamoto	4	1	5
Dhaulagiri I	Spring 1975	Japan	Takashi Amemiya	2	3	5
Everest	Autumn 1985	India	Prem Chand, Jagit Singh	5	0	5
Everest	Spring 1989	Poland	Eugeniusz Chrobak	5	0	5
Pumori	Autumn 2001	Spain	Aritz Artieda	5	0	5

Table D-53: Major accidents (5 or more killed in one or more related events)

Kang Guru, Autumn 2005

A late afternoon avalanche completely destroyed base camp at 4200m taking the lives of seven French and eleven Nepali staff (mostly Gurungs). Only four porters survived and were able to walk out for assistance. This is now the most deadly mountaineering accident in the Nepal Himalaya. (See the inset box, *Worst Disaster in Nepalese Himalaya Wipes Out French Team,* on pg. 128.)

Manaslu, Spring 1972

A huge early morning avalanche completely destroyed Camp 3 at 6500m taking the lives of four Koreans, one Japanese and ten Sherpas. Only one Korean and two Sherpas survived. This was the most deadly mountaineering accident in the Nepal Himalaya until 2005. (See the inset box, *One of Nepal's Deadliest Avalanches Hits Manaslu,* on pg. 157.)

Pisang Peak, Autumn 1994

Eleven members of a German trekking party fell to their deaths while descending from the summit of Pisang Peak. It is believed that a member of one of the three rope teams slipped dragging the team down through the lines of the other two rope teams and sweeping them all down the mountain to their deaths. This accident is excluded from the death count tables because it occurred on a trekking peak.

Gangapurna, Autumn 1971

Three Japanese and three Sherpas were swept away by an afternoon avalanche that completely destroyed their Camp 2 at 5900m. The two Sherpas sent down from Camp 3 to investigate the disappearance of the six climbers the next morning also disappeared presumably swept away by another avalanche. (See the inset box, *Double Trouble on Gangapurna,* on pg. 154.)

Everest, Spring 1996

A total of eight climbers perished as a result of a massive storm that hit the top of Everest on the afternoon of May 10, 1996. Five climbers including expedition leaders Rob Hall and Scott Fischer died on the south side while three Indians died on the north side. All died of exposure and frostbite, except for Andy Harris who was presumed to have fallen off the southeast ridge.

Everest, Spring 1922

A party of three climbers (including George Mallory) and fourteen Sherpas were swept away by an avalanche while approaching the North Col. Nine of the Sherpas slid over an ice cliff into a crevasse. Only two could be saved; the other seven Sherpas were buried by tons of snow and ice. All three members survived.

Dhaulagiri I, Spring 1969

A massive ice avalanche hit a party of six Americans and two Sherpas at noon as they were preparing to place poles to bridge a crevasse at 5335m. Only one climber Lou Reichardt survived, but he was unable to dig out the remainder of the group.

Dhaulagiri IV, Autumn 1969

A team of five Austrians and one Sherpa disappeared above 6900m on their summit attempt. Continuous bad weather prevented search and rescue attempts.

Everest, Spring 1970

Six Sherpas were killed by an ice serac collapse in the Khumbu Icefall while carrying loads for the Japanese Everest ski expedition.

Everest, Autumn 1974

French leader Gerard Devouassoux and four Sherpas were buried by the concussive blast of a nearby avalanche that dumped dislodged snow on their tents in Camp 2 at 6400m. A fifth Sherpa was simultaneously killed at Camp 1 at 5800m.

Annapurna I, Autumn 1991

Two Koreans and six Sherpas were carried 1000m down the mountain by a slab avalanche at 7500m. Only two Sherpas survived.

Makalu, Spring 2002

Six staff members from a Spanish expedition were lost in a helicopter crash while evacuating base camp. The crash site has not been found to date.

Ama Dablam, Autumn 2006

Two Swedes, one Briton, and three Sherpas were killed while sleeping in their tents when a huge ice serac broke off the "dablam" and obliterated Camp 3 in the middle of the night. This was the first fatality for Sherpas on Ama Dablam. (See the inset box, *2006 Ama Dablam Serac Avalanche,* on pg. 107.)

Annapurna I, Spring 1973

Four Japanese and one Sherpa were killed by a pair of avalanches while descending to Camp 2 from higher camps.

Dhaulagiri I, Spring 1975

An avalanche in the middle of the night buried two Japanese and three Sherpas in their tents at Camp 1 at 4500m.

Everest, Autumn 1985

A mid-October snowstorm killed five Indians after their summit bid. One fell while descending to the South Col and the other four died from exposure at the Col while attempting to wait out the storm.

Everest, Spring 1989

Fives Poles were killed by an avalanche at 6000m on Khumbutse while returning from a successful summit attempt on Everest via the west ridge and the Hornbein Couloir two days earlier.

Pumori, Autumn 2001

Five Spaniards were killed 50m above Camp 1 by a serac avalanche.

In addition to the above incidents, seven other accidents have occurred that have killed four members and/or hired personnel (six avalanches and one group fall).

The Strange Tale of Roger Buick

From the Elizabeth Hawley interviews with Russell Brice and Jim Findley – June 1998

Roger Buick was a 52-year old climber from New Zealand who attempted Everest from the north side in the spring of 1998. He was listed on the permit of Russell Brice, but was climbing entirely independently. He died from exposure on May 26 at 7400m.

The following comments are excerpted from Russell Brice's letter to Buick's solicitor on June 4, 1998.

Buick arrived at BC on 4 May and spent 3 nights there, eating in my camp for some strange reason, rather than his own Asian Trekking camp. He pitched one of his tents here, which stayed here for the entire expedition. When he departed for ABC, he left all of his personal things in my mess tent, again I am not sure why because he was not part of my team. At this stage some Americans advised him not to rush so quickly to ABC.
On the evening of 6th it started to blow at ABC. I had already been to 8300m and had installed all of my camps, so we decided to return to BC for a rest before attempting the summit. We wanted to take advantage of this time that the wind was blowing, as it is not possible to work high up on the mountain in these winds. As I mentioned I passed Roger at approximately 5600m just below the interim camp. I passed a man wearing shorts!!! and behind were 7 yaks with loads of gas for another expedition, and Asian Trekking kit bags, so I assumed that it was Roger.

Upon arrival at BC I found Roger's things in my camp, which I removed and put back into his own camp (which was manned by a Sherpa for the duration of the expedition). I later learned that Roger went to my (manned) interim camp and told the yak man there that he was a friend of mine and that he could stay. He then went to the ABC on the 8th.

On the 15th I went to C1 at the North Col (7000m), a trip that takes my Sherpas and me about 2 hours with full loads. There was a traditional afternoon snow shower, which lasted about 3 hours with a little more wind associated with this than normal, but nothing to really worry about. I did not know that Roger was in fact already at the Col in his tent. However after I had been in my tent for a while I heard Roger talking to some Sherpas (not sure who's but maybe from the Japanese team).

He told them that he thought that this storm was going to last for about 3-4 days and that he was going down to ABC. This was at about 17:00. It takes me about 1 hour to go from C1 to ABC so this was a reasonable thing to do. I have since heard that he took 7 hours, and said that he fell into 4 crevasses, and got lost in the snowstorm. I cannot understand this as there were only 4 crevasses on the entire route and there was fixed rope from the door of Roger's tent to the flat part of the glacier, and along the flat section flags marked the route.

I was working on the mountain again repairing my damaged tents with another trip to 8300m between 16-18th and returning to ABC late on the evening of 18th. Sometime during this time Roger returned to BC, trying to use my interim camp on the way down, but was refused entry by my yak man that looks after this camp for me.

During this time at BC Roger continually went to the American camp, again only a few meters from his and my camp to listen to our radio contacts and weather forecasting. The Americans and I had already agreed to work closely together before we left home. The weather forecasting was relayed by radio from the South (Nepal) side where we were sharing the costs with 4 other expeditions. Roger was imposing on our teams. They were pretty pissed off and so was I and we told him so by radio, hence a letter of apology. I thought that Roger would have known better, especially as he had spoken to Mark Whetu about such matters. Still these are all bygones. Despite this the Americans after hearing his epic descent story, advised him that Everest was not the place to start learning about climbing and that he should abandon his attempt.

I started my summit attempt on 21st leaving ABC for C1 (7000m), C2 (7500m), C3 (7900m), and C4 (8300m) and went to the summit on the 25th returning to C4. Most teams only put 3 camps in C1 (7000m), C2 (7700m) and C3 (8300m). On the morning of 25th I left my top camp to return to ABC. I assume that Roger had gone to C1 on the 25th and that he started for C2 quite late on the 26th.

I stopped at my C2 to make tea for my client. From here there is a clear view of the entire snow slope right down to C1. I spent over 1 hour here looking at a solitary figure moving up the hill. This figure was moving extremely slowly and I figured that this could only be Roger as practically every team had already left ABC. High on the mountain there were still 3 members of the American team who I had passed as they went to the top camp, and two Austrians who were going to the summit on 26th. Apart from that, everyone else was coming down, clearing the camps as they went.

As I mentioned I passed Roger at about 7200m and again I stopped at C1 and spent about 2 hours there making tea and packing. Again I could see Roger moving so slowly. In all that time, 2-1/2 hours in total, I never saw him take more than 5 steps. Besides this there were at least 8-9 other people (many Sherpas) who passed Roger and told him to turn back. We all talked about how crazy he must be not to see that he was never going to get anywhere at the speed he was moving. George, one of his team members, spent more than half an hour trying to tell him to return.

We all went down to ABC that evening. Next morning I was concerned about Roger and looked for him through my telescope and sure enough I could see his body lying on the snow slope still attached to the fixed rope. I was very busy with my own expedition, and as Roger did not move all day long, we assumed that he was dead and that there was nothing that anyone could do to help. Later that day I met with the two Austrians who confirmed that they had passed his body during the day.

The following morning 28th I left ABC early and went up to C1 in 2 hours and then went on up to Roger's body at 7400m in another 1 hour. On the way up I noticed that one of his overboots was on the rock to my right. This was strange as the prevailing wind is from right to left, so anything that he may have dropped would have gone the other way. There was quite a strong wind blowing that day, so much that I needed to wear my down suit with the hood up.

Roger was slumped over his pack, with no gloves on, wearing a lightweight ski suit and Dynafit ski touring boots. None of this clothing was adequate for the conditions one would expect on Everest. He had secured himself onto the fixed ropes by a complicated array of ascender and carabiners (not really required); his thermos was secured to him, but broken, as was his headlamp. I took photos of his body and the surrounding area for insurance purposes. Because of his position I could not roll him over, so had to cut the tape sling that held him to the rope. His body slid down for about 100m onto the rocks. I went down and moved him again so as he ended up on a long snow slope where he slid for several hundred meters.

I went back up and collected his pack, and went down to his overboot to collect that. It was at this stage that I found one of his gloves about another 50m lower, also on the rock, but with a rock sitting on top of it. About another 50m lower there is another dead body that has been there since 1986. This had become exposed over the last few years, so I thought that I would cover him over again since I was in the business of removing bodies this day. To my surprise I found new crampons marks in the snow, so I suspect that Roger had visited him on his way up. I was especially surprised to find Roger's other overboot lying in the rocks not far away.

This may all be circumstantial, but it sure does not make sense to me.

I still had a camp about 100m (vertical) above where Roger was, but this was of no use to him at the rate that he was traveling. However it took me less than an hour to return to C1, and that was with a broken crampon as I had broken one whilst pushing him over the rocks.

Again none of us can understand why he did not turn back, especially when so many people had told him not to continue. He also knew that another man had already died that day.

Since returning and looking through his equipment, I see that he was so totally under prepared for an ascent of Everest. He had several items, which are good for skiing, but are of no use on Everest. He had practically no substantial food, and only one canister of cooking gas with him. I suspect that he was planning on using everyone else's camps, except we had taken them all out the day that he was going up. He may have reached my camp at 7500m but there was nothing inside so he would have still had problems.

Jim Findley and David Hahn of the American team led by Hahn – June 4, 1998

Findlay: Buick was "a determined man in all the wrong ways" and never changed his actions despite all advice from others on numerous occasions. Hahn: "he was extremely ignorant of the mountains and never could understand how they could kill him." Hahn was one of the last to talk to Buick. Hahn, et al: he thought everyone else was doing the climb much too expensively and elaborately and he had great disdain for guides. He was convinced that in life and climbing Everest, you learn as you go along, but he took 72 hours to descend from North Col to ABC while Hahn's client took 1-1/2 hours. Is it possible that he wanted to die on Everest? Nothing else makes sense.

Oxygen and the 8000ers

This chapter analyzes the use of supplementary oxygen for the 8000m peaks in the Nepal Himalaya.

Charts O-1a-b show the percentage of ascents without the use of supplementary oxygen for each of the 8000m peaks for the 1950-1989 and 1990-2009 periods.

The 8000m peaks can be divided into three groups of peaks of similar altitude:

8091-8188	(Annapurna I, Manaslu, Dhaulagiri I, Cho Oyu)
8485-8586	(Makalu, Lhotse, Kangchenjunga)
8850	(Everest)

In general as shown in the following charts, the percentages of ascents without supplementary oxygen are the highest for the four peaks under 8200m, lower for the three peaks between 8400m and 8600m, and lowest for Everest as would be logically expected.

For members, the percentages of ascents without supplementary oxygen increase in 1990-2009 period over the 1950-1989 period for each peak except Everest and Cho Oyu (the commercially climbed peaks). For the commercial routes on Everest and Cho Oyu, the use of supplementary oxygen increases because most commercial clients are more interested in success than climbing style and route difficulty due to their general lack of experience and their relative high investment in the expedition in terms of cost and

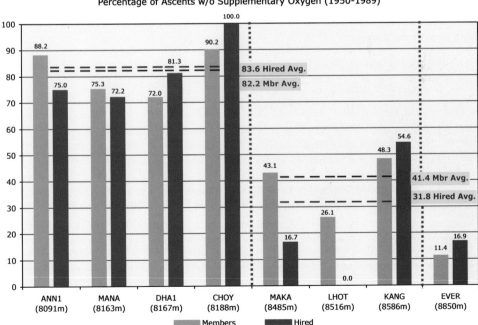

Percentage of Ascents w/o Supplementary Oxygen (1950-1989)

Chart O-1a: Percentage of ascents without supplementary oxygen for 8000m peaks from 1950-1989

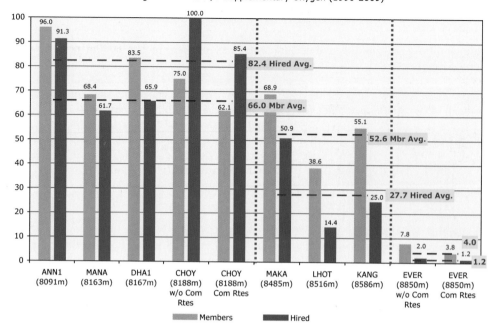

Percentage of Ascents w/o Supplementary Oxygen (1990-2009)

Chart O-1b: Percentage of ascents without supplementary oxygen for 8000m peaks from 1989-2009 with commercial routes separated out for Cho Oyu and Everest

time. Many of them cannot devote more time to their climbing adventures due to other commitments in their lives. Most commercial expeditions also require their guides (both foreign and hired) to use supplementary oxygen so that they will be stronger in the event of an emergency situation.

Members have higher percentage of ascents without supplementary oxygen on the more difficult peaks than the hired most likely because many elite climbers do not climb with hired on their summit days, either because they are not using any hired on their expeditions or are using them only for establishing the lower camps. During the 1990-2009 period, the average percentage of ascents for hired (82.4%) in the 8091-8188m group is higher than members (66.0%) only because of the heavy use of hired on Cho Oyu, the easiest of the 8000ers (see Charts O-1a-b).

Charts O-2a-b show the success rates with and without supplementary oxygen for members and hired above high camp on summit bids for the 8000m peaks from 1990 to 2009.

For members, the use of supplementary oxygen is most beneficial for the highest of the 8000ers, especially for Everest where the use of oxygen boosts the success rate from 30.2% to 74.6%. This difference is probably very conservative, considering that climbing without oxygen is usually only done by the more experienced climbers. For the lower peaks under 8200m, only on Manaslu and Cho Oyu is the use of oxygen significantly more beneficial, most likely due to the higher numbers of less experienced climbers attempting those two peaks.

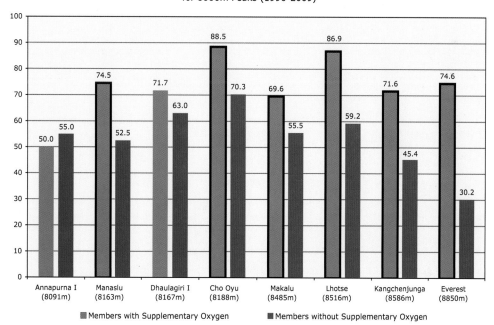

Success Rates With and Without Supplementary Oxygen for Members Above High Camp
for 8000m Peaks (1990-2009)

■ Members with Supplementary Oxygen   ■ Members without Supplementary Oxygen

**Chart O-2a: Success rates with and without supplementary oxygen for
members above high camp for 8000m peaks from 1990-2009
(the columns outlined in black in this and the following charts are statistically significant)**

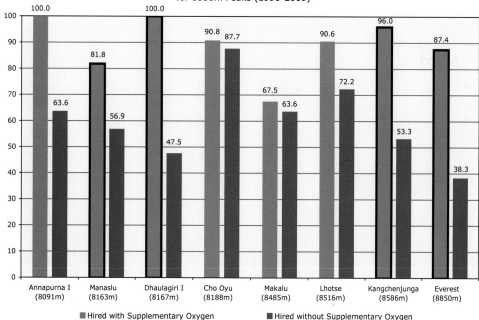

Success Rates With and Without Supplementary Oxygen for Hired Above High Camp
for 8000m Peaks (1990-2009)

■ Hired with Supplementary Oxygen   ■ Hired without Supplementary Oxygen

**Chart O-2b: Success rates with and without supplementary oxygen for
hired above high camp for 8000m peaks from 1990-2009**

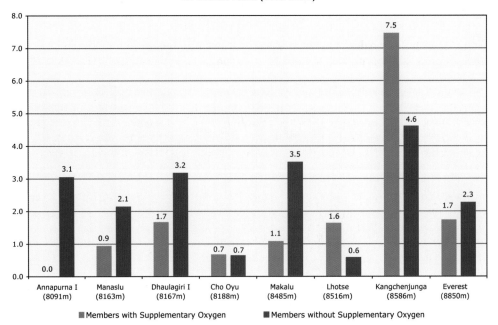

Death Rates With and Without Supplementary Oxygen for Members Above High Camp
for 8000m Peaks (1990-2009)

■ Members with Supplementary Oxygen   ■ Members without Supplementary Oxygen

Chart O-3a: Death rates with and without supplementary oxygen for members above high camp for 8000m peaks from 1990-2009

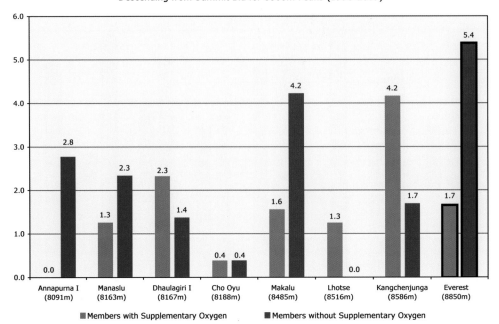

Death Rates With and Without Supplementary Oxygen for Successful Summiters
Descending from Summit Bid for 8000m Peaks (1990-2009)

■ Members with Supplementary Oxygen   ■ Members without Supplementary Oxygen

Chart O-3b: Death rates with and without supplementary oxygen for successful members descending from a summit bid for 8000m peaks from 1990-2009 (the columns outlined in black are statistically significant)

For hired personnel, the use of supplementary oxygen is most beneficial for Everest and Kangchenjunga. Dhaulagiri and Manaslu show significant benefits, but the numbers of hired above high camp on those two peaks is still relatively low.

Chart O-3a shows the death rates with and without supplementary oxygen for members above high camp on summit bids for the 8000m peaks from 1990 to 2009.

For members, the use of supplementary oxygen does not appear to affect the death rates, as none of the differences are statistically significant. On Everest, climbers using oxygen have a death rate of 1.7% whereas climbers without oxygen have a death rate of 2.3%, not significantly higher. Kangchenjunga show the opposite, where climbers with oxygen fare worse than those without, but again these rates are not statistically significant, but only anecdotal.

However as shown in Chart O-3b, if you include only those members who attained the summit, then the death rate for those climbing Everest without supplementary oxygen becomes significant, indicating that climbing without oxygen at the very highest altitudes is particularly hazardous. The death rates on the lower 8000m peaks are still not significant.

The death rates for hired are not meaningful due to the very small numbers of hired deaths that have occurred above high camp on summit bids.

As shown in the following Charts O-4 and O-5, one possible reason that climbers without oxygen do not have higher death rates is that many of those attempting to summit turn back early due to coldness and potential frostbite before they get into more serious difficulties with oxygen starvation and AMS, perhaps a sign that the human body is giving out its own early warning signals.

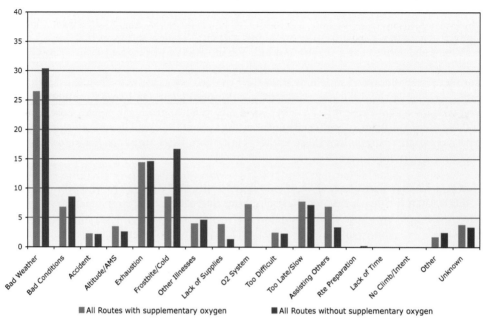

Above High Camp Termination Percentages for Unsuccessful Summit Bids
With and Without Supplementary Oxygen for All Routes on 8000ers (1990-2009)

■ All Routes with supplementary oxygen ■ All Routes without supplementary oxygen

**Chart O-4: Above high camp termination percentages for unsuccessful summit bids
with and without supplementary oxygen for all 8000er routes from 1990-2009**

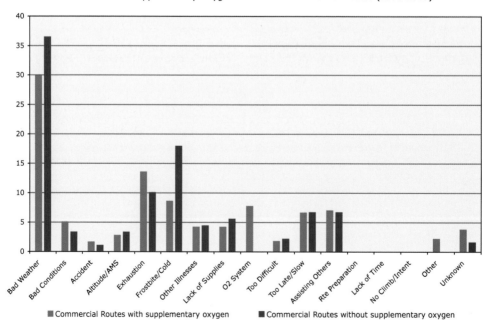

Above High Camp Termination Percentages for Unsuccessful Summit Bids
With and Without Supplementary Oxygen for Everest Commercial Routes (1990-2009)

■ Commercial Routes with supplementary oxygen ■ Commercial Routes without supplementary oxygen

**Chart O-5: Above high camp termination percentages for unsuccessful summit bids
with and without supplementary oxygen for Everest commercial routes from 1990-2009**

Appendix A: Peak Summary

The table in this appendix summarizes the peak data for the period from 1950 to 2009. The columns are defined as follows:

Peak ID – Peak ID used in *The Himalayan Database*
Region – geographical region codes for peak location (see map below)
Exp Cnt – number of expeditions to the peak
... Above BC – number of members, women members, or hired personnel that went above base camp or advanced base camp
... Smts – number of members, women members, or hired personnel that summited
Mbr Smt Rate – success rate for members (Mbr Smts / Mbrs Above BC)
... Deaths – number of members, women members, or hired personnel that died
... Death Rate – death rate for members and hired (e.g., Mbr Deaths / Mbrs Above BC)
Exp Days Avg. – average number of days for all expeditions to peak
Suc Exp Days Avg. – average number of days for all successful expeditions to peak
Smt Days Avg. – average number of days to summit for all successful expeditions to peak
Min Smt Days – minimum number of days to first summit (fastest expedition)
Max Smt Days – maximum number of days to first summit (slowest expedition)

Descriptions of all expeditions to the peaks listed in this table along with their member biodata are available in *The Himalayan Database*.

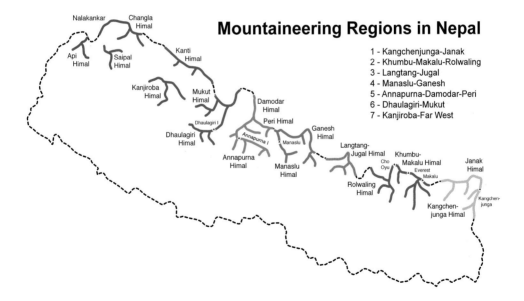

Mountaineering Regions in Nepal

1 - Kangchenjunga-Janak
2 - Khumbu-Makalu-Rolwaling
3 - Langtang-Jugal
4 - Manaslu-Ganesh
5 - Annapurna-Damodar-Peri
6 - Dhaulagiri-Mukut
7 - Kanjiroba-Far West

Peak ID	Peak Name	Alt (m)	Re-gion	Exp Cnt	Mbrs Above BC	Women Above BC	Hired Above BC	Mbr Smts	Women Smts	Hired Smts
AMAD	Ama Dablam	6814	2	742	3963	455	963	2096	222	468
AMPM	Amphu Middle	6238	2	1	6	2	0	5	1	0
ANN1	Annapurna I	8091	5	169	1111	63	413	126	6	31
ANN2	Annapurna II	7937	5	30	182	7	84	12	0	4
ANN3	Annapurna III	7555	5	31	213	22	63	20	3	11
ANN4	Annapurna IV	7525	5	75	581	70	208	75	1	37
ANNE	Annapurna I - East	8026	5	9	36	1	12	16	1	0
ANNM	Annapurna I - Middle	8051	5	7	29	1	12	12	1	4
ANNS	Annapurna South	7219	5	32	194	13	58	29	0	3
APIM	Api Main	7132	7	12	83	0	27	17	0	3
ARNK	Arniko Chuli	6034	6	2	8	3	3	8	3	0
BARU	Baruntse	7152	2	198	1137	183	352	338	40	115
BAUD	Baudha	6672	4	3	18	0	10	5	0	3
BHEM	Bhemdang Ri	6150	3	1	3	0	1	2	0	1
BHRI	Bhrikuti	6476	5	10	70	11	19	34	3	13
BHRS	Bhrikuti Sail	6361	5	2	9	2	4	8	2	4
BOBA	Bobaye	6808	7	1	2	0	2	1	0	0
BOKT	Boktoh	6114	1	2	5	0	4	3	0	0
BTAK	Bhairab Takura	6799	3	2	3	0	4	2	0	1
CHAG	Chago	6893	2	3	6	0	1	6	0	1
CHAK	Chako	6704	5	1	10	1	3	2	0	2
CHAM	Chamlang	7321	2	10	65	12	20	11	0	4
CHAN	Changla Himal	6563	7	1	4	0	4	0	0	0
CHAR	Chamar	7165	4	4	26	1	9	2	0	2
CHEK	Chekigo	6257	2	1	1	0	1	0	0	0
CHEO	Cheo Himal	6820	5	2	14	0	10	4	0	0
CHIV	Chhiv Himal	6650	5	1	5	1	0	4	1	0
CHKA	Chamar Kang	6060	7	1	5	1	1	5	1	1
CHOB	Chobuje	6686	2	6	33	4	3	11	0	0
CHOL	Cholatse	6423	2	14	69	3	6	39	2	2
CHOP	Cho Polu	6700	2	5	17	4	7	5	0	0
CHOY	Cho Oyu	8188	2	1019	5638	612	1716	2211	240	778
CHRE	Churen Himal East	7371	6	7	55	3	25	3	0	1
CHRW	Churen Himal West	7371	6	12	80	0	38	7	0	4
CHUE	Chulu East	6584	5	1	4	0	0	4	0	0
CHUG	Chugimago	6258	2	3	11	1	5	4	0	3
CHUR	Churen Himal Central	7371	6	6	39	0	28	9	0	5
CHUW	Chulu West	6419	5	1	6	0	6	6	0	0
CHWT	Changwatang	6130	7	2	9	1	8	9	1	6
DANG	Danga	6355	1	1	4	0	0	3	0	0
DHA1	Dhaulagiri I	8167	6	288	1698	133	574	354	25	60
DHA2	Dhaulagiri II	7751	6	15	99	3	57	16	0	9
DHA3	Dhaulagiri III	7715	6	3	34	0	28	13	0	1
DHA4	Dhaulagiri IV	7661	6	11	108	3	61	13	0	0
DHA5	Dhaulagiri V	7618	6	5	47	1	40	12	0	7
DHA6	Dhaulagiri VI	7268	6	7	44	0	27	18	0	4
DHAM	Dhampus	6012	6	14	91	26	23	65	17	16
DING	Dingjung Ri	6249	2	1	2	0	0	2	0	0
DINS	Dingjung Ri South	6196	2	2	5	1	1	2	0	0
DOGA	Dogari	6536	6	1	1	0	1	1	0	1
DOMB	Dome Blanc	6830	3	3	4	0	8	2	0	3
DOMK	Dome Kang	7264	1	3	16	3	10	2	0	3
DORJ	Dorje Lhakpa	6966	3	27	150	19	69	50	2	26
DRAN	Drangnag Ri	6757	2	3	21	0	13	4	0	2

Peak ID	Mbr Smt Rate	Mbr Deaths	Women Deaths	Hired Deaths	Mbr Death Rate	Hired Death Rate	Exp Days Avg.	Suc Exp Days Avg.	Smt Days Avg.	Min Smt Days	Max Smt Days
AMAD	52.89	17	2	4	0.43	0.42	13.2	13.4	10.0	1	38
AMPM	83.33	0	0	0	0.00	0.00	16.0	16.0	10.0	10	10
ANN1	11.34	45	3	17	4.05	4.12	29.9	31.4	28.1	3	62
ANN2	6.59	6	0	0	3.30	0.00	34.0	44.3	40.2	19	63
ANN3	9.39	8	0	1	3.76	1.59	28.2	30.2	26.2	16	46
ANN4	12.91	3	1	1	0.52	0.48	20.5	24.7	21.1	8	64
ANNE	44.44	1	0	0	2.78	0.00	31.4	33.6	28.3	15	44
ANNM	41.38	1	0	2	3.45	16.67	33.7	33.7	28.4	10	53
ANNS	14.95	6	0	2	3.09	3.45	27.4	34.6	28.3	19	38
APIM	20.48	4	0	0	4.82	0.00	26.3	23.0	17.7	14	19
ARNK	100.00	0	0	0	0.00	0.00	2.5	2.5	2.0	2	2
BARU	29.73	4	0	6	0.35	1.70	12.9	14.8	10.3	1	33
BAUD	27.78	1	0	0	5.56	0.00	36.5	35.0	28.0	28	28
BHEM	66.67	0	0	0	0.00	0.00	0.0	0.0	0.0	0	0
BHRI	48.57	0	0	0	0.00	0.00	5.8	5.6	3.9	1	8
BHRS	88.89	0	0	0	0.00	0.00	5.5	5.5	3.0	3	3
BOBA	50.00	0	0	0	0.00	0.00	24.0	24.0	17.0	17	17
BOKT	60.00	0	0	0	0.00	0.00	2.0	2.0	1.0	1	1
BTAK	66.67	0	0	0	0.00	0.00	23.0	43.0	19.0	19	19
CHAG	100.00	0	0	0	0.00	0.00	40.0	40.0	24.0	24	24
CHAK	20.00	0	0	0	0.00	0.00	18.0	18.0	15.0	15	15
CHAM	16.92	0	0	0	0.00	0.00	23.0	25.4	21.4	15	28
CHAN	0.00	0	0	0	0.00	0.00	8.0	0.0	0.0	0	0
CHAR	7.69	1	0	0	3.85	0.00	13.0	0.0	0.0	0	0
CHEK	0.00	0	0	0	0.00	0.00	0.0	0.0	0.0	0	0
CHEO	28.57	0	0	1	0.00	10.00	37.0	37.0	35.0	35	35
CHIV	80.00	0	0	0	0.00	0.00	14.0	14.0	10.0	10	10
CHKA	100.00	0	0	0	0.00	0.00	3.0	3.0	2.0	2	2
CHOB	33.33	2	0	0	6.06	0.00	16.2	21.0	18.3	3	36
CHOL	56.52	0	0	0	0.00	0.00	19.3	19.4	13.1	2	23
CHOP	29.41	0	0	0	0.00	0.00	12.3	13.5	19.0	19	19
CHOY	39.22	36	3	9	0.64	0.52	25.6	26.0	21.0	1	52
CHRE	5.45	1	0	0	1.82	0.00	34.0	28.5	25.5	10	41
CHRW	8.75	2	0	2	2.50	5.26	29.2	28.3	24.5	4	39
CHUE	100.00	0	0	0	0.00	0.00	0.0	0.0	0.0	0	0
CHUG	36.36	0	0	0	0.00	0.00	0.0	0.0	0.0	0	0
CHUR	23.08	0	0	0	0.00	0.00	24.5	29.3	24.7	19	30
CHUW	100.00	0	0	0	0.00	0.00	0.0	0.0	0.0	0	0
CHWT	100.00	0	0	0	0.00	0.00	11.0	11.0	8.5	5	12
DANG	75.00	0	0	0	0.00	0.00	22.0	22.0	19.0	19	19
DHA1	20.85	50	6	15	2.94	2.61	30.4	31.7	26.9	3	118
DHA2	16.16	1	0	3	1.01	5.26	33.6	39.3	32.0	28	36
DHA3	38.24	0	0	0	0.00	0.00	42.7	47.5	36.0	29	43
DHA4	12.04	9	0	5	8.33	8.20	52.0	53.0	47.0	46	48
DHA5	25.53	4	0	0	8.51	0.00	62.5	62.5	49.0	37	61
DHA6	40.91	0	0	0	0.00	0.00	32.5	32.5	28.0	16	43
DHAM	71.43	0	0	0	0.00	0.00	12.7	12.7	3.6	1	13
DING	100.00	0	0	0	0.00	0.00	0.0	0.0	0.0	0	0
DINS	40.00	0	0	0	0.00	0.00	13.0	9.0	8.0	8	8
DOGA	100.00	0	0	0	0.00	0.00	31.0	31.0	29.0	29	29
DOMB	50.00	0	0	0	0.00	0.00	0.0	0.0	0.0	0	0
DOMK	12.50	0	0	0	0.00	0.00	26.3	23.0	21.0	21	21
DORJ	33.33	2	0	0	1.33	0.00	19.7	20.9	17.3	7	36
DRAN	19.05	0	0	0	0.00	0.00	18.3	19.5	17.5	16	19

Peak ID	Peak Name	Alt (m)	Re-gion	Exp Cnt	Mbrs Above BC	Women Above BC	Hired Above BC	Mbr Smts	Women Smts	Hired Smts
DROM	Drohmo	6881	1	5	19	0	5	2	0	0
DUDH	Dudh Kundali	6042	7	2	11	4	5	8	2	5
DZAS	Dzasampatse	6295	2	1	2	0	0	2	0	0
EVER	Everest	8850	2	1274	9131	774	7303	2544	250	1983
FANG	Fang	7647	5	9	79	0	31	3	0	3
FIRN	Firnkopf	6730	7	2	11	0	9	0	0	0
FIRW	Firnkopf West	6745	7	1	3	0	2	2	0	1
FREN	Friendship Peak	6576	2	2	27	0	0	24	0	0
GAJA	Gajang	6111	5	1	1	0	1	0	0	0
GAMA	Gama Peak	7149	6	2	11	0	10	4	0	2
GAN1	Ganesh I	7422	4	8	51	6	41	3	1	0
GAN2	Ganesh II	7118	4	9	57	1	24	4	0	5
GAN3	Ganesh III	7043	4	6	42	1	9	9	0	2
GAN4	Ganesh IV	7104	4	9	65	1	17	20	1	2
GAN5	Ganesh V	6770	4	5	28	0	8	12	0	7
GAN6	Ganesh VI	6908	4	2	16	0	8	4	0	0
GANC	Ganchempo	6387	3	14	53	4	20	15	2	4
GANG	Gangapurna	7455	5	23	149	7	59	32	2	6
GAUG	Gaugiri	6110	5	5	8	1	5	7	1	4
GAUR	Gaurishankar	7135	2	23	155	6	35	4	0	2
GHAN	Ghhanyala Hies	6744	1	1	5	0	1	0	0	0
GHEN	Ghenge Liru	6596	3	1	1	0	2	1	0	2
GHUN	Ghustang North	6529	6	4	9	0	17	9	0	6
GHUS	Ghustang South	6465	6	1	1	0	5	0	0	0
GIME	Gimmigela Chuli East	7007	1	2	24	0	6	6	0	6
GIMM	Gimmigela Chuli	7350	1	6	64	1	24	17	0	8
GLAC	Glacier Dome	7193	5	25	177	11	74	48	2	13
GURJ	Gurja Himal	7193	6	8	66	9	27	19	3	11
GURK	Gurkarpo Ri	6889	3	6	36	2	13	4	0	0
GYAC	Gyachung Kang	7952	2	12	90	3	42	21	0	5
GYAJ	Gyajikang	7074	5	9	68	13	23	34	3	13
GYAL	Gyalzen	6733	3	4	10	4	13	6	2	7
HCHI	Hunchi	7029	2	8	39	1	20	10	0	4
HIME	Himalchuli East	7893	4	24	194	3	91	23	0	4
HIMJ	Himjung	7092	5	1	3	0	0	0	0	0
HIML	Himlung Himal	7126	5	42	268	39	76	87	9	33
HIMN	Himalchuli North	7371	4	3	24	0	8	3	0	4
HIMW	Himalchuli West	7540	4	5	27	0	15	7	0	0
HIUP	Hiunchuli	6441	5	2	12	2	0	5	0	0
HNKU	Hongku Chuli	6833	2	1	2	0	3	0	0	0
HONG	Hongde	6556	6	3	9	0	9	4	0	2
IMJA	Imjatse	6165	2	6	12	0	7	7	0	6
JANK	Janak	7041	1	3	6	0	4	2	0	0
JANU	Jannu	7711	1	47	271	5	112	65	0	9
JETH	Jethi Bahurani	6850	7	3	16	0	4	3	0	0
JOBO	Jobo Rinjang	6781	2	2	4	0	1	0	0	0
JOMS	Jomsom	6120	5	1	5	1	1	4	1	1
JONG	Jongsang	7462	1	5	65	0	6	3	0	0
JUNC	Junction Peak	7108	6	1	9	0	8	0	0	0
KABN	Kabru North	7338	1	4	36	0	3	10	0	0
KABR	Kabru Main	7412	1	1	27	0	0	4	0	0
KABS	Kabru South	7318	1	2	52	0	2	6	0	0
KAKU	Kang Kuru	6344	5	1	2	0	0	2	0	0
KAN1	Kande Hiunchuli N I	6521	7	2	9	0	6	0	0	0

200 Appendix A

Peak ID	Mbr Smt Rate	Mbr Deaths	Women Deaths	Hired Deaths	Mbr Death Rate	Hired Death Rate	Exp Days Avg.	Suc Exp Days Avg.	Smt Days Avg.	Min Smt Days	Max Smt Days
DROM	10.53	0	0	0	0.00	0.00	17.6	8.0	7.0	7	7
DUDH	72.73	0	0	0	0.00	0.00	5.0	5.0	3.0	3	3
DZAS	100.00	0	0	0	0.00	0.00	22.0	22.0	15.0	15	15
EVER	27.86	139	7	71	1.52	0.97	44.8	45.5	40.4	7	75
FANG	3.80	2	0	1	2.53	3.23	39.3	59.5	40.5	35	46
FIRN	0.00	1	0	0	9.09	0.00	23.5	0.0	0.0	0	0
FIRW	66.67	0	0	0	0.00	0.00	10.0	10.0	8.0	8	8
FREN	88.89	0	0	0	0.00	0.00	9.0	7.0	5.0	5	5
GAJA	0.00	0	0	0	0.00	0.00	14.0	0.0	0.0	0	0
GAMA	36.36	0	0	0	0.00	0.00	45.0	45.0	42.0	42	42
GAN1	5.88	1	0	0	1.96	0.00	25.6	41.0	34.0	34	34
GAN2	7.02	3	0	0	5.26	0.00	35.7	31.0	28.0	27	29
GAN3	21.43	1	0	0	2.38	0.00	27.5	31.5	26.0	17	35
GAN4	30.77	4	0	0	6.15	0.00	24.1	27.0	24.0	16	40
GAN5	42.86	4	0	0	14.29	0.00	28.8	31.0	25.7	22	30
GAN6	25.00	0	0	0	0.00	0.00	50.0	50.0	43.0	42	44
GANC	28.30	0	0	0	0.00	0.00	17.2	19.3	16.0	6	28
GANG	21.48	5	0	6	3.36	10.17	27.2	37.4	30.6	19	44
GAUG	87.50	0	0	0	0.00	0.00	4.4	3.0	2.0	2	2
GAUR	2.58	1	0	0	0.65	0.00	27.2	34.0	31.7	30	34
GHAN	0.00	0	0	0	0.00	0.00	13.0	0.0	0.0	0	0
GHEN	100.00	0	0	0	0.00	0.00	10.0	10.0	5.0	5	5
GHUN	100.00	0	0	0	0.00	0.00	26.3	26.3	22.5	17	28
GHUS	0.00	0	0	0	0.00	0.00	0.0	0.0	0.0	0	0
GIME	25.00	0	0	0	0.00	0.00	23.5	23.5	20.5	16	25
GIMM	26.56	3	0	0	4.69	0.00	31.5	36.7	29.7	26	37
GLAC	27.12	0	0	0	0.00	0.00	21.3	23.3	19.9	7	53
GURJ	28.79	4	1	0	6.06	0.00	23.6	24.9	20.7	9	28
GURK	11.11	0	0	0	0.00	0.00	12.8	14.0	12.0	12	12
GYAC	23.33	2	0	0	2.22	0.00	31.2	31.0	25.0	21	32
GYAJ	50.00	0	0	0	0.00	0.00	12.0	15.2	10.4	5	18
GYAL	60.00	0	0	0	0.00	0.00	29.3	35.7	22.3	19	26
HCHI	25.64	0	0	0	0.00	0.00	23.1	22.3	19.7	17	24
HIME	11.86	10	0	3	5.15	3.30	40.8	44.0	38.6	28	49
HIMJ	0.00	1	0	0	33.33	0.00	18.0	0.0	0.0	0	0
HIML	32.46	0	0	0	0.00	0.00	14.6	16.0	10.7	4	26
HIMN	12.50	3	0	0	12.50	0.00	31.3	32.5	29.5	25	34
HIMW	25.93	0	0	0	0.00	0.00	35.6	35.3	30.7	21	40
HIUP	41.67	0	0	0	0.00	0.00	19.0	19.0	17.0	17	17
HNKU	0.00	0	0	0	0.00	0.00	41.0	0.0	0.0	0	0
HONG	44.44	0	0	0	0.00	0.00	4.5	4.5	2.5	2	3
IMJA	58.33	0	0	0	0.00	0.00	2.0	2.0	1.0	1	1
JANK	33.33	0	0	0	0.00	0.00	26.3	26.0	25.0	25	25
JANU	23.99	6	0	1	2.21	0.89	32.5	36.5	33.2	6	60
JETH	18.75	0	0	1	0.00	25.00	29.0	22.0	20.0	20	20
JOBO	0.00	0	0	0	0.00	0.00	15.5	0.0	0.0	0	0
JOMS	80.00	0	0	0	0.00	0.00	7.0	7.0	5.0	5	5
JONG	4.62	1	0	0	1.54	0.00	29.0	0.0	0.0	0	0
JUNC	0.00	0	0	0	0.00	0.00	0.0	0.0	0.0	0	0
KABN	27.78	0	0	0	0.00	0.00	14.0	14.0	13.0	13	13
KABR	14.81	0	0	0	0.00	0.00	0.0	0.0	0.0	0	0
KABS	11.54	0	0	0	0.00	0.00	22.0	0.0	0.0	0	0
KAKU	100.00	0	0	0	0.00	0.00	4.0	4.0	3.0	3	3
KAN1	0.00	1	0	0	11.11	0.00	28.0	0.0	0.0	0	0

Peak ID	Peak Name	Alt (m)	Re-gion	Exp Cnt	Mbrs Above BC	Women Above BC	Hired Above BC	Mbr Smts	Women Smts	Hired Smts
KAN2	Kande Hiunchuli N II	6471	7	2	9	0	1	2	0	0
KANB	Kangbachen	7902	1	5	53	0	18	14	0	1
KANC	Kangchenjunga Cntrl	8482	1	7	50	1	28	25	0	0
KAND	Kande Hiunchuli	6627	7	5	28	5	12	2	0	0
KANG	Kangchenjunga	8586	1	108	833	50	388	194	6	43
KANS	Kangchenjunga South	8476	1	5	47	0	12	22	0	0
KANT	Kanti Himal	6859	7	4	17	0	8	5	0	3
KARY	Karyolung	6511	2	5	27	3	10	15	2	3
KCHO	Kangcho Nup	6043	2	3	8	0	12	8	0	3
KGRI	Khangri Shar	6811	2	2	8	0	6	0	0	0
KGUR	Kang Guru	6981	5	31	180	19	73	54	2	27
KHAT	Khatang	6790	2	5	49	7	3	23	1	1
KHUM	Khumbutse	6639	2	1	1	0	0	1	0	0
KIRA	Kirat Chuli	7362	1	7	58	4	3	0	0	0
KJER	Kanjeralwa	6612	7	4	20	2	9	5	0	3
KJRN	Kanjiroba North	6858	7	1	6	0	2	0	0	0
KJRS	Kanjiroba South	6883	7	6	38	2	17	17	0	5
KNAG	Kang Nagchugo	6737	2	1	2	0	0	2	0	0
KOJI	Kojichuwa Chuli	6439	7	2	8	0	3	0	0	0
KOTA	Kotang	6148	1	12	85	8	37	15	0	4
KTEG	Kangtega	6783	2	23	112	12	22	42	6	3
KTOK	Kangtokal	6294	6	3	10	0	1	7	0	1
KTSU	Kangtsune	6443	7	1	6	1	3	0	0	0
KTUN	Khatung Kang	6484	5	3	16	5	7	2	1	0
KUBI	Kubi Kangri	6721	7	2	14	5	5	7	0	0
KUML	Kumlung	6355	5	1	2	0	0	2	0	0
KWAN	Kwangde	6186	2	1	5	0	0	0	0	0
KYAS	Kyashar	6770	2	5	12	0	0	3	0	0
LAMJ	Lamjung Himal	6983	5	8	60	7	24	29	4	12
LAMP	Lampo	6460	4	1	4	0	4	0	0	0
LANG	Langtang Lirung	7227	3	42	265	19	83	40	3	8
LANR	Langtang Ri	7205	3	7	35	1	16	17	0	3
LASH	Lashar I	6842	1	1	2	0	1	2	0	0
LEON	Leonpo Gang	6979	3	7	50	0	47	13	0	3
LHAS	Lha Shamma	6412	7	2	11	6	10	4	4	3
LHOM	Lhotse Middle	8410	2	1	12	0	4	9	0	0
LHOT	Lhotse	8516	2	192	1071	68	668	305	18	95
LIK1	Likhu Chuli I	6719	2	2	8	1	3	1	1	1
LOBE	Lobuje East	6119	2	1	3	0	4	0	0	0
LOBW	Lobuje West	6145	2	2	10	2	2	5	0	2
LSHR	Lhotse Shar	8382	2	32	250	8	108	21	0	3
LSIS	Langshisa Ri	6412	3	11	60	9	12	22	2	6
MACH	Machhapuchhare	6993	5	1	5	0	3	0	0	0
MAK2	Makalu II	7678	2	45	242	23	106	61	4	17
MAKA	Makalu	8485	2	223	1411	86	589	264	16	61
MANA	Manaslu	8163	4	275	1624	132	684	323	30	112
MANN	Manaslu North	6994	4	9	69	8	25	15	1	5
MANP	Manapathi	6380	6	2	5	0	1	5	0	1
MELA	Melanpulan	6573	2	1	2	1	0	2	1	0
MERA	Mera Peak	6470	2	4	8	0	5	7	0	4
MERR	Merra	6334	1	6	12	1	3	7	0	2
MING	Mingbo Ri	6187	2	1	8	0	2	0	0	0
MOJC	Mojca	6024	1	1	2	0	0	2	0	0
MUKT	Mukut Himal	6639	6	2	8	0	5	2	0	2

Peak ID	Mbr Smt Rate	Mbr Deaths	Women Deaths	Hired Deaths	Mbr Death Rate	Hired Death Rate	Exp Days Avg.	Suc Exp Days Avg.	Smt Days Avg.	Min Smt Days	Max Smt Days
KAN2	22.22	0	0	0	0.00	0.00	22.5	28.0	22.0	22	22
KANB	26.42	0	0	0	0.00	0.00	35.3	39.5	30.5	21	40
KANC	50.00	0	0	0	0.00	0.00	39.5	47.8	42.0	19	71
KAND	7.14	0	0	0	0.00	0.00	16.3	20.0	18.0	18	18
KANG	23.29	25	4	7	3.00	1.80	40.7	42.3	36.8	12	71
KANS	46.81	0	0	0	0.00	0.00	43.8	47.5	41.3	18	72
KANT	29.41	0	0	0	0.00	0.00	12.3	18.0	16.0	16	16
KARY	55.56	0	0	0	0.00	0.00	18.3	23.0	18.5	15	22
KCHO	100.00	0	0	0	0.00	0.00	0.0	0.0	0.0	0	0
KGRI	0.00	0	0	0	0.00	0.00	11.5	0.0	0.0	0	0
KGUR	30.00	8	1	11	4.44	15.07	15.4	16.9	13.7	7	36
KHAT	46.94	0	0	0	0.00	0.00	17.5	21.5	19.0	16	22
KHUM	100.00	0	0	0	0.00	0.00	54.0	54.0	48.0	48	48
KIRA	0.00	0	0	0	0.00	0.00	22.4	0.0	0.0	0	0
KJER	25.00	0	0	0	0.00	0.00	15.5	28.0	18.0	18	18
KJRN	0.00	1	0	0	16.67	0.00	39.0	0.0	0.0	0	0
KJRS	44.74	0	0	0	0.00	0.00	25.8	25.8	20.6	7	43
KNAG	100.00	0	0	0	0.00	0.00	59.0	59.0	26.0	26	26
KOJI	0.00	0	0	0	0.00	0.00	4.5	0.0	0.0	0	0
KOTA	17.65	1	0	0	1.18	0.00	12.5	13.0	9.5	6	13
KTEG	37.50	0	0	1	0.00	4.55	17.7	18.3	15.3	3	27
KTOK	70.00	0	0	0	0.00	0.00	10.7	10.7	8.3	3	16
KTSU	0.00	0	0	0	0.00	0.00	39.0	0.0	0.0	0	0
KTUN	12.50	0	0	0	0.00	0.00	7.0	0.0	0.0	0	0
KUBI	50.00	0	0	0	0.00	0.00	49.0	49.0	39.0	39	39
KUML	100.00	0	0	0	0.00	0.00	9.0	9.0	8.0	8	8
KWAN	0.00	0	0	0	0.00	0.00	0.0	0.0	0.0	0	0
KYAS	25.00	0	0	0	0.00	0.00	10.3	18.0	15.0	15	15
LAMJ	48.33	0	0	0	0.00	0.00	31.6	31.2	28.7	19	38
LAMP	0.00	0	0	0	0.00	0.00	7.0	0.0	0.0	0	0
LANG	15.09	12	0	4	4.53	4.82	26.1	33.2	29.8	12	58
LANR	48.57	0	0	1	0.00	6.25	18.7	23.5	20.0	6	29
LASH	100.00	0	0	0	0.00	0.00	23.0	23.0	13.0	13	13
LEON	26.00	1	0	2	2.00	4.26	34.9	38.7	32.7	24	40
LHAS	36.36	0	0	0	0.00	0.00	0.0	0.0	0.0	0	0
LHOM	75.00	0	0	0	0.00	0.00	60.0	60.0	55.0	55	55
LHOT	28.48	11	1	1	1.03	0.15	38.2	37.2	32.0	4	58
LIK1	12.50	0	0	0	0.00	0.00	13.0	17.0	15.0	15	15
LOBE	0.00	0	0	0	0.00	0.00	0.0	0.0	0.0	0	0
LOBW	50.00	0	0	0	0.00	0.00	9.0	9.0	8.5	3	14
LSHR	8.40	10	0	0	4.00	0.00	44.8	51.6	43.3	31	63
LSIS	36.67	3	0	0	5.00	0.00	15.0	13.7	10.7	5	21
MACH	0.00	0	0	0	0.00	0.00	0.0	0.0	0.0	0	0
MAK2	25.21	10	0	3	4.13	2.83	26.0	30.7	24.0	12	52
MAKA	18.71	23	0	14	1.63	2.38	36.4	36.6	31.8	5	65
MANA	19.89	45	4	14	2.77	2.05	29.6	31.0	27.2	6	63
MANN	21.74	0	0	0	0.00	0.00	19.4	24.3	20.8	8	28
MANP	100.00	0	0	0	0.00	0.00	37.0	37.0	19.0	19	19
MELA	100.00	0	0	0	0.00	0.00	20.0	20.0	15.0	15	15
MERA	87.50	0	0	0	0.00	0.00	0.0	0.0	0.0	0	0
MERR	58.33	0	0	0	0.00	0.00	11.5	11.0	5.3	4	8
MING	0.00	0	0	0	0.00	0.00	5.0	0.0	0.0	0	0
MOJC	100.00	0	0	0	0.00	0.00	34.0	34.0	33.0	33	33
MUKT	25.00	0	0	0	0.00	0.00	0.0	0.0	0.0	0	0

Peak ID	Peak Name	Alt (m)	Re-gion	Exp Cnt	Mbrs Above BC	Women Above BC	Hired Above BC	Mbr Smts	Women Smts	Hired Smts
MUST	Mustang Peak	6229	6	1	5	1	3	4	0	3
NAG1	Nangpai Gosum I	7321	2	1	0	0	0	0	0	0
NAG2	Nangpai Gosum II	7287	2	1	6	1	1	0	0	0
NALA	Nalakankar North	6062	7	1	1	0	4	1	0	1
NALS	Nalakankar South	6024	7	1	9	4	5	9	4	5
NAMP	Nampa	6829	7	4	21	3	3	4	0	0
NAUL	Naulekh	6262	2	1	2	0	1	2	0	1
NCHU	Nupchu	6044	1	1	9	1	6	6	0	3
NEPA	Nepal Peak	7177	1	5	57	5	5	3	1	0
NGO2	Ngojumba Kang II	7643	2	3	22	1	8	7	0	1
NGOJ	Ngojumba Kang I	7916	2	6	47	3	29	5	0	2
NILC	Nilgiri Central	6940	5	3	18	0	10	8	0	2
NILN	Nilgiri North	7061	5	13	78	9	24	19	1	7
NILS	Nilgiri South	6839	5	7	35	0	2	6	0	0
NORB	Norbu Kang	6005	7	2	8	3	5	7	3	4
NUMB	Numbur	6958	2	15	91	1	31	21	0	7
NUMR	Numri	6635	2	1	7	2	0	3	1	0
NUPE	Nuptse East I	7795	2	8	28	1	4	2	0	0
NUPT	Nuptse	7864	2	38	174	8	63	15	0	3
OHMI	Ohmi Kangri	6839	1	3	29	4	9	10	0	4
OMBG	Ombigaichen	6340	2	1	2	0	2	2	0	2
PAN1	Panpoche 1	6620	4	1	6	0	0	0	0	0
PANB	Panbari	6905	5	1	6	2	0	5	2	0
PAND	Pandra	6850	1	1	4	0	0	3	0	0
PANG	Pangbuk Ri	6625	2	3	7	0	4	0	0	0
PANT	Panalotapa	6687	2	1	2	0	0	2	0	0
PARC	Parchamo	6279	2	6	30	3	1	11	2	0
PASA	Pasang Lhamu Chuli	7351	2	9	49	3	14	22	0	3
PBUK	Pabuk Kang	6244	1	1	2	0	1	0	0	0
PETH	Pethangtse	6739	2	6	14	0	8	14	0	8
PHUR	Phurbi Chhyachu	6637	3	1	15	3	3	14	2	2
PIMU	Pimu	6344	2	3	10	1	1	6	0	0
PISA	Pisang	6091	5	1	1	0	0	1	0	0
PK29	Peak 29	7871	4	8	87	4	46	2	0	0
PK41	Peak 41	6648	2	2	5	0	1	2	0	0
POKR	Pokharkan	6372	5	3	14	3	10	4	0	7
PUMO	Pumori	7165	2	226	1296	103	278	413	30	67
PUNC	Punchen Himal	6049	4	2	9	0	3	0	0	0
PURK	Purkhang	6120	5	2	17	2	12	8	2	6
PUTH	Putha Hiunchuli	7246	6	39	291	34	95	114	16	42
PUTR	Putrung	6500	5	1	7	0	1	0	0	0
PYRM	Pyramid Peak	7140	1	6	28	1	7	12	0	0
RAKS	Raksha Urai	6609	7	5	31	3	10	3	1	1
RAMC	Ramtang Chang	6802	1	4	8	0	0	5	0	0
RAMT	Ramtang	6601	1	4	32	2	7	0	0	0
RANI	Rani Peak	6693	4	2	10	0	6	9	0	5
RATC	Ratna Chuli	7035	5	8	71	10	27	20	2	16
RATH	Rathong	6682	1	4	62	0	16	24	0	0
ROCN	Roc Noir	7485	5	8	66	1	21	19	0	0
ROKA	Rokapi	6468	7	1	3	0	1	2	0	0
SAIP	Saipal	7030	7	11	63	5	26	15	0	3
SAMD	Samdo	6335	4	3	13	0	3	6	0	0
SARI	Saribung	6328	5	12	74	18	21	63	13	16
SHAL	Shalbachum	6707	3	2	14	0	8	4	0	2

Peak ID	Mbr Smt Rate	Mbr Deaths	Women Deaths	Hired Deaths	Mbr Death Rate	Hired Death Rate	Exp Days Avg.	Suc Exp Days Avg.	Smt Days Avg.	Min Smt Days	Max Smt Days
MUST	80.00	0	0	0	0.00	0.00	5.0	5.0	3.0	3	3
NAG1	0.00	0	0	0	0.00	0.00	4.0	0.0	0.0	0	0
NAG2	0.00	0	0	1	0.00	100.00	26.0	26.0	23.0	23	23
NALA	100.00	0	0	0	0.00	0.00	5.0	5.0	3.0	3	3
NALS	100.00	0	0	0	0.00	0.00	6.0	6.0	4.0	4	4
NAMP	19.05	1	0	0	4.76	0.00	28.0	31.0	26.5	18	35
NAUL	100.00	0	0	0	0.00	0.00	0.0	0.0	0.0	0	0
NCHU	66.67	0	0	0	0.00	0.00	15.0	15.0	13.0	13	13
NEPA	5.26	0	0	0	0.00	0.00	22.8	19.0	17.0	17	17
NGO2	31.82	1	0	0	4.55	0.00	33.3	33.3	28.7	19	34
NGOJ	10.64	0	0	0	0.00	0.00	33.8	34.7	31.7	21	37
NILC	44.44	0	0	0	0.00	0.00	25.3	22.0	13.0	13	13
NILN	24.36	0	0	0	0.00	0.00	22.5	26.2	21.6	13	32
NILS	17.14	0	0	0	0.00	0.00	20.4	26.0	24.0	24	24
NORB	87.50	0	0	0	0.00	0.00	5.0	5.0	3.5	2	5
NUMB	23.08	0	0	0	0.00	0.00	18.7	20.6	18.3	12	28
NUMR	42.86	0	0	0	0.00	0.00	26.0	26.0	17.0	17	17
NUPE	7.14	0	0	0	0.00	0.00	40.0	47.0	42.0	42	42
NUPT	8.62	5	0	0	2.87	0.00	26.0	43.2	33.4	20	46
OHMI	34.48	0	0	0	0.00	0.00	24.0	24.0	20.0	18	22
OMBG	100.00	0	0	0	0.00	0.00	0.0	0.0	0.0	0	0
PAN1	0.00	0	0	0	0.00	0.00	47.0	0.0	0.0	0	0
PANB	83.33	0	0	0	0.00	0.00	27.0	27.0	22.0	22	22
PAND	75.00	0	0	0	0.00	0.00	22.0	22.0	15.0	15	15
PANG	0.00	0	0	0	0.00	0.00	2.0	0.0	0.0	0	0
PANT	100.00	0	0	0	0.00	0.00	0.0	0.0	0.0	0	0
PARC	36.67	0	0	0	0.00	0.00	0.0	0.0	0.0	0	0
PASA	44.90	1	0	0	2.04	0.00	21.3	23.3	20.8	13	29
PBUK	0.00	0	0	0	0.00	0.00	2.0	0.0	0.0	0	0
PETH	100.00	0	0	0	0.00	0.00	21.8	21.8	24.0	6	35
PHUR	93.33	0	0	0	0.00	0.00	31.0	31.0	29.0	29	29
PIMU	60.00	0	0	0	0.00	0.00	26.0	26.0	24.0	24	24
PISA	100.00	0	0	0	0.00	0.00	0.0	0.0	0.0	0	0
PK29	2.30	4	0	1	4.60	2.17	37.7	35.0	32.0	32	32
PK41	40.00	0	0	0	0.00	0.00	7.0	0.0	0.0	0	0
POKR	28.57	0	0	0	0.00	0.00	11.0	11.0	8.7	6	12
PUMO	31.87	32	0	9	2.47	3.24	15.9	18.1	14.6	2	45
PUNC	0.00	0	0	0	0.00	0.00	6.5	0.0	0.0	0	0
PURK	47.06	0	0	0	0.00	0.00	8.0	11.0	9.0	9	9
PUTH	39.18	2	0	1	0.69	1.05	15.1	15.6	12.1	6	36
PUTR	0.00	0	0	0	0.00	0.00	5.0	0.0	0.0	0	0
PYRM	42.86	0	0	0	0.00	0.00	22.2	30.0	26.5	15	38
RAKS	9.68	1	0	1	3.23	10.00	14.2	9.0	6.0	6	6
RAMC	62.50	0	0	0	0.00	0.00	21.7	19.0	15.0	15	15
RAMT	0.00	0	0	0	0.00	0.00	11.3	0.0	0.0	0	0
RANI	90.00	0	0	0	0.00	0.00	24.0	24.0	21.0	21	21
RATC	28.17	0	0	0	0.00	0.00	16.0	19.8	13.8	8	24
RATH	38.71	0	0	0	0.00	0.00	9.0	9.0	7.0	6	8
ROCN	28.79	0	0	0	0.00	0.00	32.6	42.4	33.8	19	44
ROKA	66.67	0	0	0	0.00	0.00	19.0	19.0	13.0	13	13
SAIP	23.81	0	0	0	0.00	0.00	26.2	30.0	25.8	19	37
SAMD	46.15	0	0	0	0.00	0.00	26.0	47.0	18.0	18	18
SARI	85.14	0	0	0	0.00	0.00	6.2	6.2	4.5	2	11
SHAL	28.57	0	0	0	0.00	0.00	0.0	0.0	0.0	0	0

Peak ID	Peak Name	Alt (m)	Re-gion	Exp Cnt	Mbrs Above BC	Women Above BC	Hired Above BC	Mbr Smts	Women Smts	Hired Smts
SHAN	Shanti Shikhar	7591	2	2	15	2	0	0	0	0
SHAR	Shartse II	7457	2	4	16	1	8	4	0	1
SHER	Sherson	6422	2	2	19	1	4	18	1	3
SHEY	Shey Shikhar	6139	7	2	6	1	3	1	0	0
SIMN	Simnang Himal	6251	4	3	13	0	0	4	0	0
SING	Singu Chuli	6501	5	1	2	0	0	2	0	0
SITA	Sita Chuchura	6611	6	6	27	2	3	7	0	1
SNOW	Snow Peak	6530	6	1	20	1	23	0	0	0
SPHN	Sphinx	6825	1	2	21	0	6	20	0	0
SPHU	Sharphu I	6433	1	1	10	0	4	10	0	4
SRKU	Serku Dolma	6227	7	1	6	0	3	2	0	1
SWAK	Swaksa Kang	6405	7	1	4	0	0	0	0	0
SWEL	Swelokhan	6180	4	2	4	0	1	0	0	0
TAKP	Takphu Himal	6395	7	1	12	4	4	0	0	0
TAPL	Taple Shikhar	6447	1	2	8	1	12	1	1	3
TASH	Tashi Kang	6386	6	6	31	8	7	13	2	3
TAWO	Tawoche	6495	2	20	78	3	9	32	0	1
TENG	Tengkoma	6215	1	7	34	6	10	19	2	6
TENR	Tengi Ragi Tau	6938	2	2	11	3	9	4	2	3
THAM	Thamserku	6618	2	13	56	2	17	14	0	2
THUL	Thulagi	7059	4	1	8	3	5	0	0	0
TILI	Tilicho	7134	5	65	453	45	108	106	11	28
TKPO	Tengkangpoche	6487	2	14	57	7	1	6	0	0
TLNG	Talung	7349	1	10	46	4	26	3	0	1
TOBS	Tobsar	6065	4	1	2	1	3	0	0	0
TONG	Tongu	6187	6	2	8	0	9	7	0	0
TRIP	Tripura Hiunchuli	6553	7	3	14	1	2	2	0	1
TSAR	Tsartse	6343	6	1	3	0	0	0	0	0
TSOK	Tso Karpo Kang	6556	7	2	11	0	5	5	0	3
TUKU	Tukuche	6920	6	45	303	40	86	73	7	14
TUTS	Tutse	6758	2	1	3	1	1	0	0	0
URKM	Urkinmang	6151	3	8	27	6	9	17	3	6
WHIT	White Peak	6395	6	4	40	0	40	28	0	2
YAKA	Yakawa Kang	6482	5	1	1	0	1	0	0	0
YALU	Yalung Kang	8505	1	18	170	7	98	47	1	6
YANS	Yansa Tsenji	6567	3	1	6	1	3	0	0	0
YAUP	Yaupa	6432	2	1	3	0	0	3	0	0
YEMK	Yemelung Kang	6024	7	2	5	1	5	5	1	2

Peak ID	Mbr Smt Rate	Mbr Deaths	Women Deaths	Hired Deaths	Mbr Death Rate	Hired Death Rate	Exp Days Avg.	Suc Exp Days Avg.	Smt Days Avg.	Min Smt Days	Max Smt Days
SHAN	0.00	0	0	0	0.00	0.00	22.0	0.0	0.0	0	0
SHAR	25.00	1	0	0	6.25	0.00	36.0	36.0	34.5	21	48
SHER	94.74	0	0	0	0.00	0.00	47.0	47.0	15.0	4	26
SHEY	16.67	0	0	0	0.00	0.00	3.5	5.0	3.0	3	3
SIMN	30.77	0	0	0	0.00	0.00	35.7	53.0	45.0	45	45
SING	100.00	0	0	0	0.00	0.00	52.0	52.0	50.0	50	50
SITA	25.93	0	0	0	0.00	0.00	12.7	12.0	7.0	7	7
SNOW	0.00	0	0	0	0.00	0.00	54.0	0.0	0.0	0	0
SPHN	95.24	0	0	0	0.00	0.00	33.5	33.5	25.5	17	34
SPHU	100.00	0	0	0	0.00	0.00	16.0	16.0	10.0	10	10
SRKU	33.33	0	0	0	0.00	0.00	43.0	43.0	32.0	32	32
SWAK	0.00	0	0	0	0.00	0.00	3.0	0.0	0.0	0	0
SWEL	0.00	0	0	0	0.00	0.00	9.5	0.0	0.0	0	0
TAKP	0.00	0	0	0	0.00	0.00	0.0	0.0	0.0	0	0
TAPL	12.50	0	0	0	0.00	0.00	18.0	18.0	15.0	15	15
TASH	41.94	0	0	0	0.00	0.00	7.8	8.4	4.4	2	7
TAWO	41.03	1	0	0	1.28	0.00	16.6	15.0	11.6	2	21
TENG	55.88	0	0	0	0.00	0.00	9.7	11.0	5.0	1	10
TENR	36.36	0	0	0	0.00	0.00	29.0	35.0	31.0	31	31
THAM	25.00	0	0	0	0.00	0.00	19.0	19.5	17.5	2	33
THUL	0.00	0	0	0	0.00	0.00	43.0	0.0	0.0	0	0
TILI	23.40	7	0	0	1.55	0.00	13.2	14.6	11.0	3	23
TKPO	10.53	0	0	0	0.00	0.00	17.7	26.0	21.0	18	24
TLNG	6.52	0	0	0	0.00	0.00	26.9	21.0	16.3	8	22
TOBS	0.00	0	0	0	0.00	0.00	3.0	0.0	0.0	0	0
TONG	87.50	0	0	0	0.00	0.00	5.0	5.0	3.0	3	3
TRIP	14.29	0	0	0	0.00	0.00	25.0	25.0	23.0	23	23
TSAR	0.00	0	0	0	0.00	0.00	13.0	0.0	0.0	0	0
TSOK	45.45	0	0	0	0.00	0.00	24.0	24.0	16.5	8	25
TUKU	24.09	1	0	0	0.33	0.00	12.6	13.2	10.9	4	20
TUTS	0.00	0	0	0	0.00	0.00	9.0	0.0	0.0	0	0
URKM	62.96	0	0	0	0.00	0.00	11.3	14.0	13.0	13	13
WHIT	70.00	0	0	0	0.00	0.00	51.3	51.3	37.3	27	43
YAKA	0.00	0	0	0	0.00	0.00	14.0	0.0	0.0	0	0
YALU	27.65	5	0	2	2.94	2.04	40.8	40.3	34.4	23	54
YANS	0.00	0	0	0	0.00	0.00	10.0	0.0	0.0	0	0
YAUP	100.00	0	0	0	0.00	0.00	54.0	54.0	0.0	0	0
YEMK	100.00	0	0	0	0.00	0.00	2.0	2.0	1.0	1	1

Appendix B: Supplemental Charts and Tables

This appendix provides supplementary information relating to the statistical signifi-cance of the data in the tables and charts presented throughout this book.

The charts and tables below include the estimated rates of ascent and death for peaks, as well as the 95% confidence intervals for each rate. The width of a confidence interval is a measure of the reliability of an estimated rate. A 95% confidence interval indicates in essence that there is a 95% probability that the true rate falls within that interval. Confidence intervals can be calculated in various ways, and we used the adjusted Wald method. For example in the ANN1 entry in the supplemental Chart A-3s below, the estimated ascent rate for Annapurna I is 11.3% with a 95% probability that the actual ascent rate lies between 9.6% and 13.4%. The information in Chart A-3s and Table A-3s correspond to the information presented in the primary Chart A-3 in the *Ascent Analysis* chapter.

Sample size plays a major role in the calculation of confidence intervals: a larger sample size reduces the width of the interval, and thus the calculated result is more certain. In Chart A-3s, the width of the confidence interval for all peaks is narrower than the interval for Kangchenjunga (comparing a sample of 39,126 against a sample of 833 members above BC), thus the mean ascent rate of 30.2% for all peaks is more certain than the mean rate of 23.3% for Kangchenjunga.

If one wants to estimate whether ascent rates differ for two peaks, a quick-and-dirty way is to see whether the confidence intervals for two rates overlap: if they do, this suggests that the two rates do not differ significantly. For a more formal evaluation of statistical significance of rates for two peaks, we use chi-square tests with Yates' correction for continuity. If the calculated p-value is 0.05, then the probability is only 5% that the observed difference between the two peaks could have occurred by chance: a probability this unlikely is considered statistically significant. If the p-value is much smaller than 0.05, then the difference between the two peaks is even less likely to have occurred by chance. Using 0.05 as the cutoff for statistical significance is arbitrary, but most statisticians use this as a standard for analysis. We did not adjust p-values for having done multiple comparisons.

Each of the confidence interval charts has one or two horizontal dashed lines, which represent the composite rate for some group of peaks. If the width of the confidence interval is very small, only one dashed line is present; otherwise, two dashed lines represent the confidence interval of the composite group. In Chart A-3s, for example, the horizontal dashed line at 30.2% represents the member ascent rate for all peaks combined. If the confidence interval for a given peak is far from that line, this suggests that the ascent rate of the peak in question is highly significantly different from the overall rate. For example, ANN1 and MAKA are well below the dashed line indicating a much lower ascent rate than the mean rate for all peaks, whereas AMAD and all 6000ers are well above indicating a much higher ascent rate. BARU and LHOT are very close to (and crossing) the dashed line, indicating a similar ascent rate to the mean rate for all peaks (thus a statistically insignificant difference). Note that the associated Table A-3s gives the formal statistical probability of that difference. In each case, the rate for a given peak is compared against the rate for all other peaks in the sample. Thus the rate for ANN1 is compared against that of all other peaks.

In the supplemental Chart D-4s that corresponds to Chart D-4 in the *Death Analysis* chapter, the sample sizes are so small that the resulting confidence intervals become vary large and indicate no statistical significance for most peaks. This makes intuitive sense because the occurrence of a single death can dramatically alter the results.

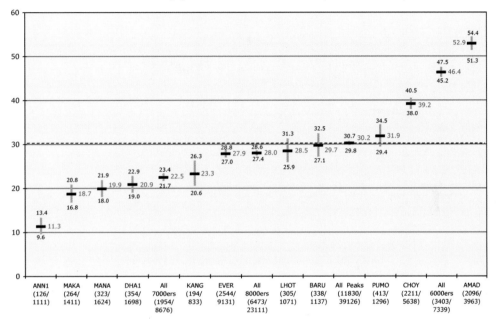

Chart A-3s: Member ascent rates for popular peaks from 1950-2009 with more than 750 members above base camp

	Members Above BC	Ascent Count	Failure Count	Ascent Rate	95% Confidence Interval		Yates' Chi Square
					Lower	Upper	p-value
Annapurna I	1111	126	985	11.3	9.6	13.4	<0.001
Makalu	1411	264	1147	18.7	16.8	20.8	<0.001
Manaslu	1624	323	1301	19.9	18.0	21.9	<0.001
Dhaulagiri I	1698	354	1344	20.9	19.0	22.9	<0.001
All 7000ers	8676	1954	6722	22.5	21.7	23.4	<0.001
Kangchenjunga	833	194	639	23.3	20.6	26.3	<0.001
Everest	9131	2544	6587	27.9	27.0	28.8	<0.001
All 8000ers	23111	6473	16638	28.0	27.4	28.6	<0.001
Lhotse	1071	305	766	28.5	25.9	31.3	0.216
Baruntse	1137	338	799	29.7	27.1	32.5	0.729
All Peaks	39126	11830	27296	30.2	29.8	30.7	
Pumori	1296	413	883	31.9	29.4	34.5	0.204
Cho Oyu	5638	2211	3427	39.2	38.0	40.5	<0.001
All 6000ers	7339	3403	3936	46.4	45.2	47.5	<0.001
Ama Dablam	3963	2096	1867	52.9	51.3	54.4	<0.001

Table A-3s: Member ascent rates for popular peaks from 1950-2009 with more than 750 members above base camp

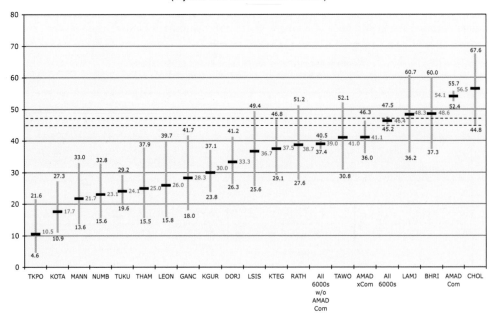

Member Ascent Rates for Popular 6000m Peaks (1950-2009)
(Adjusted Wald 95% Confidence Intervals)

Chart A-4s: Member ascent rates for selected 6000m peaks
with 50+ members above base camp from 1950-2009

	Members Above BC	Ascent Count	Failure Count	Ascent Rate	95% Confidence Interval		Yates' Chi Square
					Lower	Upper	p-value
Tengkangpoche	57	6	51	10.5	4.6	21.6	<0.001
Kotang	85	15	70	17.7	10.9	27.3	<0.001
Manaslu North	69	15	54	21.7	13.6	33.0	<0.001
Numbur	91	21	70	23.1	15.6	32.8	<0.001
Tukuche	303	73	230	24.1	19.6	29.2	<0.001
Thamserku	56	14	42	25.0	15.5	37.9	0.002
Leonpo Gang	50	13	37	26.0	15.8	39.7	0.006
Ganchempo	53	15	38	28.3	18.0	41.7	0.012
Kang Guru	180	54	126	30.0	23.8	37.1	<0.001
Dorje Lhakpa	150	50	100	33.3	26.3	41.2	0.002
Langshisa Ri	60	22	38	36.7	25.6	49.4	0.167
Kangtega	112	42	70	37.5	29.1	46.8	0.072
Rathong	62	24	38	38.7	27.6	51.2	0.277
All 6000ers w/o AMAD	3376	1307	2069	38.7	37.1	40.4	<0.001
Tawoche	78	32	46	41.0	30.8	52.1	0.402
All 6000ers	7339	3403	3936	46.4	45.2	47.5	
Lamjung Himal	60	29	31	48.3	36.2	60.7	0.860
Bhrikuti	70	34	36	48.6	37.3	60.0	0.802
Ama Dablam	3963	2096	1867	52.9	51.3	54.4	<0.001
Cholatse	69	39	30	56.5	44.8	67.6	0.115
Dhampus	91	65	26	71.4	61.4	79.7	<0.001
Saribung	74	63	11	85.1	75.1	91.6	<0.001

Table A-4s: Member ascent rates for selected 6000m peaks
with 50+ members above base camp from 1950-2009

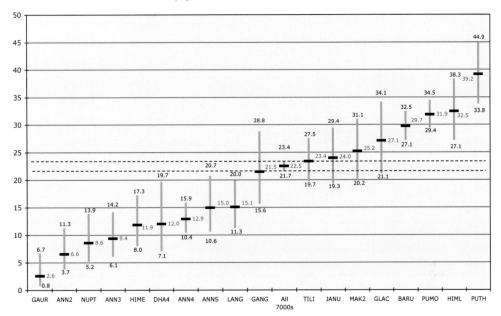

Member Ascent Rates for Popular 7000m Peaks (1950-2009)
(Adjusted Wald 95% Confidence Intervals)

Chart A-5s: Member ascent rates for selected 7000m peaks
with 100+ members above base camp from 1950-2009

					95% Confidence Interval		Yates' Chi Square
	Members Above BC	Ascent Count	Failure Count	Ascent Rate	Lower	Upper	p-value
Gaurishankar	155	4	151	2.6	0.8	6.7	<0.001
Annapurna II	182	12	170	6.6	3.7	11.3	<0.001
Nuptse	174	15	159	8.6	5.2	13.9	<0.001
Annapurna III	213	20	193	9.4	6.1	14.2	<0.001
Himalchuli East	194	23	171	11.9	8.0	17.3	<0.001
Dhaulagiri IV	108	13	95	12.0	7.1	19.7	0.013
Annapurna IV	581	75	506	12.9	10.4	15.9	<0.001
Annapurna South	194	29	165	15.0	10.6	20.7	0.014
Langtang Lirung	265	40	225	15.1	11.3	20.0	0.004
Gangapurna	149	32	117	21.5	15.6	28.8	0.834
All 7000ers	8676	1954	6722	22.5	21.7	23.4	
Tilicho	453	106	347	23.4	19.7	27.5	0.688
Jannu	271	65	206	24.0	19.3	29.4	0.609
Makalu II	242	61	181	25.2	20.2	31.1	0.349
Glacier Dome	177	48	129	27.1	21.1	34.1	0.165
Baruntse	1137	338	799	29.7	27.1	32.5	<0.001
Pumori	1296	413	883	31.9	29.4	34.5	<0.001
Himlung Himal	268	87	181	32.5	27.1	38.3	<0.001
Putha Hiunchuli	291	114	177	39.2	33.8	44.9	<0.001

Table A-5s: Member ascent rates for selected 7000m peaks
with 100+ members above base camp from 1950-2009

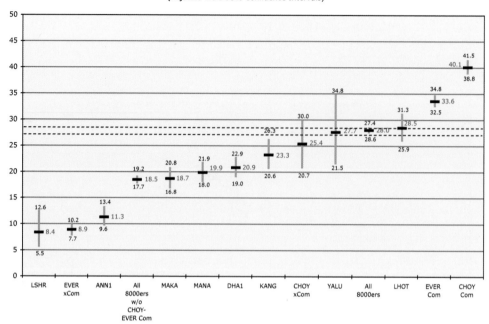

Member Ascent Rates for Popular 8000m Peaks (1950-2009)
(Adjusted Wald 95% Confidence Intervals)

**Chart A-6as: Member ascent rates for 8000m peaks
with 150+ members above base camp from 1950-2009**

	Members Above BC	Ascent Count	Failure Count	Ascent Rate	95% Confidence Interval		Yates' Chi Square
					Lower	Upper	p-value
Lhotse Shar	250	21	229	8.4	5.5	12.6	<0.001
Annapurna I	1111	126	985	11.3	9.6	13.4	<0.001
Makalu	1411	264	1147	18.7	16.8	20.8	<0.001
Manaslu	1624	323	1301	19.9	18.0	21.9	<0.001
All 8000ers w/o CHOY-EVER	8342	1718	6624	20.6	19.7	21.5	<0.001
Dhaulagiri I	1698	354	1344	20.9	19.0	22.9	<0.001
Kangchenjunga	833	194	639	23.3	20.6	26.3	0.002
Yalung Kang	170	47	123	27.7	21.5	34.8	0.999
Everest	9131	2544	6587	27.9	27.0	28.8	0.699
All 8000ers	23111	6473	16638	28.0	27.4	28.6	
Lhotse	1071	305	766	28.5	25.9	31.3	0.752
Cho Oyu	5638	2211	3427	39.2	38.0	40.5	<0.001

**Table A-6as: Member ascent rates for 8000m peaks
with 150+ members above base camp from 1950-2009**

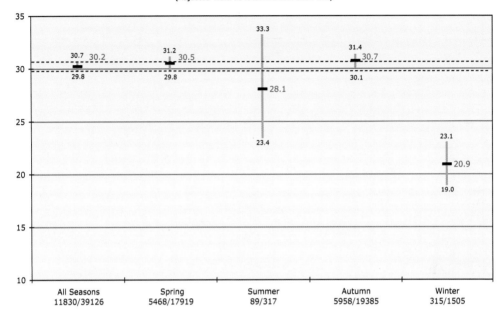

Chart A-7s: Member ascent rates by climbing season for all peaks from 1950-2009 (the ascent rate is above the column bar; the ascent and above BC counts are below)

	Members Above BC	Ascent Count	Failure Count	Ascent Rate	95% Confidence Interval		Yates' Chi Square
					Lower	Upper	p-value
All Seasons	39126	11830	27296	30.2	29.8	30.7	
Spring	17919	5468	12451	30.5	29.8	31.2	0.273
Summer	317	89	228	28.1	23.4	33.3	0.436
Autumn	19385	5958	13427	30.7	30.1	31.4	0.034
Winter	1505	315	1190	20.9	19.0	23.1	<0.001

Table A-7s: Member ascent rates by climbing season for all peaks from 1950-2009 (the ascent rate is above the column bar; the ascent and above BC counts are below)

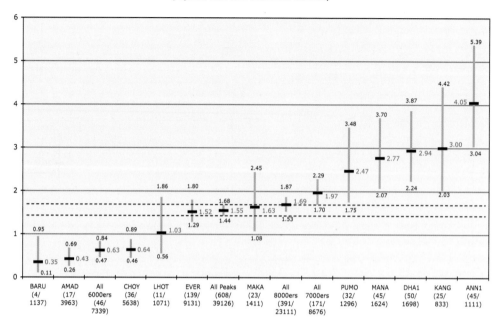

Chart D-3s: Member death rates for popular peaks from 1950-2009 with more than 750 members above base camp

					95% Confidence Interval		Yates' Chi Square
	Members Above BC	Death Count	Survival Count	Death Rate	Lower	Upper	p-value
Baruntse	1137	4	1133	0.35	0.11	0.95	0.001
Ama Dablam	3963	17	3946	0.43	0.26	0.69	<0.001
All 6000ers	7339	46	7293	0.63	0.47	0.84	<0.001
Cho Oyu	5638	36	5602	0.64	0.46	0.89	<0.001
Lhotse	1071	11	1060	1.03	0.56	1.86	0.198
Everest	9131	139	8992	1.52	1.29	1.80	0.818
All Peaks	39126	608	38518	1.55	1.44	1.68	
Makalu	1411	23	1388	1.63	1.08	2.45	0.899
All 8000ers	23111	391	22720	1.69	1.53	1.87	0.009
All 7000ers	8676	171	8505	1.97	1.70	2.29	<0.001
Pumori	1296	32	1264	2.47	1.75	3.48	0.010
Dhaulagiri I	1624	45	1579	2.77	2.07	3.70	<0.001
Kangchenjunga	1698	50	1648	2.94	2.24	3.87	<0.001
Manaslu	833	25	808	3.00	2.03	4.42	0.001
Annapurna I	1111	45	1066	4.05	3.04	5.39	<0.001

Table D-3s: Member death rates for popular peaks from 1950-2009 with more than 750 members above base camp

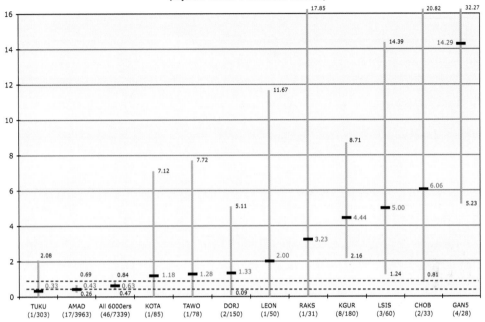

Chart D-4s: Member death rates for selected 6000m peaks with 25+ members above base camp from 1950-2009

	Members Above BC	Death Count	Survival Count	Death Rate	95% Confidence Interval		Yates' Chi Square
					Lower	Upper	p-value
Tukuche	303	1	302	0.33	0.00	2.08	0.767
Ama Dablam	3963	17	3946	0.43	0.26	0.69	0.029
All 6000ers	7339	46	7293	0.63	0.47	0.84	
Kotang	85	1	84	1.18	0.00	7.12	0.964
Tawoche	78	1	77	1.28	0.00	7.72	0.999
Dorje Lhakpa	150	2	148	1.33	0.09	5.11	0.559
Leonpo Gang	50	1	49	2.00	0.00	11.67	0.737
Raksha Urai	31	1	30	3.23	0.00	17.85	0.486
Nampa	180	8	172	4.44	2.16	8.71	<0.001
Langsisa Ri	60	3	57	5.00	1.24	14.39	<0.001
Kang Guru	33	2	31	6.06	0.81	20.82	0.004
Chobuje	28	4	24	14.29	5.23	32.27	<0.001

Table D-4s: Member death rates for selected 6000m peaks with 25+ members above base camp from 1950-2009

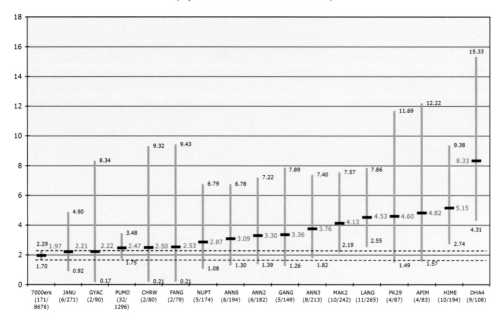

Chart D-5s: Member death rates for selected 7000m peaks
with 75+ members above base camp from 1950-2009

					95% Confidence Interval		Yates' Chi Square
	Members Above BC	Death Count	Survival Count	Death Rate	Lower	Upper	p-value
All 7000ers	8676	171	8505	1.97	1.70	2.29	
Jannu	271	6	265	2.21	0.92	4.90	0.944
Gyachung Kang	90	2	88	2.22	0.17	8.34	0.834
Pumori	1296	32	1264	2.47	1.75	3.48	0.197
Churen West	80	2	78	2.50	0.21	9.32	0.950
Fang	79	2	77	2.53	0.21	9.43	0.964
Nuptse	174	5	169	2.87	1.08	6.79	0.555
Annapurna South	194	6	188	3.09	1.30	6.78	0.381
Gangapurna	182	6	176	3.30	1.39	7.22	0.303
Annapurna II	149	5	144	3.36	1.26	7.89	0.353
Annapurna III	213	8	205	3.76	1.82	7.40	0.099
Makalu II	242	10	232	4.13	2.19	7.57	0.027
Langtang Lirung	265	12	253	4.53	2.55	7.86	0.005
Api Main	87	4	83	4.60	1.49	11.69	0.166
Peak 29	83	4	79	4.82	1.57	12.22	0.139
Himalchuli East	194	10	184	5.15	2.74	9.38	0.003
Dhaulagiri IV	108	9	99	8.33	4.31	15.33	<0.001

Table D-5s: Member death rates for selected 7000m peaks
with 75+ members above base camp from 1950-2009

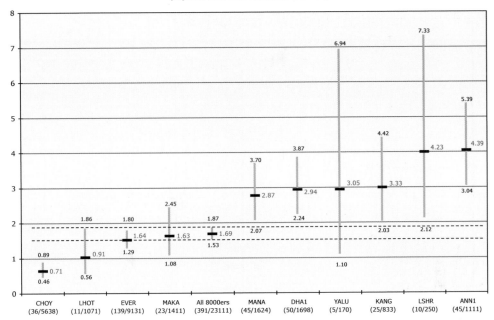

Chart D-6as: Member death rates for 8000m peaks
with 150+ members above base camp from 1950-2009

					95% Confidence Interval		Yates' Chi Square
	Members Above BC	Death Count	Survival Count	Death Rate	Lower	Upper	p-value
Cho Oyu	5638	36	5602	0.64	0.46	0.89	<0.001
Lhotse	1071	11	1060	1.03	0.56	1.86	0.108
Everest	9131	139	8992	1.52	1.29	1.80	0.118
Makalu	1411	23	1388	1.63	1.08	2.45	0.938
All 8000ers	23111	391	22720	1.69	1.53	1.87	
Yalung Kang	1624	45	1579	2.77	2.07	3.70	<0.001
Dhaulagiri I	1698	50	1648	2.94	2.24	3.87	<0.001
Kangchenjunga	170	5	165	2.94	1.10	6.94	0.332
Manaslu	833	25	808	3.00	2.03	4.42	0.004
Lhotse Shar	250	10	240	4.00	2.12	7.33	0.009
Annapurna I	1111	45	1066	4.05	3.04	5.39	<0.001

Table D-6as: Member death rates for 8000m peaks
with 150+ members above base camp from 1950-2009

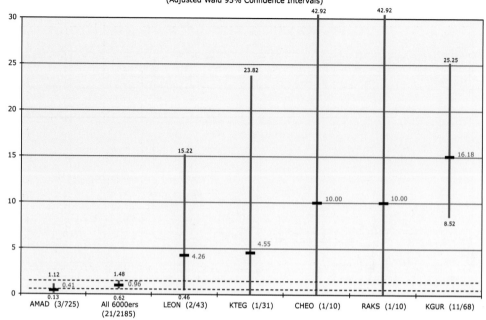

**Chart D-7s: Hired death rates for selected 6000m peaks
with 10+ hired above base camp from 1950-2009**

	Hired Above BC	Death Count	Survival Count	Death Rate	95% Confidence Interval		Yates' Chi Square
					Lower	Upper	p-value
Ama Dablam	963	4	959	0.42	0.13	1.12	0.036
All 6000ers	2185	21	2164	0.96	0.62	1.48	
Kantega	47	2	45	4.26	0.46	15.22	0.113
Leonpo Gang	22	1	21	4.55	0.00	23.82	0.526
Cheo Himal	10	1	9	10.00	0.00	42.92	0.189
Raksha Urai	10	1	9	10.00	0.00	42.92	0.189
Kang Guru	73	11	62	15.07	8.52	25.25	<0.001

**Table D-7s: Hired death rates for selected 6000m peaks
with 10+ hired above base camp from 1950-2009**

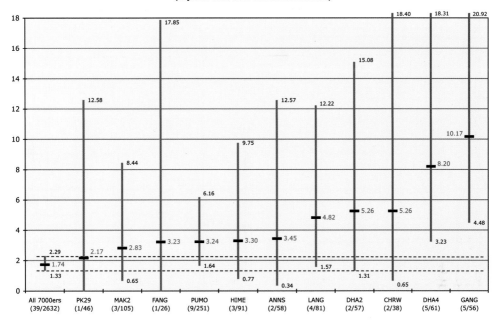

Chart D-8s: Hired death rates for selected 7000m peaks
with 25+ hired above base camp from 1950-2009

	Hired Above BC	Death Count	Survival Count	Death Rate	95% Confidence Interval		Yates' Chi Square
					Lower	Upper	p-value
All 7000ers	2923	51	2872	1.74	1.33	2.29	
Baruntse	46	1	45	2.17	0.00	12.58	0.731
Peak 29	106	3	103	2.83	0.65	8.44	0.623
Makalu II	31	1	30	3.23	0.00	17.85	0.956
Himalchuli East	278	9	269	3.24	1.64	6.16	0.079
Annapurna South	91	3	88	3.30	0.77	9.75	0.458
Pumori	58	2	56	3.45	0.34	12.57	0.621
Langtang Lirung	83	4	79	4.82	1.57	12.22	0.081
Dhaulagiri II	57	3	54	5.26	1.31	15.08	0.124
Churen Himal West	38	2	36	5.26	0.65	18.40	0.297
Dhaulagiri IV	61	5	56	8.20	3.23	18.31	<0.001
Gangapurna	59	6	53	10.17	4.48	20.92	<0.001
Gangapurna	56	5	51	8.93	3.54	19.79	<0.001

Table D-8s: Hired death rates for selected 7000m peaks
with 25+ hired above base camp from 1950-2009

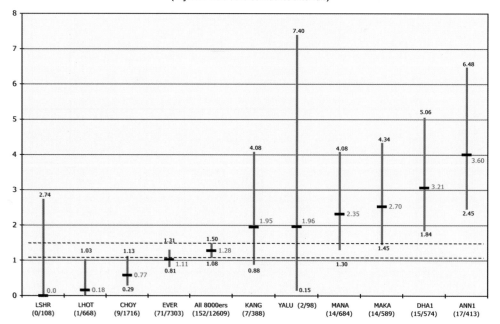

Chart D-9as: Hired death rates for 8000m peaks with 75+ hired above base camp from 1950-2009

	Hired Above BC	Death Count	Survival Count	Death Rate	95% Confidence Interval		Yates' Chi Square
					Lower	Upper	p-value
Lhotse Shar	108	0	108	0.00	0.00	2.74	0.478
Lhotse	668	1	667	0.15	0.00	0.95	0.017
Cho Oyu	1716	9	1707	0.52	0.26	1.02	0.008
Everest	7303	71	7232	0.97	0.77	1.23	0.006
All 8000ers	12609	152	12457	1.21	1.03	1.41	
Kangchenjunga	388	7	381	1.80	0.81	3.78	0.389
Yalung Kang	98	2	96	2.04	0.15	7.69	0.767
Makalu	684	14	670	2.05	1.20	3.45	0.058
Manaslu	589	14	575	2.38	1.39	4.00	0.013
Dhaulagiri I	574	15	559	2.61	1.56	4.32	0.003
Annapurna I	413	17	396	4.12	2.55	6.56	<0.001

Table D-9as: Hired death rates for 8000m peaks with 75+ hired above base camp from 1950-2009

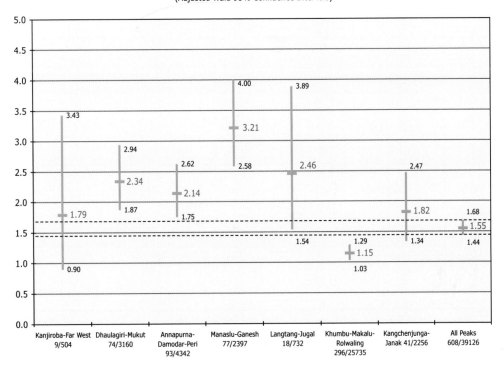

Member Death Rates by Geographical Region (1950-2009)
(Adjusted Wald 95% Confidence Intervals)

Chart D-10as: Member death rates by geographical region for all peaks from 1950-2009 (the death rate is above the column bar; the death and above BC counts are below)

	Members Above BC	Death Count	Survival Count	Death Rate	95% Confidence Interval		Yates' Chi Square
					Lower	Upper	p-value
Kanjiroba-Far West	504	9	495	1.79	3.43	0.90	0.808
Dhaulagiri-Mukut	3160	74	3086	2.34	2.94	1.87	<0.001
Annapurna-Damodar-Peri	4342	93	4249	2.14	2.62	1.75	0.001
Manaslu-Ganesh	2397	77	2320	3.21	4.00	2.58	<0.001
Langtang-Jugal	732	18	714	2.46	3.89	1.54	0.065
Khumbu-Makalu-Rolwaling	25735	296	25439	1.15	1.29	1.03	<0.001
Kangchenjunga-Janak	2256	41	2215	1.82	2.47	1.34	0.340
All Peaks	39126	608	38518	1.55	1.68	1.44	

Table D-10as: Member death rates by geographical region for all peaks from 1950-2009

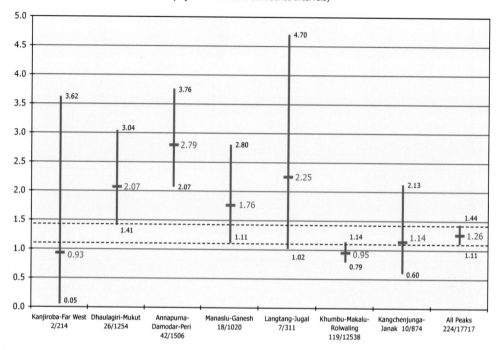

Chart D-10bs: Hired death rates by geographical region for all peaks from 1950-2009 (the death rate is above the column bar; the death and above BC counts are below)

	Hired Above BC	Death Count	Survival Count	Death Rate	95% Confidence Interval		Yates' Chi Square
					Lower	Upper	p-value
Kanjiroba-Far West	214	2	212	0.93	3.62	0.05	0.899
Dhaulagiri-Mukut	1254	26	1228	2.07	3.04	1.41	0.011
Annapurna-Damodar-Peri	1506	42	1464	2.79	3.76	2.07	<0.001
Manaslu-Ganesh	1020	18	1002	1.76	2.80	1.11	0.184
Langtang-Jugal	311	7	304	2.25	4.70	1.02	0.189
Khumbu-Makalu-Rolwaling	12538	119	12419	0.95	1.14	0.79	<0.001
Kangchenjunga-Janak	874	10	864	1.14	2.13	0.60	0.865
All Peaks	17717	224	17493	1.26	1.44	1.11	

Table D-10bs: Hired death rates by geographical region for all peaks from 1950-2009

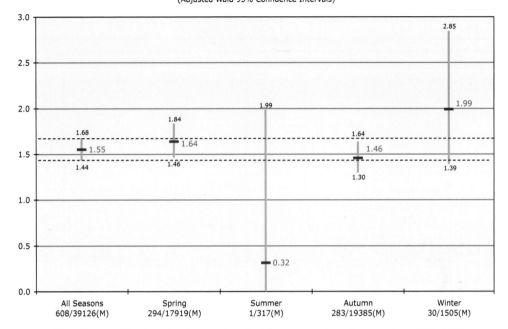

Chart D-11as: Member death rates by climbing season for all peaks from 1950-2009 (the death rate is above the column bar; the death and above BC counts are below)

	Members Above BC	Death Count	Survival Count	Death Rate	95% Confidence Interval		Yates' Chi Square
					Lower	Upper	p-value
All Seasons	39126	608	38518	1.55	1.44	1.68	
Spring	17919	294	17625	1.64	1.46	1.84	0.217
Summer	317	1	316	0.32	0.00	1.99	0.118
Autumn	19385	283	19102	1.46	1.30	1.64	0.147
Winter	1505	30	1475	1.99	1.39	2.85	0.194

Table D-11as: Member death rates by climbing season for all peaks from 1950-2009

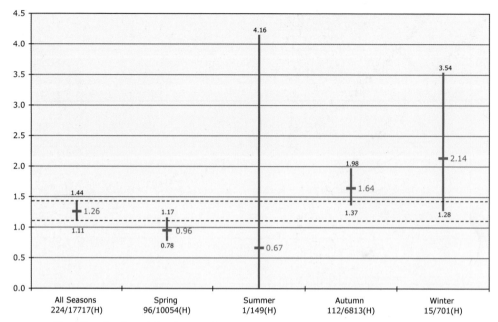

Chart D-11bs: Hired death rates by climbing season for all peaks from 1950-2009
(the death rate is above the column bar; the death and above BC counts are below)

	Hired Above BC	Death Count	Survival Count	Death Rate	95% Confidence Interval		Yates' Chi Square
					Lower	Upper	p-value
All Seasons	17717	224	17493	1.26	1.11	1.44	
Spring	10054	96	9958	0.96	0.78	1.17	<0.001
Summer	149	1	148	0.67	0.00	4.16	0.777
Autumn	6813	112	6701	1.64	1.37	1.98	<0.001
Winter	701	15	686	2.14	1.28	3.54	0.052

Table D-11bs: Hired death rates by climbing season for all peaks from 1950-2009